Portrayals of Americans
on the World Stage

Portrayals of Americans on the World Stage

Critical Essays

Edited by KEVIN J. WETMORE, JR.

McFarland & Company, Inc., Publishers
Jefferson, North Carolina, and London

LIBRARY OF CONGRESS CATALOGUING-IN-PUBLICATION DATA

Portrayals of Americans on the world stage : critical essays /
edited by Kevin J. Wetmore, Jr.
    p.   cm.
Includes bibliographical references and index.

ISBN 978-0-7864-4419-9
softcover : 50# alkaline paper

   1. Drama — History and criticism.   2. Americans in literature.
3. National characteristics, American, in literature.
4. United States — In literature.   I. Wetmore, Kevin J., 1969–
PN1650.A44P67   2009
809.2 — dc22   2009017887

British Library cataloguing data are available

Cover images ©2009 Shutterstock

Manufactured in the United States of America

McFarland & Company, Inc., Publishers
  Box 611, Jefferson, North Carolina 28640
  www.mcfarlandpub.com

To the memory of Forest Wetmore

Acknowledgments

This book is the product of many hands, many ideas, and many conversations. Thanks are due to the American Society for Theatre Research, as this project began life as a seminar at the 2007 ASTR conference. Thanks to the original participants, some of whom have work in this volume, and to the scholars and students in the audience for their feedback, questions and comments. Thanks to Adam Versanyi, Claire Conceison and Carol Sorgenfrei.

Thanks to the individual contributors, all of whom worked very diligently and speedily to bring the volume to completion. To an individual, they were open to criticism and suggestion and it has been an honor and pleasure to work with them.

Thanks are due as well to Loyola Marymount University and the Department of Theatre, under whose aegis this volume was compiled. Thanks as always to my colleagues, associates and family for their patience and guidance while this volume was completed.

Contents

Introduction:
Staging the Ugly American /
America the Beautiful

Kevin J. Wetmore, Jr.

"For we must consider that we shall be as a city upon a hill.
The eyes of all people are upon us."
    —John Winthrop, "A Model of Christian Charity" (1630)

No one can deny that from its inception America has had a strong self-image as a distinct and unique nation that uses its power for good in the world. John Winthrop, as demonstrated in the epigraph, saw the potential in the colonies of the New World to be a "city upon a hill" which Ronald Reagan later amended to "a shining city upon a hill." Certainly its natural beauty and history lead citizens of the United States to perceive "America the Beautiful" as a beacon of democracy. The American Dream sees the United States as a land of opportunity to which individuals from other nations and cultures were free to come to pursue their dreams, dreams which often centered on the realization of business or fiscal accomplishments.[1]

In contrast with this image is another one, also originating within the United States, although quickly embraced around the world: the ugly American. In 1958 William J. Lederer and Eugene Burdick published *The Ugly American*, a novel about American bureaucrats in Southeast Asia who are boorish, ethnocentric and corrupt, and who seek to benefit American businesses more than the indigenous people with whom they work. Ironically, the title character, Homer Atkins, is physically unattractive, but his behavior is the opposite of the well-dressed bureaucrats. The novel was made into a film in 1963 with Marlon Brando as Atkins. The term, however, has since come

1

to refer to Americans (usually abroad but also at home) who are offensive, loud, self-centered, willfully ignorant, and compare their foreign environments negatively with "home." Thus, American uniqueness has been defined at home and abroad in positive and negative terms.

From its origins the American theatre has also sought to define American uniqueness and develop this self-image of the United States as different from all other nations and Americans as different from all other people. The first play ever written by an American to be performed in public by a company of professional actors, *The Contrast* by Royall Tyler, first performed in New York City in 1787, sets up its very mission in its title. The contrast is between Colonel Manly, the noble and patriotic American, and Mr. Dimple, an effete, lying coward who prefers to act as Europeans do. Jonathan, Manly's servant, is the first in a long line of stage Yankees, and his simple, direct assessment of all situations has become a model for the hardworking, unpretentious American hero. From the very beginning of its drama, America has constructed itself as distinct and different from (and just as often as superior to) all other nations, and has sought to project this image through its drama and, later, media such as film and television.

These media projections have also shaped the modern perception of Americans in ways Tyler could not have foreseen. A 2007 BBC poll of British citizens ranked Homer Simpson as "the greatest American ever" ("D'oh" A16). Dr. Martin Luther King, Jr., and Abraham Lincoln came in second and third, respectively, with less than ten percent of the vote each. America is now seen in the world through its popular culture — a culture whose image of the United States is not always the positive one Tyler would have preferred, nor particularly flattering.

This volume engages the representation of America and Americans through the drama and theatres of other nations and the construction and dissemination of the American Other on the world stage. This construction often takes one of three forms. First is the American play presented abroad. For example, *Death of a Salesman* was produced in communist China in 1983.[2] While the play is an American one, the new context and the transculturation of production change how the play is perceived from its original American context. Second is the play written by a non–American but set in the United States. Often this type of drama deals with immigrants from the source nation challenged by life in the United States and the conflicted identity that has been created by the hyphen, such as Edgar White's *Lament for Rastafari*, which is about a West Indian family moving first to London and then to New York City. Third is the play written by a non–American featuring American characters visiting or living as expatriates in the source culture, such as Richard Nelson's play *Some Americans Abroad*, concerning American academics (mostly professors of English literature) in the United Kingdom. Claire Conceison's 2004 *Significant Other: Staging the American in China* remains one of the few book-length studies of the representation of Americans in world drama. She observes that in modern Chinese drama, the Americans are usually represented as "abroad," in other words, out of their indigenous context and living in or visiting China. The American abroad is a "privileged marginalized Other rather than a dominated colonized object" (Conceison 3). Unlike the plays of the second type, in which immigrants remain a dominated colonized Other living within a United States that is indifferent to them and their identity at best and hostile at worst, in plays of the third type, the stage American occupies a place of "privileged marginalization" (Conceison 4).

In the essays which follow, several recurring themes appear. One of the major issues in foreign drama about the United States concerns hybrid/hyphen identity: Melissa Rynn Porterfield, Thomas B. Costello, and Khai Thu Nguyen, for example, look at the relationship between Serbian Americans, Irish Americans and Vietnamese Americans, respectively, and their homelands and their new homeland of the United States. Costello, as noted below, also introduces the idea of the "American American," a character defined by his Americanness with no other indication of other identity.

Another issue is the complex negotiations between "America" and "Americans," and the idea that the nation is more (and less) than the sum of its individual people. This reflects the reality of the difference in perception of Americans and perception of the United States in international polls. Traditionally, Americans have been more liked and respected than America, although in the Iraq War era that has also changed. A 2006 headline in the *New Orleans Times-Picayune* noted, "World Opinion of U.S. Sinking: Dislike of Everything American on the Rise" (Wood). The Pew Globe Attitudes poll showed "an ominous turn," in the words of David Wood:

> In the past, while Europeans, Asians and Arabs might have disliked American policies or specific U.S. leaders, they liked and admired Americans themselves.... [Now] [m]ajorities around the world think Americans are greedy, violent and rude, and fewer than half in countries like Poland, Spain, Canada, China and Russian think Americans are honest.

The Pew Global Attitudes Project was published 13 June 2006. It noted that America's image had declined internationally and that other major nations are perceived much more favorably. And while Americans are viewed less favorably than they were, they are still viewed more favorably than the United States as a nation. The report found that much of the image slip had to do with unfavorable reactions to the "War on Terror," American aggression in Iraq, the policies and scandals of the Bush administration and the belief that

American actions had made the world less, not more, stable.[3] These attitudes have begun to be reflected in world drama.

Umehara Takeshi's "Superkyogen" play *Ōsama to kyōryū* (The King and the Dinosaur), for example, was written in 2002 and performed in 2003, two weeks after the beginning of the Iraq War. The play is a satire of and critique of international relations, with a particular focus on the United States. In the play, King Tottora is the ruler of Sunland, the most powerful nation in the world. He wants to retain his nation's hegemony so he summons "Mr. Money," who wears a hat resembling the U.S. dollar sign. Mr. Money teaches the King the magic word "globalization" which brings all the Mr. Monies from all over the world to Sunland. In addition, the King needs military might to protect his wealth, so he summons personified weapons and forces such as "Mr. Battleship," "Mr. Fighter Jet" and "Mr. Nuclear Bomb."[4] The King eventually wins the "No-Hell" Peace Prize when he accidentally hits the wrong button, intending to bomb the world but instead covering it in manure. Certainly this play is not a flattering portrait of the United States, and is directly reflective of the events following 9/11.

Another theme evident in the essays which follow is the idea that America is represented globally through its popular culture. America (read: Hollywood) produces numerous images of the United States and Americans through film, television programs, and music which are distributed throughout the world. This culture is perceived as "America," and yet as Heide Fehrenbach and Uta G. Poiger observe, "There is no monolithic American culture but perhaps only a stream of image-ideals" (xxix). That stream of image-ideals is pervasive throughout the world and America is defined by and through the popular images its exported culture depicts. These images further influence when they are localized and recreated by the importing culture. To give but a single example, the internationalization of hip-hop and the repeated use of American-style gangster imagery in the hip-hop music coming out of England, France, Germany, Russia, Japan, China, Kenya, Nigeria and South Africa reflect a specific image-ideal of urban America which, like many image-ideals, is not based on a reality but on a romanticization of urban African American culture. Within the importing culture are therefore complex negotiations, acceptances of and resistances to this stream of images, recognizing their artificiality and resenting their competition with local and national culture, yet also idealizing the United States and its people and appealing especially to younger generations. As one character in a recent South African play complained, "Our Coloured youth are far too Americanised, but what we see on TV is not reality. Americans are selling us their garbage and we're buying it!"[5] Not only are they buying it, they are recycling it, localizing it, and creating a return image-ideal.

The last major theme is the presence of the United States in world theatre through the Broadway musical, America's contribution to world drama. Developing as an indigenous form since 1866 with *The Black Crook*, considered to be the first book musical, the musical is often a reflection of contemporary American cultural concerns. From *Camelot* to *Hair* to *Rent* to *The Producers*, the musical is America on stage. Part III of this volume concerns itself with examples of the process of not only translation but transculturation, moving the cultural context of the musical.

This volume contains fourteen essays engaging the dramas of Europe (Western and Eastern), Asia, Latin America, and Africa from the beginnings of the thirteen colonies through the present day. The contributors are both established figures in the field and emerging scholars, and many are from the cultures about which they write.

Part I, "Historical Depictions of America and Americans on World Stages," contains four essays which consider the different manners in which Americans have been depicted during the first two centuries of the United States' existence. In "Satire and Sentiment: Images of America and Americans in German Drama to 1800," Sabine Macris Klein demonstrates the German fascination with Native Americans and perception of them as "noble savages." Klein depicts America as a site of German colonial fantasies and projections and arguably one of the first instances of the fictionalizing of the American Other almost as soon as there was an America in the sixteenth century. Klein's essay also establishes drama as an early medium in which the relationship between New and Old Worlds could be explored and in which "America" is seen in opposition to Europe. The emergent United States would define itself against Europe, but conversely, as Klein notes, Europe would also define itself against the United States. Yet, there is also, as she observes, no uniform vision of the United States. The complexity and variety of the American experience serves as source material for international drama.

In "Throwing Insults Across the Ocean: Charles Mathews and the Staging of 'the American' in 1824," Maura L. Jortner details two productions that resulted from the visit of British actor Charles Matthews to the United States in 1824: *Trip to America* and *Jonathan in England*. These two plays represent two of the three models discussed above: the foreigner in the United States finding his ways and customs exotic and strange and the American in the homeland, serving as synecdoche for his or her people. In the former drama, Matthews plays himself in a stage travelogue — presenting the American as simple or strange — and reinforcing existing stereotypes held by the British. In the sequel, an American character from the first play comes to England. What is most interesting, as Jortner reports, is that the first play succeeded tremendously and was very popular, but the second play was highly problematized and complicated by the politics of slavery it depicted. The forces that would lead to British abolition of slavery in 1833 and to the American Civil War were already present in England when Mathews staged the play, causing controversy.

Moving to the twentieth century, the next essay considers an historical drama from 1909 depicting events from over fifty years earlier. In 1635, the Tokugawa Shogunate promulgated an edict closing Japan to the outside world, and Japan remained closed for the next two centuries. In 1853, President Millard Fillmore sent Commodore Matthew C. Perry with a fleet of ten ships and two thousand men to begin commercial relations with Japan. In other words, America threatened Japan with its military might in order to begin trade in what might be perceived as one of the first major steps toward globalization. In "Gunboat Diplomacy on the *Kabuki* Stage: Okamoto Kidō's Construction of America and Japan's Deconstruction of *Pacific Overtures*," Kevin J. Wetmore, Jr., first considers Okamoto Kidō's *Amerika no Tsukai*, a play marking the anniversary of the Treaty of Yokohama and the first American ambassador to Japan, Townsend Harris. Kidō is also concerned about orientalism and about a Japanese woman whom scholars believed was Harris's mistress, but in his play he seeks to construct a new model of Japanese nationalism that welcomes sacrifice but not by becoming subservient to the United States. Behind the gender conflict is an assertion of equality between nations and people. In 1976, three Americans wrote a musical about the opening of Japan by the West. *Pacific Overtures* was conceived as a *Kabuki*-esque presentation of the events surrounding the opening of Japan told from the Japanese perspective. In 2000, Japan finally mounted a production of the play in which the director and cast deconstructed America's reconstruction and actually presented the narrative from a Japanese perspective. One of the key ways in which this was done was through a transformation of the *mise-en-scene* from *Kabuki* to *nō*. Wetmore concludes that part of the change in perspective grows from a desire to transform a tired indigenous drama via the techniques of a foreign drama, from Kidō's use of western dramaturgy in his play to Broadway's embracing of the surface aspects of *kabuki*.

Also recognizing that in theatre not all language is spoken, Jessica C. Locke considers the work of Mexican playwright Rodolfo Usigli and the notion of "gesture." In "'Gringo' Agency and Revolutionary Disillusionment in Rodolfo Usigli's *El gesticulador*" she reflects upon the figure of the "gringo," a term referring to people from the United States, primarily non-native speakers of Spanish, which is often perceived as pejorative. The "gringo" might also be seen as a variation on the "Ugly American." Locke explores the perception of the gringo and of the United States in Mexican drama, and also introduces us to the emblematic figure of the American academic, a stock character in international drama concerning Americans, and capable of being its own form of Ugly American.

In Part II, "Contemporary America and Americans in World Theatre," six essays engage the topic of the United States in world drama in recent decades. "Srbljanović's Ugly American: Simultaneously Constructing Serbian and American Identities" by Melissa Rynn Porterfield analyzes the perception of the United States in the work of Serbian playwright Biljana Srbljanović. Complicating Serbia's relationship to the United States are the transformations of its ethnic and national identity, especially during the Bosnian war of the 1990s. Srbljanović represents the "lost generation" after the war, seeking to define a new identity in the wake of the breakup of Yugoslavia. In her plays, Porterfield notes, America is a synecdoche for the West in general, especially due to its leading role in NATO and Bill Clinton's decision to become involved in the siege of Sarajevo. Srbljanović's *Belgrade Trilogy*, set partly in Los Angeles, deals with Slavic immigrants, lost Slavic identity, and the embracing of a new identity in the United States. It also engages the frequently-voiced concern of foreigners that the United States is a violent society and that violence is part of everyday life in major urban areas. Related to this American violence on the micro-scale is American violence on the macro-scale: Srbljanović sees the United States as an international bully, using physical force to enforce its hegemony.

Thomas B. Costello scrutinizes how American characters shape the perception of American identity, as well as Irish identity, immigrant identity and even Irish drama itself in contemporary Irish drama. Focusing primarily on Brian Friel, although many other playwrights are also considered, "The American Hyphen in Modern Irish Theatre: Irish-, Academic-, and American-Americans in the Plays of Brian Friel and Beyond" categorizes the tropes and types of Americans present in the plays: the returned immigrant, the academic American (as also seen in Locke's essay), and what Costello calls the "American-American." The American-American's "primary function is to embody a sense of America, whether as a cultural, political, or philosophical other," although this figure can also be more complex than a simple metaphor or stock character, especially in production. For example, in *Someone Who'll Watch Over Me* by Frank McGuinness, Adam (the American American) is, as Costello states, frequently played by an African American. The "American-American" can show the complexity and diversity of American society as much as the stereotypical understanding of the United States and its citizens.

Race and the history of ethnic relations are key issues in understanding American history. Neilesh Bose argues that the historic treatment of people of color in the United States represents a form of colonialism and imperialism in and of itself. In "Of Human Rights and Playwriting Against Empire" he gives a close reading of Utpal Dutt's *The Rights of Man*. After an overview of Dutt's career and the context of South Asian drama, Bose probes Dutt's play, an exploration of race relations and power dynamics in the United States. The 1969 examination of the trials of the Scottsboro Boys — nine African American men accused of raping a white woman — in Alabama in the thirties indicts the American judicial system as a kangaroo court in which no genuine justice was possible for the accused. Dutt (and Bose) relates the racism of America to the political realities in postcolonial India and, as the title of Bose's essay suggests, human rights and imperialism towards black and brown people by Westerners.

In the second of three essays on Americans in Japanese drama (all of which in some manner connect to musicals, interestingly enough), Nobuko Anan examines Japan's postwar national self-image as shaped by the United States. In "Reconsideration of Japanese Women's Bodies: KATHY's Parody of *Singin' in the Rain*" she perceives in a stage production of the Hollywood musical as adapted by KATHY, a performance collective that presents Americanized Japanese women employing the name of a stereotypical American woman, a variety of different challenges to Japanese identity, and especially Japanese women's identity following World War II. Anan theorizes Japanese identity following Murakami Takashi, the founder of the postmodern "Superflat" art movement, who sees Japan as "Little Boy," which is not so coincidentally the name of one of the atomic bombs the United States dropped on Japan at the end of the war. Anan also considers KATHY's performance as *modoki* (a Japanese theory of mimesis) and as a form of dubbing, demonstrating the separation of body and voice which further causes separation of identity.

In the United States there were two great influxes of Africans: the Middle Passage, in which Africans were involuntarily transported to the New World for the purpose of chattel slavery, and the post-slavery, post-independence immigrants of the twentieth century, especially students. Marking the newly discovered relationship between these two groups during the post-war period was Lorraine Hansberry's *A Raisin in the Sun*. Of particular interest for the purposes of this study is the character of Joseph Assagai, who serves as link between Africa and African America. At the dawn of the civil rights movement there arose a new interest in Africa by Americans of African descent. Similarly, in the same period, Africans began to attend American universities, as Assagai does in the play, and African and African American discover mutual interest and ignorance about one another. Kevin J. Wetmore, Jr.'s, "Motherland and Mothers-in-Law: African-American Wives in African Plays" investigates African plays in which Africans take African American wives. The metaphor of marriage may also be applied to the relationship between the peoples of the African diaspora: joined together but not always comprehending or working together smoothly.

It is sobering for Americans to think that the war known in the United States as the Vietnam War is called *Kháng chiến chống Mỹ* in Vietnamese: "The War of Resistance against America," perhaps better translated as "The American War." The theatre can be a place to shape perspective, and, like Costello's and Porterfield's essays, Khai Thu Nguyen's essay is concerned with the hyphenated American, in this case Vietnamese. To be a Vietnamese American is to see both the Vietnam War and the American War. In "Marking the Nation from the Outside: Vietnamese Americans as Abject in the Vietnamese Play *Dạ Cổ Hoài Lang*" Nguyen considers the construction of postwar national identity in Vietnam and its relationship to the Vietnamese diasporan community in the United States. She argues that the Vietnamese American is an abject figure, in Kristeva's sense, and that "the play *Dạ Cổ Hoài Lang* demonstrates the process of abjection in the formation of national identity in postwar Vietnam, in which the Vietnamese American plays an abject that is both jettisoned and constitutive of Vietnamese identity." The play is further shaped by the dual need to define Vietnamese national identity and simultaneously integrate both global capitalism and transnational empathy and identity with Vietnamese living outside the nation. In the end one must ask how the Vietnamese American reconciles Vietnamese and American identities, particularly when they are defined against one another.

Part III focuses on America's contribution to world drama: the Broadway musical. In "America through Musicals on the World Stage" four essays consider the production of American musicals in new cultural contexts, how those contexts change the musicals, and how those musicals shape foreign understanding of the United States.

In the spring of 1992, the inhumane and savage four-year siege of the Bosnian capital, Sarajevo, began, 25 years after the premiere of *Hair*, a rock musical about the counterculture, celebrating American youth culture, presenting a pro-drugs and free-love, anti–Vietnam War message and engaging the generational conflict of the sixties. Nenad "Neno" Pervan asks why the citizens of Sarajevo would risk their lives to rehearse, perform and attend an American hippie musical and what does *Hair* have to say to or do with Bosnia during the siege? The "original American tribal love-rock musical's" message of "peace, flowers, freedom and happiness" provided an alternative model of relations between different groups to the siege and to ethnic cleansing. American hippies, their opposition to the Vietnam War, and their embracing of the notion of one "tribe" regardless of ethnic or religious origin, became a model in Sarajevo for the citizens to resist the oppression of the Serbs.

The third essay on Japanese understanding of the United States through drama focuses on the all-female *Takarazuka*. Women play men's and women's roles, but the gender deconstructions are used to simultaneously destabilize and reinforce Japanese notions of gender. Jessica Hester, in "Japanese Women/ American Men: National Identities and the Takarazuka Revue," offers a brief consideration of American musicals and musicals about America on the Takarazuka stage. Following the anti–American musicals offered during World War II, the Takarazuka seized upon American musicals during the post-war period, featuring the emulation of American celebrities and offering up a variety of depictions of the United States: *West Side Story*; the only musical version of *Gone with the Wind*; and *Swing Butterfly*, a variation on Puccini's *Madame Butterfly*, the original American/Japanese opera using a distinctly American musical style. As with previous chapters, Hester demonstrates how Japanese identity is demonstrated by the differences with the performed American identity.

In "Taiwan Style *I Love You, You're Perfect, Now Change* by Lancreators," Llyn Scott delves into the Taiwanese production of the second longest running Off-Broadway musical (the longest still remains *The Fantasticks*). She discovers that *I Love You*, as produced by the Lancreators company, became something new and different when translated and transculturated. When an American musical is performed abroad by non–Americans, localization is transformation. Scott also elucidates the challenges in producing American musicals in Taiwan in particular and in foreign cultures in general.

Following along the same theoretical and historical lines, Ji Hyon (Kayla) Yuh surveys how Korean audiences understood *The Producers* and *Assassins* when they were produced in the Republic of Korea (known in the United States as South Korea). In her essay "The Great White Way Revived in Seoul: Korean Productions of *The Producers* (2006) and *Assassins* (2005)," Yuh notes that what was missing in the Korean productions was all the cultural information and the jokes that would have been readily apparent to American and especially New York audiences. In an absence of knowledge and experience with Jews and Jewish culture, for example, especially as they relate to the entertainment industry in the American preconception, Koreans did not understand the Jewish jokes, among other cultural and topical references. Instead, the play, contractually obligated to remain unchanged from the American production, played to a romanticized Korean understanding of the United States as the "Land of Opportunity." Contrasted with this is the Korean reception of *Assassins*, which, as Yuh demonstrates, is not only a play about the dark side of the American Dream (in America, anyone can grow up to be the president and anyone can grow up to try to kill the president), but also challenged Korean assumptions about the United States while confusing audiences less familiar with the details of American history around which the musical is organized. If not familiar with the individual presidents and their respective assassins and attempted assassins, the play loses much of its ability to generate meaning. This aspect combined with a less-than-idealized America on stage made *Assassins* less successful in Korea than other American musicals.

These fourteen pieces taken together produce a unique distorted mirror in which the United States may see itself, not as it sees itself, but as others have seen it. Often critical, sometimes flattering, sometimes even insulting, these portraits of the United States in international drama give us a much more complicated, multivocal, multivariant understanding of Americans and their representation on world stages.

NOTES

1. The American theatre, we might note, has celebrated the American Dream and responded to this notion critically. One of the most celebrated plays of the twentieth century was Arthur Miller's *Death of a Salesman*, showing the dark side of the American dream and the effect it has on one who holds the dream but lacks the ability to attain it.

2. See Miller's fascinating *"Salesman" in Beijing* (London: Metheun, 1984) for a first-person account of this production.

3. For full details of the report, see the Pew Global Attitudes Project Report, available at <http://pewglobal.org/reports/display.php?pageID=825>. Accessed 12 December 2008.

4. For more information on the production, see Jonah Salz's "Super-*kyōgen*: Radically Traditional Utopian Comedies" and Eric Rath's "Godzilla Meets Super-*Kyogen*, or How a Dinosaur Saved the World."

5. The play is *A Coloured Place* by Malika Ndlovu, first performed in 1996 and published in *African Women Playwrights*, edited by Kathy A. Perkins (Urbana: University of Illinois Press, 2009).

PART I. HISTORICAL DEPICTIONS OF AMERICA AND AMERICANS ON WORLD STAGES

1

Satire and Sentiment: Images of America and Americans in German Drama to 1800

Sabine Macris Klein

German literature has long reflected a fascination with the subject of America and things American. In the nineteenth and twentieth centuries, this translated into a particularly strong interest in Native Americans, who became the fantasized subjects of dime novels, paintings, Western movies, the overwhelmingly popular fiction of Karl May, and hobbyist groups devoted to Indian impersonation. In the seventeenth and eighteenth centuries, Germans were intrigued with America as a land of potential empire and extension of national power, as a new frontier to confront a racial other, and as a site for experimenting with radical new political and social ideas. It was a fascinating land of possibilities. Yet, this vision of America as *tabula rasa* problematically negates the history of America's native population.

Analyzing the image of America in German literature has become a fairly prolific area of study.[1] Interestingly, however, in the dozens of books and articles examining the topic, drama is given minimal attention. Yet stage performances played a potent role in shaping the idea of America in the German cultural imagination, particularly after the mid-eighteenth century. The most complete coverage of the subject of the image of America in German drama is provided in Harold Jantz's article, "Amerika im deutschen Dichten und Denken," found in *Deutsche Philologie im Aufriss*. Susanne Zantop's *Colonial Fantasies: Conquest, Family, and Nation in Precolonial German, 1770–1870* also discusses some depictions of America in eighteenth-century German drama. This essay will flesh out and extend the start made by Jantz and Zantop by examining a survey of the largely idealistic, often sentimental, views of America developed during the seventeenth and eighteenth centuries.

Germany had only a brief history as a colonial power, from the 1880s until the end of World War I, but that did not stop German writers from developing a vivid set of colonial fantasies about the Americas and Americans. Some plays of the seventeenth century openly envision America as a site for colonial empire. The more sentimental plays of the eighteenth century tend to sublimate messages of colonial aspirations within love stories between European white men and Native American women of color, or tales of brotherly friendship between men of European and Native American backgrounds. At the same time there is clearly sincere admiration among Enlightenment and Romantic thinkers for the freedom and naturalness of America, the plays of this era nonetheless still retain a perception of the cultural superiority of the Europeans over their native brothers and wives. Furthermore, the images of America developed during the seventeenth and eighteenth centuries in Germany, were actively participating in a broad, Europe-wide effort to fictionalize and fantasize the lives of the American Other.

In the seventeenth century, appearances of American themes in German drama were rare, however major renaissance playwrights did include a few American characters among their work. The image of America begins with negative associations of rebellion and Puritan extremism in Andreas Gryphius's *Murdered Majesty or Carolus Stuardus* (1657), which dramatizes the execution of the English King Charles I. The radical Puritan, Anglo-American Hugh Peter is the driving force of the play and its primary villain, leading the Christ-like figure of King Charles inevitably to his beheading. Peter delivers the axe, which he sees as an instrument of Divine Justice, to the executioner with the exhortation: "Look, Hero! Here is the hatchet that God calls upon you to wield; / Be quick and set yourself to Charles's fruitless oak" (92). In *Carolus Stuardus*, the rebellious and revolutionary spirit that comes to be associated so frequently with America is here portrayed as a detrimental force, bringing about the martyred death of a saintly king. The American background of Hugh Peter is not mentioned in the text of the play, but Gryphius makes clear in his published notes that he knew the historical figure had founded a Puritan church in New England and had been chosen by his parish to return to London in support of Oliver Cromwell and the Commonwealth (141).

In the 1660s, Daniel Casper von Lohenstein includes brief depictions of America at the end of his tragedies, *Cleopatra* and *Sophonisbe*. These are meant to assert the political prowess of Lohenstein's patrons, the Austrian ruling family of Habsburg. The plays advocate Emperor Leopold's aspirations to bring Spain under Hapsburg influence, which would in turn give Austria power over Spanish colonies in the Americas. In *Cleopatra*, America is mentioned briefly at the play's close, as a future site of the Habsburg Empire, which is offered as a modern parallel to the Roman Empire to which Cleopatra has succumbed. In the final speech of the play, the allegorical figures of the Rhein and Donau rivers address their sister rivers, the Nile and the Tiber:

> The present world is too small for him [Emperor Leopold].
> A world will be created,
> Upon which the sun will not set,
> And Thule will no longer be the Earth's boundary mark.
> That, which Columbus and Magellan,
> The other Tiphys, will discover,
> How distant the two Indias stretch,
> Will fall adoring to the feet of our emperor's house [Lohenstein 152].

Although not named as such, Lohenstein is clearly including America as a desired outpost of Austria colonial ambitions.

In a parallel final scene to the tragedy *Sophonisbe*, Lohenstein creates an allegorical character of America, who is invited to join her sister continents, Europe, Africa, and Asia: "Welcome, sister! Stand by us! / Help us to tear off the laurel wreath" (353). The wreath in question has just been passed between four allegorical characters representing the empires of Assyria, Persia, Greece, and Rome. America joins her fellow continents for a final chorus claiming the victory crown for Austria.

Images of America in seventeenth-century German drama were few and brief. Interest in America then blossomed in the early eighteenth century as Germany sent its first large wave of emigrants to settle in Pennsylvania. The demand for information about America exceeded the availability of reliable knowledge on the subject, so writers (including playwrights) began to fictionalize events or embroider historic accounts to satisfy the German public's taste for American novelty. Travel accounts and novels set in America began appearing more frequently. Daniel Defoe's *Robinson Crusoe* (1719) became a European sensation and was quickly translated into multiple languages. Plays set in the Americas or including American characters began appearing in England and France, by authors such as William Davenant, John Dryden, Aphra Behn, Louis François Delisle, and Voltaire.[2]

In the eighteenth century, German playwrights seemed particularly interested in exploring conceptions of the primitivism of Native Americans. Whether they were portrayed satirically as in the anonymous *The Savage* (*Der Wilde*, 1732) or as the idealized noble savage in international theatrical successes such as the Inkle and Yariko dramas of mid-century or Kotzebue's *The Virgin of the Sun* (*Die Sonnenjungfrau*, 1789), the primitivism of Native Americans was presented as a point of stark contrast to the customs of their European counterparts.

Caroline and Johann Neuber presented *The Savage* in Hamburg in 1732. No script survives, but there is a brief description from an advertising pamphlet.

A new comic play
The Savage
Or
The Unaffected Impressions of a Wild American
Of the Customs of our Time
Among other things there will appear:
The savage's description of his homeland.
The wonder at the ship, on which he has been brought to Germany, similarly at our wares and trade, and without money, etc. etc.
The curious customs of the savages for engagements and weddings
The savage's particular pleasure in the secret of the mirror, which he cannot understand, and more of the same [Reden-Esbeck 113].

It is clear from the description of the plot events and the character list that the Neubers were producing either a translation or adaptation of an enormously popular French play, *The Savage Harlequin*, written by Louis François Delisle in 1721.[3] The Delisle play was, in turn, inspired by the historical visit of four members of the Mohawk tribe to London in 1710, and more directly by a subsequent essay in Joseph Addison and Richard Steele's *The Spectator*. A year after the Mohawks' return to America, Addison published a satirical review of English customs from the perspective of one of the visitors (Honour, *European Vision* 198–199). Another source for Delisle's play was the travel account of Louis Lom d'Arce, Baron of Lahontan, *New Voyages to North America*, which described Huron courtship and marriage rituals (Honour, *New Golden Land* 122).

The Neuber adaptation renames all of the characters from the Delisle play, referring to the Native American protagonist as Peter, rather than Harlequin. The central Native American character is at times the butt of jokes, as when he tries to discover the magic behind the mirror. More typically, however, it is European customs that are the source of comedy. Courtship, sexual morality, financial and legal practices are all satirized in comparison to the idealized naturalness (and foreignness) of the Native American. For example, in Delisle's script, when Harlequin tries to exit a shop with a pile of merchandise for which he has not paid, the sea captain Lélio tries to explain to him the basic principles of a financial market system.

LÉLIO: There are two kinds of people among us, the rich and the poor. The rich have all the money, and the poor have none.
HARLEQUIN: Very good.
LÉLIO: So that the poor can have it, they are forced to work for the rich, who give them money in proportion to the work they do.
HARLEQUIN: And what do the rich do while the poor work for them?

LÉLIO: They sleep, they promenade, and spend their lives in diversions and good cheer.

HARLEQUIN: It's comfortable for the rich then [Castillo 184].

Harlequin also marvels that a woman cannot make love to a man, simply because she has decided this is what she wants. He explains how in Huron custom, a woman's desire would be signaled by the woman wordlessly blowing out a lit match brought to her by the interested male. When young Violette blows out Harlequin's match, he immediately takes her in his arms. The others separate him from her, protesting, "That's not how it's done." Harlequin asks, "Why? Isn't she her own mistress and can do whatever brings her pleasure, as long as it harms no one?" The American character has license to say outrageous things because of his foreignness. Susan Castillo describes this protagonist as "a curious blend of the Wise Fool of traditional European drama, the buffoon who because of his lowly status is allowed to speak uncomfortable truths, and the Noble Savage" (185). Delisle's play (and the Neuber adaptation) with its comic popularity and novelty did much to pave the way for Rousseau's serious thoughts on the basic goodness of man in a natural state.

The tale of Inkle and Yarico, though little remembered today, was a popular culture phenomenon in eighteenth century Europe. Over sixty discrete versions were published as short stories, epic poems or dramas in multiple languages, not including translations (Felsenstein 1–2). Inkle is a young English sailor, who after being shipwrecked on a Caribbean Island, is cared for by a young native woman, Yarico. After Inkle manages to contact a passing ship, he returns to England, selling the now pregnant Yarico to slave traders in Barbados on his way home. Originating as an anecdote in Richard Ligon's *History of the Island of Barbados* (1657), the story first fired the wider public imagination in 1711 as an essay in Addison and Steele's *The Spectator*.

The first German stage version of the Inkle and Yarico story was performed in 1766, as a translation of the French play *La Jeune Indienne* by Sebastien Chamfort. Six German translations, entitled *Die junge Indianerin* (*The Young Indian Woman*), were made of Chamfort's play over the next half century in addition to twelve original German dramatizations of the Inkle and Yarico story (Price 94–125). The top theatre managers of the era—Heinrich Koch, Ernst Friedrich Jester, Konrad Eckhof, and Abel Seyler—all included the play in their repertoires. Indeed, Heinrich Leopold Wagner asserted in his review of a Frankfurt performance of *The Young Indian Woman* in 1777 that "there is no company, big or small, that has not produced it" (Price 94–97). A young Johann Wolfgang Goethe announced to his sister his intention to write an Inkle and Yarico drama in 1766, but there is no evidence to confirm that he ever did.

The tale evinced a remarkable plasticity in its widely differing versions.

Often a happy ending for the story would be included, with Yarico buying Inkle back and the two lovers being rejoined. But tragic endings were also seen. One play shows Inkle without enough money to buy Yarico back. Instead she commits suicide after telling Inkle she forgives him. In another version Inkle is struck down by lightning (Price 102, 112). Inkle was depicted as succumbing to a variety of European cultural pressures (the need for money, a fiancée at home, a brother or friend trying to persuade him to sell Yarico) that seemed to work against his desire to be with Yarico and the simplicity of their life alone on the island. The juxtaposition of Yarico's "natural" innocence and goodness contrasted against Inkle's vacillation between noble and self-serving impulses created a sentimental conflict that greatly appealed to German audiences.

The Inkle and Yarico plays are first in a series of German dramas that depict a white, male European establishing his connection to the "New World" through a sexual relationship with a young, native woman. As Susanne Zantop notes, it is not only in Germany, but across Europe, that eroticism and colonial desire go hand in hand.[4] "In all of these earlier conquest fantasies, the innocent, child-like American [woman] fell in love with the irresistible European [man] and relinquished her 'savage ways' in order to live with and serve the stranger faithfully" (122). The sexual relationship of the European man with the native woman in eighteenth-century German drama (typically marriage) affirms the European's right to claim the woman's land as his own. At the same time it places the native woman in the culturally subservient position of wife and displaces the native male altogether. "The fateful conflation of land with woman, which had formed part of the European imaginary since the Discovery, lends credence to such an interpretation. Clearly, the progress from intruder to lawful owner of the land, from 'rapist' to loving 'husband' is the sustaining myth in all of the marriage romances discussed" (136–137). August von Kotzebue's *The Virgin of the Sun* was another extremely popular example of a German play fitting this pattern.[5]

The prolific late eighteenth-century playwright August von Kotzebue frequently chose to set his plays in exotic, foreign locations. The popularity of *The Virgin of the Sun* (1789) led him to write a sequel, *The Spanish in Peru* (1796). Kotzebue's two intensely sentimental melodramas, like the Inkle and Yarico plays, center around a selfless, innocent, beautiful, young Native American woman — Cora — who has fallen in love with a white European man, with serious consequences. This time, however, the man in question — Dom Alonzo Molina — acts far more honorably toward the native characters than had Inkle. Offended by the cruel behavior of the Spanish, Alonzo has left Pizarro's army to serve as an advisor to the Incan King Ataliba. A love triangle evolves between Cora, whose service in the temple of the sun binds her to a life of chastity, Rolla, a former military commander under Ataliba, and Alonzo. All three act nobly toward one another. After Rolla learns that Cora has fallen in love with Alonzo, and that they have both been sentenced to death for breaking Cora's vow of chastity, Rolla tries to help them escape. The first play ends with the king forgiving all three of their crimes. In the sequel, *The Spanish in Peru*, Rolla dies a hero after having rescued Cora and Alonzo's child from Pizarro's soldiers. Rolla is a strong example of the noble savage character type in German drama. He repeatedly risks his own life to selflessly serve Cora and Alonzo in both plays, despite the fact that she had chosen Alonzo over him. Rolla's nobility and altruism are set in sharp contrast with the European Pizarro, who is described in the plays as a barbaric villain. Rolla is idealized, but as Zantop points out, this idealization is limited to a position of exclusion. "Rolla becomes a brother only by the restraint of his own desires and the self-sacrificial, selfless support he is willing to extend to the Euro-American couple" (133).

Once again, Kotzebue's play provides an example of the recirculation of images of America across Europe. *The Virgin of the Sun* was based on a French novel, *Les Incas*, by Jean-Françoise Marmontel. Kotzebue's play was extremely popular and soon inspired adapted translations in England, by Richard Brinsley Sheridan and Charlotte Smith, and one in America by William Dunlap.

The noble savage was perhaps the most popular American character type at this time, but German dramatists shaped the idea of America along other lines as well. Friedrich Maximilian Klinger's influential play *Sturm und Drang* (1776), set during the American Revolution, presented the freshly emerging country as a land of newness and passionate turmoil. The emotional central character, a young Englishman who has renamed himself Wild, despairs of living and travels to America to find death in the Revolutionary War. Wild explains to his two friends, Blasius and LeFeu, his reasons for bringing them first to Spain and then America: "You know that I led you out of Russia to Spain, because I believed the king [of Spain] was going to start a war with the Mogul. But the Spanish nation was as lazy as ever. So I packed you up again, and now you're in the middle of the war in America. Ha! Let me feel it in my depths, to stand on American soil, where everything is new, everything is significant. Oh!" Wild continues shortly thereafter: "Now we are in the middle of the war here. The only ecstasy I know is to be in the middle of a war" (Klinger 102–103). Curiously, Wild's motive for coming to America is to find war, not because he feels a particular ideological attraction to American revolutionary ideals.

Wild gives up his drive to seek death in war, however, once he rediscovers the woman he had fallen in love with as a young teenager, Jenny, the daughter of his father's archrival. As the reunited couple exult in the emotional bliss of being together, Wild exclaims, "I found you, found you in America; where I sought death, I find peace and blessedness in those sweet eyes" (Klinger 120–121). Soon after, Wild commits himself to fight for Jenny's new fatherland. For him, America has changed from a place defined by the lure of death, to a place promising new life. At the same time, Wild's sense of America seems vague and rather disconnected to the specific place. He speaks more rapturously about Jenny's eyes and the moonlit garden they stand in, than he does about America.

In contrast to *Sturm und Drang*, Karl Gotthelf Lessing's *The Mistress* (*Die Mätresse*, 1780) relies quite heavily on the image of America as a Utopian land of romantic social and political ideals. Karl Gotthelf Lessing is best remembered today as the early biographer of his famous older brother, Gotthold Ephraim Lessing, however he was also a successful dramatist in his own right. In *The Mistress*, American ideals are represented in the character of Otto von Kronfeld, the black sheep of his family who went off to America as a destitute young man. Otto worked for a kindly Pennsylvania Quaker farmer who eventually made him his heir. He returns decades later to Europe as a wealthy man to rescue his brother, Hans, from bankruptcy. Here, Otto is the self-made man and America is the land of opportunity where he is able to establish himself.

There are two sets of principles espoused in this play, defined as American and European. The first is represented by Otto as the "American uncle" who has returned home, the European is represented by Hans and his wife, Maria, and Otto's nephew, the proud Count von Mannhof. The title character of the play is Juliane, a young, hardworking woman from respectable, bourgeois family who had been seduced years earlier by Mannhof, and is raising her illegitimate son, Karlchen, in a cottage near Otto's estate. The action of the play largely concerns Juliane's fate once Mannhof and others realize that they share a son.

The American Otto manifests many romantic ideals. He lives a life close to nature, where he values people for their virtues rather than their wealth or social prestige. Otto acts and speaks according to his heart, not the dictates of society: "My mouth is my heart and my heart is my mouth" (Lessing 56). While living in America, Otto's heart leads him to reject racial prejudice and marry an African woman. "A slave trader brought her to me. She was beautiful, black, like the lustrous raven, and slim as a reed. I gave what the man asked, but he asked for very little to be rid of her. Her mind, her mind! And her heart! As my wife, brother, everyday I discovered new charms." Otto grieved for her intensely after she died in childbirth: "If tears could have woken her from the dead, she would have risen again" (Lessing 31–32).

Where Otto views his marriage as an undeniable action of the heart, his sister-in-law rejects his behavior as debauchery and loose living that would bring shame to the family if any of their European neighbors were to hear of it. In contrast to Otto, Maria values people primarily for their money and social position. She condemns Otto as "a brutal man! Completely without breeding. One would have to be ashamed of him, if he didn't have money" (Lessing 64). Maria encourages her daughter, Elizabeth, to marry the Count von Mannhof despite the fact that he has had a mistress, instead of the man she loves who has a title of lesser nobility. As way of persuasion, Maria reminds her daughter that as a countess she would keep company with princes and eat from golden plates.

Otto's American/romantic views on education, class difference and politics stand in marked contrast with the conservative/European stances of Hans, Maria, and Mannhof. Hans insists that only a university education qualifies a man to make sound judgments about serious matters, whereas Otto is content to rely on life experience and common sense. When the subject of politics is raised, Hans aligns himself with European monarchy and Otto with American democracy. Otto is offended at Hans's reference to Americans as rebels.

> OTTO: Rebels! So am I a rebel, too, since true American blood flows in me? And if I had not lost my wife, I would never have returned to you.—Rebels!
> HANS: Yes, yes, rebels; unthankful children against their tender mother.
> OTTO: The devil take the mother that wants to grow rich and powerful at the expense of her children.

Here Otto clearly declares his allegiance to American democracy, as well as romantic principles in support of the rights of the common man. Otto also shows that it was through his wife—a woman of color, but not native to America—that he had felt ultimately connected to America.

Otto helps resolve the major problems presented in the play, applying poetic justice from a romantic perspective, so that all those who live by their hearts and common sense are rewarded. After Mannhof refuses to marry Juliane because of her lower social status, Otto disinherits him. In Mannhof's place, Juliane, Karlchen and Elizabeth are made Otto's heirs, and Elizabeth is left free to marry the man she loves.

By the latter half of the eighteenth century, America and its people came to be viewed quite idealistically in German drama. The promise of a new land, a land of natural laws, a land that had rejected the tyranny of European bureaucracy and monarchy with violent revolution had an inevitable appeal for German romantic writers. This was quite different from the seventeenth-century views of America as a land of dangerous rebellion or potential colonial empire-building presented in Gryphius and Lohenstein. Yet, the sexual fantasies embodied in many of these plays still relay the colonialist desire.

The topic of America was often a site for Germans to negotiate issues of race or introduce domestic social criticism. The image of Native Americans is one that was shaped by a pan-European mesh of sources, translated and interwoven for audiences in Germany and other countries.[6] Native American characters presented in eighteenth-century German drama were frequently inspired by French or English originals. Toward the end of the eighteenth century, however, this became an increasingly two-way exchange. Images of America presented in Germany's romantic plays and melodramas inspired translation and imitation among its European neighbors and back to America, as well.

There was no uniform vision of America in German drama during the seventeenth and eighteenth centuries. It had many faces. America was depicted as a land of opportunity, a land of lawlessness and savagery, a land of naturalness and nobility, a land waiting to be conquered and controlled, a land of turmoil, a land of future promise, a land of radical new ideas, a land of equality, a land of villains, and a land of heroes. Yet all these images had as much to say about what Germans thought of themselves and the rest of Europe, as they did about America. However America was defined, it was always set in opposition to the Europeans. Whether the final result was flattering or critical, in the end, Germans used their images of America to define themselves.

NOTES

1. The words German, Germany, America and American are imprecise and evolving terms. For the purposes of this essay, I use the terms in a broad sense. I am including in this survey drama written in German-speaking countries. I also include plays that depict America and Americans from beyond the current borders of the United States. It should be noted that the German conception of the word "America" shifted during the time period under discussion. Increasingly, after the creation of the United States of America in 1776, residents of the United States who were of European background were referred to as "Americans" while Native Americans were referred to as "Indians." The word "America,'"too, shifted its meaning after 1776 for German speakers. Before the United States broke away from Britain, the term America was used to denote locations in South, North or Central American continents; after 1776, "America" typically referred to the new country of the United States of America.

2. *Native Americans as Shown on the Stage, 1753–1916* by Eugene H. Jones has a helpful index of plays written in Europe or America between 1658 and 1982 that include Native American characters.

3. Much of Neuber's repertoire was made up of translations or adaptations of French plays.

4. Zantop builds on the observations of Anne McClintock and Robert Young with regard to British colonialism.

5. The Pocahontas story is yet a further example of this dramaturgical pattern. There is a German play entitled *Pocahontas*, written c. 1784 by Johann Wilhelm Rose, but I

have been unable to locate a copy. While this very early Pocahontas play was written and performed, the story of Pocahontas did not prove as popular a dramatic subject in Germany as the Inkle and Yarico or the Cora and Alonzo stories (*The Virgin of the Sun*).

6. See Peter Hulme's discussion of the European-wide effort to shape colonial fantasies.

2

Throwing Insults Across the Ocean: Charles Mathews and the Staging of "the American" in 1824

Maura L. Jortner

Charles Mathews, a renowned English comedian, traveled to America in 1822. His trip was relatively short. It included only six cities and was complete in less than a year. Mathews had gained fame in England after an 1808 performance of *The Mail Coach Adventure*, a one-man show that had wowed audiences at the Haymarket Theatre and then throughout the British provinces as it toured the country. Mathews' career continued to gain speed throughout the 1810s and he was well loved, if starting to falter financially, by the early 1820s. Many Americans were thrilled to see such a famous actor perform in their theatres. A few English stars had come "across the pond" previously, but such a transatlantic tour was still a bit of a novelty. Thus, Americans crowded into theatres to see the famous Mathews perform. The applauded him wildly, filled his pockets with silver, and laughed heartily at the humorous depictions set before them.

Mathews most popular brand of humor dealt with national peculiarities and eccentricities. Mathews was a satirist of those he observed. Says Francis Hodge, author of *Yankee Theatre*, "In his [Mathews'] one man, vaudeville-type performances he had lightly ridiculed through songs, skits, and monologues the Scots, Welsh, Irish, many of the English country types, and the French, German, and Dutch" (61). Thus, although Americans enjoyed his portrayal of various "foreign" types, they were less thrilled when he planned to leave the country. There was speculation that Mathews would soon be parodying them on stage as soon as he returned to the King's shores — a speculation that was, first of all, not that far off base, and, second of all, not terribly comfortable for many Americans who still cared deeply about how they were perceived by the international community.[1]

One newspaper printed these comments, perhaps in an effort to combat such an anxiety:

> On Monday evening this extraordinary actor [Mathews] takes leave of the American audience, to return to the comforts of his home and family.... He returns with profit, if not improvement; and though it may be expected that some of our national peculiarities will form the subject of future entertainments, we are persuaded that he has discerned some traits worthy of his esteem and respect. We should not complain if these peculiarities are presented in a rational and amusing way to an English audience; for Mathews has been entertaining us with many amusing hits and laughable absurdities at the expense of his own countrymen. We have, therefore, no right to expect an exemption from professional sallies and satires [Memoirs III 409–410].

Predictably, Mathews did satirize the American public. Seemingly as soon as he stepped off of the boat, he (along with playwright Richard B. Peake) began constructing two plays stemming from his recent trip. Also perhaps predictably, both plays focused on the "foreign" aspects of America. This paper will examine these two pieces. The first, aptly called *Trip to America*, works as a travelogue: it stages America as an unfamiliar, foreign space, in which strange, incomprehensible, and at times ridiculous inhabitants abide. *Jonathan in England, or Jonathan Doubikins*, the second work, which premiered six months later, tackles the subject of American foreignness from a different perspective: it depicts an American traveling in England. Thus, in one we will see how America is made foreign; in the second, we will see the American as foreigner. Both, we will find, rely on an Imperial vision, one which centers "home," "the norm," and "the respectable subject" clearly on one side of the Atlantic.

International travel became a popular pastime for elite English subjects in the nineteenth century. Men and women swarmed out of England to explore the world around them, to see the "strange" foreign cultures surrounding their own. Some had European destinations in mind; they observed French fashions, feasted on Italian cuisine, personally discovered the ancient ruins of Greece, and stared mystified at the destitute medieval castles of neighboring Scotland and Ireland. Others ventured further out, to America, India, or Africa.[2] Wherever they went, they kept diaries or personal journals. Personal travel writing became a fad. Everyone who could afford the travel took up the habit, and all noted their most personal thoughts. The main point was to be able to remember every intimate detail of the trip to explain the experience to others.

As the years passed, however, a more public purpose superseded the mnemonic function of these accounts. That is, many of these travel accounts were published, and made their authors hundreds of pounds. Thus, English subjects began to travel and write accounts for this express purpose. In other words, little by little, a genre emerged: travel writing. Some travel journals were scientific in nature, others focused on the social sciences, and still others were politically minded.[3] Whatever the style, however, these works were immensely popular, and they were immensely popular for a number of reasons: Travel accounts satisfied a growing curiosity about the international world, a growing need to see England as superior, and a growing number of lower class subjects who needed relatively inexpensive entertainment. Given their popularity and complex cultural functions, it is not surprising to find the travelogue jumping from "page to stage" in the early 1820s.

Trip to America, a simple travelogue, opened on March 26, 1824, to glowing reviews. The action of *Trip to America* is straight-forward, though somewhat disjointed, as accounts of travel often seem. The play begins with Mathews addressing the audience as himself, explaining his motivation for crossing the Atlantic. He jokes that he wants to find some "yellow boys" (Klepac 101) and soon after, still on board the ship, he hears that yellow fever is sweeping through New York.[4] He engages in dialogue with a young man (a Yankee) who confuses the actor with his many "Americanisms," and likewise worries him by speculating on the severity of the fever in the city. The ship finally lands at Hoboken, staying clear of the greatly feared malady.

Once aground, Mathews meets other two other English travelers, Jack Topham, a mischievous young man, and his uncle, Barnaby Gray. The three, all played by Mathews, travel to an inn, and soon discover how difficult it is to deal with an American landlord. The landlord insists that he has no responsibility to feed the travelers since the meal was served at four o'clock. Yet Mathews, being hungry, persists. He was not yet at the inn, he says, and thus could not partake of the meal when it was served. The landlord still refuses. Mathews ends the bit by expressing his general exasperation with American landlords.[5] Nothing is easily got in America and the service is of the worst kind.

Mathews then imaginatively travels to Bristol and Baltimore via stagecoach, and is able to meet a few Americans, with whom he is sharing the small compartment. His kind theatrical reception at Baltimore is described, and many anecdotes are shared. On board a steamboat he meets an Irishman, Pat, who sees a real turtle and confuses it with a mock turtle[6] and then he journeys via stagecoach to New York.[7] On this coach Mathews meets a young man who is attempting to write a jest book (he has the title and preface ready; he wants "only ... the body of the work" [Klepac 104]). While in New York, Mathews witnesses an African-American actor, a tragedian, who performs

Hamlet and sings the "Opossum Song" in the midst of the famous "To be or not to be" soliloquy. A review of the American militia follows, "in the style of the field day of the London volunteers of former celebrity" (*The Examiner* March 29, 1824), whose inspection and actions are abruptly ended by an onslaught of mosquitoes.

Part II is more pointed. Mathews desires a servant, but he can find none to help him. He asks Daniel Doolittle (a Yankee figure) if he would be his servant, but Doolittle is confused. In America servants are referred to as "help," so he does not understand the famous actor's request — nor does he desire to be so insulted as to become a servant. The actor then visits Bunker Hill and inspects the inscriptions on the Monument which are said to read: "This monument was built of brick, / Because we the English did lick" (Klepac 110). Next, Mathews meets the "genuine" Yankee of the piece, Jonathan, who tells him two long stories of his Uncle Ben. He meets a Frenchman, Mr. Mallet, who cannot get mail at the post-office since the persons in charge cannot spell his name[8] and then sings an air about General Jackson, which showcases classic American bluster. He criticizes an American judicial trial, highlighting its inefficiency and touches on the "horrid" practice of tobacco spitting. Lastly, Mathews meets an African-American slave, Maximilian, who attempts to serve him dinner. Through ventriloquism Mathews (the actor playing himself at the table) convinces the black man that a child is speaking to him from a snuff-box on the table and this so scares him that he drops a dinner dish.[9] Concluding Part II, Mathews claims that he has collected "as much of American manners and American gold as he thought tantamount to his purpose" (Klepac 117), so he decides to return home to share his adventures in America with his countrymen.[10]

The monopolylogue, "All Well at Natchitoches," centered on the Yankee, Jonathan, and his slave, Agamemnon.[11] In this one-act Agamemnon has run away from Jonathan, who is a slave-owner. Jonathan is upset because he has made a bad purchase — he has been cheated. Uncle Ben, who sold him the slave, said that Agamemnon was a very useful "help," yet Jonathan cannot get him to do even the smallest task. He has been swindled and wants his $60.25 promptly returned. The play ends with Jonathan finding Agamemnon hiding in the well[12] and Mathews expressing generally benevolent sentiments.[13]

Trip to America was similar to contemporary travelogues in format and style. It took the form of a trip across the foreign country and showcased the American culture for all to see (and then to judge). It openly mocked American manners and practices and displayed characters as either strange and exotic, or just plain simple and confusing. It relentlessly portrayed American culture through an outsider's point of view. Likewise, filled with an air of

English authority, the play presented such depictions as fact and laid out the occurrences therein as authentic truth-claims.[14]

Likewise, it drew on the type of humor found in travelogues and accounts of America. Mathews was telling no new jokes in his shoes. Americans were parodied in a specific way in current travelogues, and Mathews' representation of them did not veer from established tropes. Americans were queer types, too serious for their own good. They were naive and a bit dimwitted, blatantly voicing American jingoism whenever possible and bragging in a non-stop fashion. Too stringently clinging to their belief in independence and egalitarianism, they were a stubborn and dull people. Mathews' work hit all the same jokes and the English public surely understood this brand of humor. It was, indeed, the general audience awareness of such current depictions of Americans that made his renditions of these specific characteristics so humorous.

Trip to America was similar to travelogues in terms of general themes as well. Jane Louise Mesick and Max Berger, in their respective works, *The English Traveller in America, 1785–1835* and *The British Traveler in America, 1836–1860*, claim that English travelogues most often focused on religion, manners and customs, national temperament, slavery, egalitarianism, and capitalism.[15] Unsurprisingly, most of these American themes/national differences are covered in *Trip to America*. Though relatively unconcerned with religion,[16] Mathews' work both uncovered and displayed American foreign manner and customs. *Trip to America* worked to display — if not to exploit — the unique and strange American ways. Likewise, his play also gave information on the American character. The play itself was a type of catalogue, meant to stand in for the whole American experience.[17]

As for slavery, egalitarianism, and capitalism, Mathews expressed a typical English reaction to these American institutions. What is most interesting about his critique is that all of the hard-hitting assaults came through the Yankee character. The Yankee was a popular character on the stage and in the popular culture at large in the nineteenth century. Jonathan, as this character was called, represented the United States, much as we today might think of and/or use Uncle Sam. This character most often worked as a vehicle of nationalism. That is, in America, stories told about him, anecdotes featuring him, political cartoons centering on him, or — pertinent to our cause — plays starring him, were attempting to exhibit America in a positive light. Although Jonathan was a country bumpkin of sorts, his naiveté often worked in his favor. Frequently his "bumpkinness" highlighted foreign snobbery or somehow showcased the hazards of holding anti–American biases. Within American works, Jonathan's faults were lovable; his shortcomings were endearing and/or shown to be not shortcomings at all. He was the idealized, if comic, American.[18]

Key to Mathews' critique was casting Jonathan as a slaveholder. This Yankee not only keeps a slave, but he also mistreats him. His behavior is abominable. But most importantly, Mathews makes sure that Jonathan is clearly linked to "America." For example, in the monopolylogue, the dialogue is clearly pointed; references to freedom and equality directly follow those on slavery:

"Well, Uncle Ben, I calculate you have a Nigger to sell?" "Yes, I have a Nigger, I guess. Will you buy the Nigger." "O, yes! If he is a good Nigger, I will, I reckon; but this is a land of liberty and freedom, and as every man has a right to buy a Nigger, what do you want for your Nigger?" "Why as you say, Jonathan," says Uncle Ben, "this is a land of freedom and independence, and as every man has a right to see his Niggers, I want sixty dollars, and twenty-five cents..." [Klepac 119–120].

The Yankee clearly misses the point. Apparently too imbedded in his American viewpoint, Jonathan does not see the hypocrisy of his sentiments. He juxtaposes notions of independence and egalitarianism directly with his right to keep (and mistreat) a slave.

In Mathews' *Trip to America*, like in American works, the Yankee becomes the representative American. But in this play, he does so in a negative sense; he becomes the embodiment of American political practice and/or thought, and as such he bears the brunt of perceived American hypocrisy. In short, the Yankee becomes a vehicle for transatlantic communication and is used to critique American institutions and beliefs. According to Francis Hodge, Jonathan was the "most successful" character in this play (69), but he was also the most critical: "[Jonathan] reflected Mathews' deep pessimism about the Great Experiment" (77).

Mathews' Yankee had few redeeming qualities. He was an unpolished, hard bargainer. Never thinking of others, but only concerned with turning a profit, Jonathan was the embodiment of the (imagined) trends and fallout of American capitalism. He was an ignorant country fellow, stupid and devious; likewise, he was deeply selfish and racist. Depicting Jonathan as such, Mathews threw a sharp political barb at the New World.[19]

Though today the scholar may read *Trip to America* as staunchly anti–American, the nineteenth-century English public did not see it this way. Newspapers and reviewers alike commended it. Many even suggested (as perhaps Mathews did in the last line of the play) that this work might function as a cultural bridge. Naively, they thought this work would bring the two countries together. For example, *The Morning Advisor* reported:

Mr. Mathews last night resumed his exertions at this House, bringing out the long-looked-for *Budget* from America. It is entitled "*A Trip to America*" and is avowedly founded on the Author's — and the Performer's — observations and adventures during his late "Trip" to the United States. It is an exceedingly interesting production. The subject was new, and it was also difficult; for there were many who calculated that nothing was to be done except the Americans were turned into ridicule. Mr. Mathews, greatly to his credit — has done no such thing. When he visited America he thought for himself; and though he has collected together a rich fund of entertainment, which at the same time gives forcible ideas of the manners of the Americans, we much mistake if Mr. Mathews has not done a vast deal to promote that good understanding between the two Countries, which interested and selfish persons only would desire to interrupt.... The house continued excessively crowded to the last and so happily chosen were many of the peculiarities of American manners and language that they were afterwards loudly repeated. Our conversations will now be inundated with Americanisms — with "I guess," and "I calculate".... The whole went off admirably, and is a production that does Mr. M. great honour [March 26, 1824].

The Morning Advisor was not alone in doling out praise to Charles Mathews. The Globe and Traveller and The Examiner also came out with raving reviews of the performance. The British public was thrilled with this performance. They saw in Trip to America a quaint bunch of characters, none of which could possibly anger Americans. They saw innocent humorous depictions. Americans, they thought, would surely appreciate Mathews' wit.

English praise of Trip to America most certainly spawned from the subjects' national/cultural positioning vis-à-vis Charles Mathews, for the rhetoric imbedded in any travel narrative relies on a distinct and known insider/outsider construction. Contextualizing the notion of "home," Kristi Siegel, in the introduction to Issues in Travel Writing: Empire, Spectacle, and Displacement, surmises:

> Travel implicitly calls the notion of "home" into question because that is typically the standard from which experiences are measured. By definition, then, exotic would be "other than home." In journeys outward — away from home — other landscapes, countries, and cultures are often viewed in terms of how they compare to one's home ["Travel" 4].

It is this measurement against a standard that creates and codifies a power structure within a travel narrative. Home is the familiar, therefore becomes codified as "the right," "the correct," and more "appropriate" mode of living. The "exotic," then, by mere juxtaposition, is cast as "the backwards," "the inferior," and "the morally degenerative."

One can clearly see the cultural imperialism present when the otherwise obscured binaries are outlined in this fashion. In travel writing, one is dealing with a sense of home and a sense of "Self," neither of which is questioned within the genre. Indeed, the genre requires what might be called an "imperial I." The traveler — the "I" of the narrative — sees the strange — the "Other"— and records it for his/her fellow countrymen and women. The sense of authority within this recording is not to be questioned; if it were, the genre would disintegrate, fall in upon itself. Authority to look, to analyze, and to explain is required by the genre itself. The sense of "home"/"not-home," "travel," "Self"/"Other," "I," "Them," and "We" maintains the framework of the genre.

Simultaneously, this authority creates imagined geographic power structures, which relate to the real world. Melanie Hunter summarizes this power struggle in her essay "British Travel Writing and Imperial Authority": "The ever-confounded 'genre' of travel writing, when viewed through the lens of post- or neocolonialism, becomes intimately bound up with the struggle between the metropolitan centers of power ... and the (post-)colonial margins" (29). The genre requires an authoritative narrator, one speaking from and within a sense of "home;" likewise, it demands a misunderstood, misrepresented, and exotic Other. These narrative contexts structure world politics and reify world geography as understood by the power centers as well as the margins. Therefore, "[w]hen one is considering the subject of travel and of travel writing," Hunter continues, "one must also consider the matter of perspective, of location, of circumstance and privilege" (30). If one, then, does stop to consider these matters, it becomes clear that in 1824 America was the underdog. The New World was the margin, the periphery to London's center. What is more, when one considers the fact that Mathews was performing in England, the power structure shows itself to be even more uneven. Mathews was examining, seeing, and judging America through his imperial viewpoint. He was doing so, likewise, from within the center. His critique was aimed across the Atlantic at the post-colonial margin.

Similar to contemporary travelogues, Mathews' work focused on the "strangeness" of both Other people and of Other places. He, like the traveler in written accounts, was always the "Self" experiencing the "foreign." In his work *Charles Mathews at Home*, Richard Klepac explains the way the comedy works in general and the way it functioned specifically in Mathews' *At Home*: "Comedy may consist in an eccentric facing a normal world or a normal character involved in confusion. These scripts contain both. Mathews is the normal character leading his audience through a world of confusion. The sub-protagonists are the eccentric characters in a relatively normal world" (30). Klepac's use of the word "normal" here makes the point all the more clear. As Mathews staged his imaginative travels, he enacted the part of himself. He would begin and end the piece as himself, dressed in his own attire, and welcoming the audience into his imagined home. Likewise, he would end the piece as himself as well, happy to be returning to England. It was this character, this persona, to which the English public could relate. He was a version of them on stage. His reactions were akin to what their own would be; he typified the common English subject.

Since *Trip to America* was a one-man show, Mathews also played the part of the Other. Directly after being the "Self," he would enact the "eccentric." He would portray the Frenchman, the Irishman, the African-American slave, and when he did so, these Others were immensely laughable. The Frenchman was overly excitable, easily misunderstood (with his "funny" accent), and always feisty. The Irishman was a fool, not understanding the basic world around him, or extremely and frequently intoxicated. The slave was the wise fool, the uneducated who spoke the truth, or he was simply a ridiculous clown. These "Others" were indeed farcical, but as Klepac makes clear, it was not only their particular eccentricities that generated laughs; it was also the "Self's" reaction to them. One can only imagined Mathews' reactions to the volatile, fiery Frenchman, for example. His calm, rational, "normal" English temperament juxtaposed to such an impulsive individual must have been quite amusing, enhanced by the virtuosity Mathews displayed in simultaneously playing both parts.

Mathews' work was filled with imperialistic rhetoric. Not only was Mathews staging the "Other" as humorous, laughable, and odd (strictly because of the differences they exhibited from the London public), he was, along with his audience, clearly positioned as the "Self," the normal. Physically traveling to other lands — in this case, to America — and then staging his findings, he brought the foreign "home"; he brought the "strange" and "exotic" to London where it was displayed for all. He was staging travel narratives. In a real way, then, he conquered these "Others" (which he placed on view), both metaphorically and physically. Just as we might think of his traveling and staging these peoples as symbolically conquering other cultures/lands for England, we also might think of Mathews, the actor, physically conquering these "Others," for he supposedly embodied them in a way unlike any other performer.

According to all accounts, Mathews brought foreigners to life even better than they could themselves. For example, one reviewer said of him:

> In imitation he was the greatest master of his art; for he not only imitated the face, voice, gestures, modes of expression, and other peculiarities of the originals who sat for him, but their characters, opinions, sentiments, and minds. As a superior author does not describe his dramatis personae, but as it were, himself becomes really each in turn, so did Mathews transform himself into all the various personages whose vivid portraiture and living likeness it pleased him to present to view [from an unnamed document found in Mathews' Memoirs IV 427–428].

Assuming (as this reviewer does) that Mathews knew not only the manners, but also the minds of the persons he portrayed, the reviewer demonstrated how deep the imperialist notions of Selfhood ran in the culture at this time.[20] Mathews felt confident in symbolically conquering "Others" on stage and his reviewers assumed that he could perform these persons with intimate accuracy even though he had quite possibly never even spoken to them.[21]

As previously suggested, English audience enjoyed Mathews' *Trip to America* because of their relation to the actor. It was, conversely, perhaps the difference between the portrayed "Self" (Mathews) and the foreigners (Americans) which led to Americans' feelings about the play. Americans, to say the least, were upset by the piece. They were furious with the content in *Trip to America*. They judged it an unfair portrayal of their country and were particularly angry because they had so lined the comedian's pockets with their hard-earned money. They had been generous to him (as they were to all touring English stars) and never expected to be repaid with such animosity. Angry comments were printed in domestic newspapers. A few Americans even found a way to get their thoughts published abroad. The clearest example of their indignation, though, came ten years later, when Mathews returned to America for a second acting tour. In early 1834 Mathews needed money. His career was faltering in England[22]; the obvious choice was to return to America, where he had earned so much capital in 1822. If he assumed that any scandal provoked by *Trip to America* had died down by this time, he was sorely incorrect. On a November evening Mathews arranged to play *Trip to America*. That night a sign was anonymously — and ominously — hung on the theatre door. It read:

> We understand chs. [Charles] Mathews is to play on Monday evening, the 13th inst. The scoundrell [sic] ought to be pelted from an American stage after his writing that Book which he did about six years ago called Mathews Carricature [sic] in America. This insult apont [sic] Americans ought to be met with the contempt it deserves. After using the most vilest language against the "TOO EASILY DUPED YANKeeS" as he calls us, he thinks thus to repay our kindness towards him. But we hope they will show him that we are not too easily duped this time, as we were then. And drive the ungrateful slanderer from our stage forever [as recounted by Klepac 20].[23]

Too, a crowd threatened violence.[24] The manager and Mathews waited backstage and braced for the worst. Although it was 1834, ten years after *Trip* originally opened, many Americans still keenly felt the grievances of this play.[25] Some were ready to riot over it.[26]

But if American citizens were angered by *Trip*, their ire would inflate to new levels with *Jonathan in England; or Jonathan Doubikins. Jonathan Doubikins* was constructed after *Trip to America*'s hugely successful run.[27] It hit London theatres less than six months after *Trip to America* showed, but it was so unsympathetic a portrayal of Americans that it not only re-angered New World citizens but also evoked indignation from English subjects as well. It made *Trip to America* look an innocent and playful sketch comedy by comparison.

Jonathan Doubikins, the second piece harvested from Mathews's tour of the United States, premiered at the English Opera House September 3, 1824. Richard B. Peake, a playwright who often assisted Mathews, collaborated on the project. The play begins when Jonathan Doubikins, the same character from *Trip to America*, arrives in England. He has been sent overseas for general "improvement" (*The Courier* September 4, 1824), but instead of embracing the culture around him and/or learning from Britons, he decides to use his time abroad to do research. He announces that when he returns to New York he will publish a travelogue based on his experience in England. In the beginning of the play, he and his slave, Agamemnon, arrive in Liverpool where they find Mr. Ledger, a merchant to whom Jonathan has been consigned. Ledger gives him a letter of recommendation for Sir Leather Grossfeeder, a rich Londoner. The night before Jonathan is to leave for London, two postillions rob the larder in his room. They have been in service at the inn for some time and feel cheated by the landlady; thus, for weeks they have squirreled away small items for their trip as just compensation. They open a compartment to remove their stash.

It is dark, the middle of the night. Jonathan hears the two thieves, but cannot understand what they are doing. He thinks they are after his money, which he has been flashing around (in typical American fashion) for all to see. He yells for help, and the two scurry off into the darkness. In the commotion, though, they inadvertently exchange letters with Jonathan. They now hold a letter of introduction to Mr. Grossfeeder, while Jonathan has one identifying him as a common lackey. The landlady enters to see what Jonathan is yelling about, though she can find no apparent reason for the tumult he is causing. Affronted by her lack of concern, he leaves the establishment for London. When Jonathan travels to London, with the wrong letter in hand, he is thought to be a postillion. The "usual mistaken-identity game now begins," says Hodge (73). For a brief time general confusion and mischief fills the play: the lackey travels to London as well and enjoys Jonathan's reception, although he is confused by the new employer's generosity and wonders why he is not required to do any work. Likewise, Sir Grossfeeder considers his new employee (Jonathan) the most insolent servant he has ever taken on. The play also features a rather standard subplot: a young girl, Mary, the ward of Mr. Grossfeeder, is unable to marry her beloved, William. In the end, Grossfeeder submits, the two are happily united, and Jonathan's real identity is discovered. Thus, says Hodge, "The plot is ... entirely conventional" (74).

Once again, Mathews relies on the incorporation of the travelogue to emphasize the comedy, albeit in a very different format than in *Trip to America*. As previously noted, Jonathan appears as a traveler in England. Though unfamiliar with the persons or customs and though planning to stay for a limited time, he is obsessed with writing his own travelogue. He enters all occurrences, and keeps notes on all he meets in a small notebook, which he keeps close to him at all times. This is a "revenge diary" (Hodge 74) of sorts; he makes his purpose clear, saying, "I'll touch 'em [the English] up in an atarnal manner that's what I will. My blud is up. I'm pretty considerable darn'd mad about that Mathers who I hear has taken me off at the playhouse, but I'll make the whole kingdom smart for it when my book is published" (ibid). Jonathan shows his peculiar, unwieldy, and uncultured American temperament here. First of all, he cannot even pronounce Mathews' name correctly. Though angered at the comedian, he cannot remember the famous man's name. He is quick to seek revenge, and undeniably painted as a hot-blooded yokel.

Jonathan writes everything down, and makes overtly sweeping generalizations about the English culture and people from his limited experience. Though he has just arrived on English shores and "han't put [his] foot ashore five minutes" (Peake 1),[28] he notes the lack of American luxuries and conveniences. Finding the Waterloo Hotel, for instance, he assesses its inadequacies:

> This here's the Waterloo Tavern — I see never a bar to it — [takes up a book and pencil] I'll lose no time in beginning my remarks on the state of the British nation — I've done the title page already — "Remarks on the state of the British nation, by Jonathan W. Doubikins, United States"— no bar, en! [Writes] "The taverns in the British nation, haven't got no bars" [Peake 1–2].

Moments later, unsatisfied with the chair brought to him by the innkeeper, he notes in his book, "No comfortable chairs throughout the whole Kingdom of England," pointedly adding, "There's rather a slap for them, the sarpents!" (Peake 2). Upon being introduced to the innkeeper, Tidy, he notes, "Tidy, oh! Tidy! That's information. [Takes his book and writes] All the head waiters in England are called Tidy" (3). Jonathan continues the work in this fashion, continually noting all that he finds inconvenient while abroad, making exaggerated and supercilious critiques in his soon-to-be published travelogue.

One might read Jonathan's furious note taking and mischievous plans to publish a revenge travelogue as Mathews mocking Americans' anger over *Trip to America*. Americans worried when he left the country. Later they were upset to see their countrymen and culture paraded on stage in a satire of national habits and manners. Was Mathews mocking the American reaction to his work? Was he suggesting that everyone who felt an amount of irritation over his show had to have been as immature and childish as this Yankee? If this were the case, he was surely combating the American public's feelings rather harshly, painting Jonathan as a yokel out for revenge.

The second way to read this mockery is to interpret Jonathan's actions as a condemnation of Americans' reactions to travelogues about their country. The American public was not nearly as concerned with reading travelogues as the British public was; on the whole, they were not interested in writing travel accounts either. What they were interested in was combating what they considered to be misinformation within such accounts. They felt that Americans were depicted incorrectly in many works, and they voiced their opinions publicly. Some authors published criticisms of English writing and traveling practices within English journals[29]; a few even wrote mock travelogues to show how the genre itself led to problems of representation.

Jonathan is obviously getting his information wrong. He is continually making incorrect assumptions and over-generalizing. Likewise, he has started his writing immediately upon entering the country. He has taken no time to get to know the people, nor has he experienced the country at all before he begins his revenge narrative. The point is that Jonathan believes that all travelogue writers employ the same practices. He thinks that if his country was not represented exactly as he would have it within a certain travelogue, then the writer must have used like techniques, and he is going to seek his revenge as cruelly and swiftly as possible. The implication is that Americans are not only vengeful, but naïve as to the "real" task a travelogue writer undertakes. Mathews' sense of both Self and national superiority become clear here. He assumes that the English writers could not — could never perhaps — have been mistaken, but that Americans must be simply acting in too sensitive a fashion.

The Yankee's worst fault in this work, however, goes far beyond poor writing and observation techniques. He is, again, a slaveholder. "It is the Jonathan-Agamemnon controversy over slavery and freedom," Hodge remarks, "that gives the play significance" (74). Similar to *Trip to America*, Jonathan's assertions on New World freedom and independence are clearly juxtaposed to American slavery practices. For example, after having gotten into an unprovoked argument with Mr. Ledger, Jonathan becomes angry. Taking his aggression out on Agamemnon, he spouts: "...[A] pretty considerably darned out of the way beginning I've made in this country, and you, you great stick of black liquorice [sic] — you great round piece of black spermacetti [sic] — to stand by and hear your boss abused" and he strikes the slave (Peake 4). Agamemnon cries at the blow. Tidy overhears the commotion and asks Jonathan to leave the inn. At this Jonathan bellows: "Du you call this a land of liberty, where I cannot larrup my own nigger without being ordered out of the house? Du explain to me the principles of the British constitution!" (ibid). But without waiting for a reply, Jonathan tries to sell Agamemnon to the landlord. The dialogue is telling:

DOUBIKINS: Here, you, Tidy, what will you give me for this black?
TIDY: Give you, sir?
DOUBIKINS: Yes, he is mine, you Tidy.
AGAMEMNON: Please buy me, you Tidy—me berry good nigger—I can fiddle like nightingale!
TIDY: You appear quite strange to our customs, sir.
DOUBIKINS: Your customs have got all my trunks and luggage—pretty considerable awful beginning, I guess, for quite a stranger—have you a pony that I might swop with you for the nigger? [ibid].

When Tidy throws Jonathan out of the inn for such behavior, the Yankee exclaims, "If I don't tell my Uncle Ben of this — to be turned out by an underlin — a help — a sarvant — a sarvant of sarvants is a slave to the devil! Come along you black scoundrel — if I don't complain to Congress — there'll be a war between the tu countries, and all on my account, oh yes" (ibid). Mathews and Peake were obviously interested in throwing a substantial blow at the American myth of egalitarianism and independence.

Jonathan's behavior continues in this way throughout the script. Later that night, for example, when Mrs. Lemon asks if the "black gentleman" would like a bed, Jonathan laughs and says, "I saw a nation nice place below for the black gentleman to sleep in — the water trough — I guess this black gentleman never slept in a bed in his life" (Peake 8). Jonathan is rough with his slave and he is mean-spirited towards him. At the same time, he also brags about his country's freedom, sings "Yankee Doodle," and touts jingoistic American sentiments. The point is clear. America is no land of freedom and equality so long as slavery is practiced.

This may have been "the first antislavery play," says Hodge (74), for Jonathan's worst qualities come out when he deals with his slave; conversely, Agamemnon is kind and pitiable. What's more, the slave seems far nicer than Jonathan. He gets along with everyone he meets and even treats his master — undeserving as he is — with respect. Hitting the political point home, Mathews and Peake constructed an ending that displays Agamemnon's triumph over Jonathan. A British (black) servant tells Agamemnon that he is able leave the Yankee immediately, for once he set foot on English soil he became a free man. Agamemnon's response is strategically trenchant: "Free—free! What is dat? In me hear de name in America—but me don't know what it is" (Peake 13), and once he is convinced of his freedom, he exclaims, "Oh, nice country, England—God sabe de king. Rule Britannia!" (ibid). In Agamemnon's mind (and surely in the audience's minds by this time in the play), England is far better country than America. It offers more freedom, more liberty, and more equality.

Not only is Jonathan a slaveholder, he is also a stingy capitalist. He is constantly concerned with money. When the two lackeys are trying to steal the lager from their hiding place, Jonathan is only worried about his own life and dollars. He is cowardly, quaking underneath the bedcovers, squeaking, "Oh, my dollars!" (Peake 9). He thinks the two might be planning to kill Agamemnon, but instead of showing any real concern for his slave, he quickly resigns himself to the idea: "Cut a piece of fat out of poor Aggy? What's to be done?" (ibid). Likewise, once he knows he is safe, the first thing he checks on is his money. His first lines after the incident are: "Oh, yes — my dollars are safe" (ibid). Immediately following these, come curses flung at Agamemnon for not waking up. He also throws about derogatory remarks concerning England. "Here's a cursed country," Jonathan says, "I will have my throat cut" (ibid). The joke is, of course, that the men are not stealing from him at all; it has all been his egocentric money-obsessed imagination.

Jonathan's (in)famous Uncle Ben also showcases this Yankee fault.[30] He has sold Agamemnon to Jonathan, first of all, under false pretexts. As in *Trip to America*, Jonathan has been cheated out of good money. His Uncle told him the slave was well behaved, but Jonathan finds him to be most belligerent. Likewise, Uncle Ben's sneaky, dishonest American tactics almost ruin Mary's future. Mr. Ledger is concerned because he received a clipping from a Baltimore paper saying that a certain American company he put stock in has gone bankrupt. Mary's fortune is lost. Fortunately for Mary, her fiancé William still wants to marry her. In the end, however, this entire newspaper story is uncovered as false. Jonathan's uncle wrote the article because he wanted to invest in the company and if he publicized the news that the company had gone bankrupt stock prices would drop. Jonathan summarizes his uncle's actions as "darned cute" and excuses his behavior to the astonished English subjects, "Lawks! Did your uncles never tell white lies? I reckon" (Peake 15). Although the untruth is discovered before any real mischief transpires, the older Yankee is clearly as money-obsessed as his nephew. Such plot devices clearly criticize American economic "norms."[31]

As in *Trip to America*, in *Jonathan Doubikins* the Yankee bears the brunt of English discontent with their "transatlantic cousins." Jonathan is not only a brute, but unaware of the culture surrounding him. As a traveler, he is rude and begrudging. As a non-fiction writer, he is dishonest, fraudulent, and belittling. As slaveholder, though, he is even more pointed. As the Yankee, Jonathan becomes nearly representative of all Americans. He is the foreigner and he personifies what Mathews and Peake consider America's political hypocrisy. Completely reversing the function of the Yankee character (as found in American plays), Mathews used this figure not only to satirize, but also to condemn American claims to egalitarianism, independence, and capitalism. What makes *Jonathan in England; or Jonathan Doubikins* particularly interesting to the theatre historian — and what gives it greater significance as to understanding how the American was constructed as foreigner — is its origin. Mathews and Peake did not constructed *Jonathan Doubikins* from imagination, but, rather, from a little known American work called *The Yankey in England*, written by Colonel David Humphreys. Humphreys was a Harvard wit and fairly well connected in the theatrical world, but although he seems to have passed the script to a few artistic luminaries,[32] the only production his play received was an amateur showing in his hometown in 1815. It is unclear how Mathews obtained his copy, but what is clear is that he did indeed have one, for Mathews and Peake not only used Humphreys' vocabulary list as a guide for the Yankee's language, but even published a version of it for the audience[33]; they structured the action of their play in a manner similar to that of the American version, and even stole dialogue verbatim from the unpublished work. But their actions were more than simple plagiarism, which was a relatively accepted practice at this time. Re-writing the Yankee's part at key moments, they specifically reversed the Yankee's function and, thus, turned Humphreys' play upside down. If one examines these key interventions, one finds how the Yankee turned from a vehicle of nationalism in Humphreys' play into the means of critiquing Americans in Mathews' version.

Jonathan was a foreigner in both plays; that is, he is unfamiliar with England within both works. But there is a clear difference between the plays in terms of his foreignness. In Humphreys' play, the Yankee is a version of the "Self" on stage, though he is in a foreign land; in Mathews' play, the Yankee is clearly the unwanted foreigner in an understood and known land. For example, Humphreys' work begins with the Yankee arriving on English shores, as does Mathews.' In Mathews' work, however, the Yankee's foreignness turns him into a blight rather than an idealized, if comedic, American. The Waterloo Hotel is featured in *The Yankey in England* and in *Jonathan Doubikins*. In both works Jonathan is confused by the customs he witnesses at this inn. In *The Yankey in England*, however, Jonathan's antics are simple cultural misunderstandings. Humphreys uses Jonathan's frame of mind, his very simplicity, to light-heartedly mock the English. Jonathan, for instance, cannot understand why the headwaiter will not take the time to answer his never-ending stream of questions. The Yankee barrages the worker with far too many inquiries, and Americans would have understood this as part of the Yankee's rural inquisitive nature. He is annoying, but not mean-spirited. He just does not understand that not everyone wants to take hours to answer his every query. Thus, when the waiter cuts Jonathan off, telling him that he will no longer speak with him, it is the waiter who looks rude, hot-tempered, and snobbish. Jonathan is the victim; the waiter is the impatient brute.

In *Jonathan Doubikins*, on the other hand, Jonathan gets himself thrown out of the hotel from his rude behavior, constant interruption, and slave-dealing. What is more, he deserves it. In Mathews' hands, the Yankee is the fiend. When Jonathan enters the hotel he yells to Tidy "Here, landlord! Landlord... Give me a chair!" (Peake 2). "No sir, here's the waiter," Tidy replies. Yet, although he has the wrong worker, Jonathan continues to barrage the Tidy. The dialogue following is compelling:

> JONATHAN: Little chap — head waiter — not tall enough to tie my tail, I calculate. D'ye hear? I'm just come from Varmount State, and ... I'm pretty plaguily tired tramppoosing the Atlantic — give me a chair!
>
> TIDY: Shall I show you to a room, sir?
>
> JONATHAN: Why, this is a room, isn't it? This will do well enough for me, till I goes to bed. Let me make an inquiry of you. I'll ax you a bit of a question, if there's nobody agin it?
>
> TIDY: Well, sir.
>
> JONATHAN: Is your boss a member of Congress?
>
> TIDY: My boss, sir? I don't comprehend.
>
> JONATHAN: Come, none of your gum — now, you are but an underlin,' tho' you are so uppish...— where's the chair?
>
> TIDY: Here's a chair, sir...
>
> JONATHAN: Pretty particular, damn'd considerable uncomfortable chair I ever sat on. Havn't you a one with a rocker?
>
> TIDY: These are the only chairs we use, sir.
>
> JONATHAN: Are you sartin sure of that?
>
> TIDY: Yes, sir.
>
> JONATHAN: Well, never mind...
>
> TIDY: You will doubtless excuse me taking the liberty, sir, but there is no smoking allowed in the Waterloo Hotel.
>
> JONATHAN: Oh! The dickens — I'm stunded!
>
> TIDY: It is considered a filthy custom, more honoured in the breach than in observance — this hotel is remarkably clean.... You still have got the cigar, sir.
>
> JONATHAN: Oh, yes. I'm like the Fultem steamboat. I can't go on without smoking, I guess... [Peake 2].

In Mathews' hands, the Yankee is rude, uninformed, and aggressive. He overwhelms the poor Tidy and refuses to modify his behavior in accordance to local customs.

There are other, more exact examples. In *The Yankey in England*, Doolittle, the Yankee of the piece, begins the play washed up on English shores after a shipwreck. He is described as "wet, in a sailor's dress, munching a piece of bread and sobbing" (Humphreys 19). He was on his way to London when an English vessel captured his American ship. Mistaking him for a British boy, the sailors press him. Perhaps fortunately, a storm suddenly comes up and the vessel is lost at sea, though close to shore. Doolittle is able to swim to safety. Thus, he begins the play sopping wet and bemoaning his fortune, which is now lost. All of his possessions are gone and he does not know how he will survive in this strange land. This is a young Yankee, merely a boy, and he has suffered tremendously on his transatlantic journey. Emphasizing British tyranny, Humphreys gives details of Doolittle's plight. He describes the Yankee's impressment at the hands of British sailors, evoking strong pity in the reader or audience. Explaining his capture to the General, for example, Doolittle claims that his captain could do little but give in to English demands:

> Opposition! What a rot could he du, when they turned right at us their great black bumbs and guns? Says they, "Cum tu, or we will shute." "Shute, and be darned, if you dare," says he; "but if you spill the deacon's ile, I'll make you rue it." And when they got abord, says they, "We want nun of your Yankey rue, or pork and lasses; but we will have that likely British boy" (meaning me) "whose name is not on your shipping paper, and who has no legal pertection." Says I, "I won't stur a step:" but I guess I was forced tu; and they got me so tight into their limboes and bilboes, that when I got my body loose, I looked nation poorly for a lengthy while afterwards ... [and then they pressed me]; and squeezed me tu into the hole of a ship, in the hinder part, named the poop. I bawled as bad as I could, and told them it was a tarnation shame to treat a true born Yankey in that sort of way. But they didn't mind it enny more than they du what the minister says in a gale of wind, as soon as ever the storm is over [Humphreys 42].

Imagining little Doolittle in tears on the English vessel certainly would have affected an American audience. Humphreys's little Yankee is a figure to be pitied; he has endured quite a trial at sea and now he has to try to survive in a foreign land.

Juxtaposed to this innocent Yankee, Mathews's Jonathan enters the stage space with a cigar in his mouth, furious that his luggage was lost on the long sea journey. He has also suffered a trying voyage, but his troubles stem from his obsession with money, rather than from a terrifying experience with British customs. Wanting to save money on his nephew's voyage, Uncle Ben has sent Jonathan over with the freight. Thus, he has been tossed and tussled in with the cargo, but no one is to blame save another Yankee. When Jonathan bemoans his fate, using the same words as Doolittle: "Oh, Jonathan, Jonathan, you'd a better a staid at home with your mother, brother Josiah, sister Deborah, cousin Jemina, poor little Aminadab, and the rest; not forgetting old granny, bent somewheres about half double — I'm dispurd sick of being in strange parts, tho' I hadn't put my foot ashore five minutes — I wish I was at hum again..." (Peake 1), the audience held little sympathy for him. Humphreys originally wrote these lines imagining a completely different scenario; Mathews' Jonathan complains with little cause. He is simply angry and rude.

Changes such as these make Mathews's intent and rhetorical position clear. Plainly voicing anti–American sentiment, Mathews reverses the rhetoric throughout Humphreys's play. *The Yankey in England* worked as a vehicle of nationalism. In the Englishmen's hands, however, it became a vehicle of political condemnation. It showed the Yankee in a very different light. Instead of the cute, little American who symbolized the new nation, in Mathews' hands, Jonathan became a vindictive pest. He became more than a Yankee in England, he became the worst kind of traveler — the foreign Other in England who had no taste, no tact, and no manners.

Interestingly, the English audience did not see *Jonathan Doubikins* as innocent, comic fun, as they did *Trip to America*. The main complaint: *Jonathan Doubikins* proposed that Agamemnon, the black slave, would be free upon entering English borders. One reviewer summarized the situation thusly:

> *Jonathan* is accompanied by his fat "*Nigger*" *Agamemnon*, and while talking of the Star of Columbia that protects them from Tyranny and Oppression in England, goes about seeking somebody to buy his black nigger. This was innocent enough;— however the black here gets his liberty. He is told that on putting his foot on English ground he is free; so he told his Master that "he had put his foot in it, and was free — but in America 'em knew not what *free* meant." Now *we* are not exactly the people who ought to sneer at other countries where the Slave Trade may happen to exist. The House justly was indignant at the point, and loudly hissed it [*The (London) Morning Advisor* September 4, 1824; original emphasis].

Mathews' criticism of America, it seems, went too far, and English audiences rejected the piece. The comedy crossed a line. At this key moment in the play — when Agamemnon rejoiced at his freedom found on English shores — English audiences saw Americans not as Others, but as political beings similar to themselves. The binary between foreigner and Self that Mathews' humor banked on, fell apart. The politics regarding slavery were too similar within the two countries for comfort. One reviewer, commenting on the "excited ... disapprobation" of the audience, noted: "Some jokes are too true to be forgiven" (*Globe and Traveller* September 4, 1824).

Mathews's comedy had struck a nerve, and his English patrons would not let it pass unnoticed. He had assumed that there existed a key difference between English subjects and American citizens, and, at least in this aspect, he was voted wrong. English and American customs were too close for one to be criticized without condemning the other. American practices, in other words, were not quite so foreign, and the attitude of American citizens not quite so different as Mathews had thought.

NOTES

1. If Americans had been familiar with Mathews' behavior backstage at various local theatres, they would have been even more concerned. Actor-manager Joe Cowell recalled Mathews' "irascible temperament" (Young *Famous* 773), recounting, "He was really an amiable, good-hearted man; but his nervous irritability — commenced no doubt in affectation and terminated in disease — rendered him extremely objectionable to those who were not inclined either to submit or laugh at his prejudices; and his uncontrolled expressions of disgust at everything American would have speedily ended his career, but that Price had managed to have him continually surrounded by a certain set, who had the good sense enough to admit his talent as ample amends for his rudeness. He actually came to rehearsal with his nose stopped with cotton to prevent his smelling the 'd — American chops'" (ibid.). Actor James E. Murdoch also commented on Mathews' rather snobbish (and anti–American) behavior, telling this anecdote: "One morning, in company with Mr. Mathews, I was rehearsing a farce of his in which there are only two characters. He was suffering from rheumatism, and not at all in an amiable mood. The smoke from the burning of some greasy matter found its way to the stage, at which Mr. Mathews cried out petulantly, 'Oh, dear! Oh, dear! What's that? Now that's unbearable! Such a stench! Where can it be from? Poh! Poh!' I told him that the stage-carpenter lived in the back part of the theatre, and I supposed the odor came from the kitchen. 'Ah, ah, that's it! That's it — beefsteak *done brown*. You Americans don't know how to cook; you *burn* everything up. You know the old story: 'Heaven sends meat — the devil sends cooks.' Hey? Hey?, I laughed, and we went on rehearsing. However, I had the better part of the laugh — 'in my sleeve,' as the saying is — for I knew the property-man was burning his lamp-rags under the stage (we had no gas then, but used fish oil), and the smell that had offended our olfactories was something widely different from the cooking of a beefsteak. Considering the Englishman's proverbially 'rare taste,' this did no credit to his sense of smell" (as recorded in Young *Famous* 773–74).

2. Travel to America had become very popular after the Revolutionary War, but dipped as the War of 1812 approached. After 1815 international travel not only resumed but increased in frequency. The onset of the Industrial Revolution meant that subjects were earning more money, so more could afford to travel at this time than ever before. This trend continued to increase until the 1850s.

3. Travelogues written about America focused on the social sciences as well as the political. It is interesting to note how the growing empire marked a particular country's "insufficiencies" by assigning a corresponding travelogue genre. For instance, while America was written about as a sister country, whose social and political systems demanded analysis, countries deemed more "foreign" and "primitive," like those peppering Africa, were written about in purely scientific terms. These people needed to be studied to determine how the climate affected their bodies, spiritual beliefs, and/or digestive systems, for instance.

4. This occurrence really happened. Mathews' ship did not land in New York because

just as the vessel was pulling up to port, the crew learned that there was a current yellow fever epidemic and so landed in Baltimore instead. Many of the occurrences within this play, in fact, stem from real events, through most are altered in some way to make them more dramatically interesting.

5. Mathews actually experienced a similar landlord while traveling in the United States. He was so bothered by the experience at the time that he mentioned it in a letter to his wife. It should be noted though that the landlord in question eventually relented and fed the hungry actor.

6. Making fun of the Irish was of course an old and favorite pastime of English comedic representations.

7. Of such stagecoaches, Mathews wrote to his wife: "No horrors can convey to you the horrors of traveling in this country. Though their winters are like Siberia, because their summers are like the East Indies, they only provide themselves about the heat. I don't believe there is a carriage in the country covered all over so as to keep out the air.... It is impossible ... to be warm" (Memoirs III 365; letter to his wife, from New York, dated February 7, 1823).

8. Interestingly, in his Memoirs Mathews praises Americans for their bilingual ability. Jokes made in broken English in *Trip to Paris* were far more successful in the States, he says, because the audience understood most of the French used in the script. London audiences were not able to appreciate all the humor, not being able to understand the language. So this critique is interesting — quite anti–American in sentiment, knowing his actual experience.

9. Mathews claimed, "I shall be rich in black fun" (Memoirs III 390; letter to James Smith, esq. from Philadelphia, dated February 23, 1823). While against slavery as an institution, Mathews certainly enjoyed the "constant amusement" provided by such "strange persons."

10. One should remember that interspersed with this action were "colorful mimicries, jokes, and patter-songs — half song, half dialogue" (Hodge 67–68). Though I have not noted the songs within the action, they certainly added not only to the amusement of the piece, but also to the anti–American rhetoric in the show as well. Hodge says, "Imagine the scene at Mrs. Bradish's Boarding House with its salty chatter about the boarders: "'I guess,' and 'I calculate,' here they're exclaiming,/ But still we can't blame them for that I will show;/ And 'I reckon' the Yankees we mustn't be blaming,/ For we have expressions in England, 'You know.'" (68).

11. It also included Hiram Peglar, a Kentucky shoemaker; Monsieur Capot, a French emigrant tailor; Miss Mange Wurzel, a Dutch heiress; and Mr. O'Sullivan, an Irish improver of his fortune. Hodge claims that the drama was constructed to "...show his [Mathews'] best characters in one scene" (Hodge 70).

12. Hence the title "All *Well* at Natchitoches."

13. One version of the script has him ending the play by saying, "if he can only make his friends smile when he gets back, he will never regret his Trip to America" (Klepac 120). Another account describes his ending comments as suggesting that he hopes this night of innocent entertainment will help bridge any transatlantic gaps between the two countries — that it will help heal any residual hard feelings.

14. Though a theatrical piece, Mathews had actually been to America and his audience was aware of this fact. They may have expected slight exaggeration, but — from this artist — they anticipated the truth as none other could give them. His comedies, they assessed, were amusements, but were funny because of their unveiled truthfulness.

15. Each work covers more than these listed subjects, but these seem to be the most important within the whole of their writing.

16. This omission is strange since nearly every travelogue on America concerned itself with religion at this time. Some were curious about the Quakers and appreciated their strange ways. Others were concerned with how democracy (lack of an established church) would affect religion. This is also an odd omission since Mathews was clearly struck by what he deemed odd religious practices in America. He notes in his letters that he met an African-American Methodist preacher, yet his comments are guarded, even then: "I shall be rich in black fun...It is a pity that I dare not touch upon a preacher. I know its danger, but perhaps the absurdity might give a *colour* to it — a *black* Methodist!" (Memoirs III 390; letter to James Smith, Esq. from Philadelphia, dated February 23, 1823). Did Smith, or perhaps playwright R. B. Peake, urge him to leave the subject alone? Also, to what danger is he referring? Would he have been deemed immoral if he made fun of a preacher?

17. If not the plot synopsis, a popular lithograph of *Trip to America* demonstrates this. The painting consists of all the characters Mathews played, in full costume (though they could not possibly have been this detailed in performance); below each is written a summation. (In the pursuit of brevity I will list only a few characters):

Baranaly Bray ha ha ha what a clever fellow that Jack is — the Boy'll be the death o' me he will ha ha ha. *Jack Topham* Well you Yankees ant so bad as I thought you were but I sh'd like to see one of ye eat a man, you know you always eat yr. Prisoners, at least I know you used to eat 'em all. *Jonathan W. Doubikin* (a real Yankee) I guess I'll go & call on my sweetheart Miss Mangle Wurzle I wish Uncle Ben would pay me that trifle he owes me. *Mr. Pennington* (Strictures on English Tourists) Independent Landlord — Want dinner do ye I calculate its just ½ past 4 & you want dinner 2 hours after all other Folk have dinned aye well I'll see what I can do for ye... [Klepac 49].

Each character seems to be able to be summed up by a line or two. Like a refrain, the characters come back to one particular aspect of the American character.

18. See my article ("The Yankee and the Veteran: Vehicles of Nationalism," *Journal of American Drama and Theatre [JADT]*, Spring 2001) for further explanation of this concept.

19. Mathews surely knew that the New England states were free. He had visited Massachusetts, Maryland, New York and Pennsylvania on his trip, after all. The choice to have a New Englander — specifically this Yankee character — own a slave was intentional. Not out of malice, per say, did Mathews make this choice, but from strong political convictions. He chose Jonathan, the "real" Yankee, the "authentic" American, for a reason.

20. After his death a proverb sprang up, which not only demonstrated the approval English reviewers gave him, but also which we might appreciate for its imperialist rhetoric: "Mathews — saw them; Mathews — was them" (Memoirs IV 471).

21. For example, Mathews played a Baptist minister in *Trip to America*, although he had never formally met the man. He witnessed the minister preach at a service and his performance was based solely on this impersonal interaction.

22. His career faltered due to his health and the English economy rather than his reputation. Mathews remained a popular star until his death. At this time though he needed to make a lot of money, so the obvious choice was to go to the United States.

23. Interestingly, Klepac downplays this event. He claims, "...the public was some-

what opposed to his appearances because of reports that had been told that it ridiculed the American way of life. These erroneous reports had confused *Jonathan in England; or Jonathan Doubikins* with Mathews' entertainment, *Trip to America*" (20). Klepac seems to take Mathews at his word that he was not involved in the creation of *Jonathan in England; or Jonathan Doubikins*, but if he has done so he obviously did not do enough research. Mathews, though he claimed innocence in writing *Jonathan in England; or Jonathan Doubikins*, was surely part of the process. Peake wrote him letters discussing the play and it obviously came out of his travels, since there are details in the play that seem to stem directly from his memoirs but do not appear in *Trip to America*.

24. Riots planned for theatres were often surreptitiously announced. Ladies were told not to attend or sent back home in their coaches. Likewise, the performer at fault was often notified through some covert means. Messages were sent through the manager or notices were posted on the doors. Most of the time the crowd wanted an apology or some other form of public contrition. If they got it, the show would be allowed to go on.

25. Eventually, and somewhat inexplicably, the crowd settled down. If Mathews made some kind of public apology, it is not recorded. When *Trip to America* was shown later that night, it had obviously been changed to suit an American audience. Hodge says, "On that occasion people laughed at the jokes, good, bad, and indifferent, and yawned where they found it dull" (72). Such a blasé response never could have accompanied the play in its original form.

26. There is good reason to believe that Mathews knew how angry Americans would be by his performance. A story that includes Washington Irving demonstrates the comedian's latent fear that an angry citizen would accost him. It goes: Irving happened to be in London for a showing of *A Trip to America*. He did not tell his acquaintance of his visit, but decided to surprise him at the theatre. After the performance, the writer sent word backstage to Mathews that an American wished to see him. When Irving appeared at his dressing room, Mathews was in "a state of excitement" which only calmed when he understood that his visitor was a friend. He cried "My God! Irving, is it you, my dear fellow?" At this, Irving smiled and chided him, "Confess that you expected to find a tall Kentuckian with a gun on his shoulder!'" (recounted in Hodge 72n).

27. Within the "Yankee Theatre" canon, there are four different versions of plays entitled *Jonathan in England*; therefore I will, herein, refer to this version as *Jonathan Doubikins*. The script is also noted as *Jonathan in London* by at least one 1824 newspaper. The only published form of this play available (that I have found) is called *Americans Abroad*. Although it is titled differently, it is obviously the same play. Perhaps when Peake published the work, he gave it a new title.

28. The quotations are credited to Peake because he is listed as the author on the only available published version of the script. Mathews was obviously instrumental in the formation of this work, though, so I will often note him as well in the body of the essay.

29. That is, they claimed that many English travelers did not travel enough to possibly understand the country before they set out to judge all American practices publicly. True enough, many English travelers visited only a few cities on their journeys; many more tried to interact with Americans as little as possible by bringing their servants along with them.

30. His Uncle Ben is clearly a Yankee, too, not only from his familial relation to Jonathan, but because he is noted in the script as having been baptized in New England.

31. The English public would have believed this was the norm, but, needless to say, that was not the whole truth.

32. William Dunlap mentions Humphreys in his *History of American Theatre*, and possibly even references this script.

33. Newspaper reviews mention this.

3

Gunboat Diplomacy on the *Kabuki* Stage: Okamoto Kidō's Construction of America and Japan's Deconstruction of *Pacific Overtures*

Kevin J. Wetmore, Jr.

Japan closed its doors to the west at the beginning of the seventeenth century, when the United States did not even exist. Almost two and a half centuries later, in 1853, President Millard Fillmore sent Commodore Matthew C. Perry with a fleet of ten ships and two thousand men to begin commercial relations with Japan. In his letter to the Emperor, President Fillmore listed four requests:

> The only objects for which I have sent Commodore Perry with a powerful squadron to pay a visit to your Imperial majesty's renowned city of Edo: friendship, commerce, a supply of coal, and provisions and protection for our shipwrecked people [qtd. in Perry 220–221].

Perry left the letter and went on to China, returning in 1854 to sign the Treaty of Kanagawa. In 1855 President Franklin Pierce appointed Townsend Harris as the envoy to Japan to negotiate a commercial treaty. Harris arrived in Japan in August of 1856, but was not allowed to enter Edo until November of 1857. Harris negotiated with the Japanese for the first half of 1858 and the Treaty of Shimoda was signed in July. Harris remained in Japan as Envoy until 1862 when he was relieved by a new envoy appointed by President Abraham Lincoln.[1]

Perry and Harris are arguably the two men responsible for the beginning of the relationship between Japan and the United States and the forced opening of Japan to the West for commercial purposes. Two plays have used *kabuki* to narrate the "Gunboat Diplomacy" of America in negotiating with Japan and to construct the role of these two men in the opening of Japan. Okamoto Kidō's *Amerika no tsukai* (The American Envoy, 1909) is a *shin-kabuki* play about Townsend Harris. John Wiedman and Stephen Sondheim's *Pacific Overtures* (1976/1984) tells the story of Perry from the perspective of the Japanese, but was not actually performed by the Japanese until 2000. The Japanese production of *Pacific Overtures* offered a very different critique of the United States than the American original.

Both plays are rooted in actual historical events, but contain gross historical inaccuracies in order to achieve the stated goals of their creators. Both plays engage the history of the opening of Japan through the use of *kabuki* theatre for the purpose of challenging and reinvigorating their own theatre traditions. Both plays are reflective of the context of relations between Japan from the Other's point of view: Okamoto Kidō places Harris at the center of his narrative and favors his perspective, Weidman and Sondheim use *kabuki* elements to construct Perry's arrival in Japan and the subsequent changes it brought by keeping Perry at a distance and instead focusing on two Japanese characters. In the 2000 Japanese production, and the revival in 2002 that toured the United States, the Japanese replaced *kabuki* elements with *nō* elements as a critique of both American and Japanese culture.

Okamoto Kidō (1872–1939) was born in Tokyo, studied Chinese poetry and English as a student and, in 1890 became a reporter and the drama critic for the *Tokyo Nichinichi Shimbun*.[2] Kidō, as he was called, began "publishing unperformed plays in theatre magazines" in 1896, which brought him to the attention of theatre impresario Kawakami Otojiro (Keene 420). Kawakami asked Kidō to write a play for Ichikawa Sadanji II (1880–1940), the *kabuki* actor who was also interested in modernizing Japanese theatre. While the proposed collaboration with Kawakami never occurred, in 1908 Kidō wrote *Ishin zengo* for Ichikawa Sadanji's *kabuki* company. It was the first of many collaborations between Ichikawa and Kidō, including the "major triumph" *Shuzenji monogatari* (The Tale of Shuzenji) in 1911 and a decade of historical dramas such as *Muromachi gosho*, *Sasaki Takatsuna*, *Toribeyama shinju* (Love Suicide at Toribe Mountain), and *Banchō sarayashiki* (Keene 421; Hisamatsu 314). Hisamatsu Senichi considers these plays to be "among the most outstanding of modern *kabuki* pieces," which are still performed in the modern repertoire (314). Although Kidō was also a novelist and short story writer, with over 100 works of fiction to his credit, he was a far more prolific dramatist, with 196 plays to his credit, making him the most prolific playwright of his era, and he specialized in *shin-kabuki* (Hisamatsu 314).

Shin-kabuki, a new literary form designed to modernize the *kabuki* after contact with the west, developed at the end of the nineteenth century and was pioneered by actor Ichikawa Sadanji II and "scholars and literary men who were not attached formally" to the traditional *kabuki* theatres (Leiter 356). Tsubouchi Shōyō, famed father of the literary *shingeki* movement, translator of Shakespeare, and founder of the *Bungei Kyokai* (Literary Theatre) wrote *Kiri hitoha* (A Paulownia Leaf) in 1884, considered by many to be the first work of *shin-kabuki*. He was followed by such writers as Mori Ogai, Matsui Shoyo, Takayasu Gekko, Hasegawa Shin, Mayama Seika and the prolific Kidō. Samuel L. Leiter in his *Kabuki Encyclopedia* considers Kidō "the representative writer" of *shin-kabuki*, one so famed as the master of the form that current scholars can refer to a period as "the golden age of Kidō" (286). *Shin-kabuki* was an attempt by *kabuki* actors and modern writers to develop a modern Japanese theatre based upon *kabuki*. It is written to "be acted by *kabuki* actors on a *kabuki* stage," yet takes as its subject matter the contemporary period and attempts to depict modern life (Powell 2). Samuel L. Leiter offers perhaps the most succinct definition of this hybrid form: "These works are written according to modern European dramatic standards, but are staged with *Kabuki*'s production apparatus" (365); naturalistic drama to be performed in a stylized theatre.

In 1909, the same year that Ichikawa Sadanji joined Osanai Kaoru to found the groundbreaking home of the *shingeki* movement, the *Jiyū Gekijō* (Free Theatre), Kidō wrote *The American Envoy* for the fiftieth anniversary of the opening of the port of Yokohama.[3] Kidō not only wrote the play for the commemoration but also to correct what he saw as a false historic record. Thirty-eight years after Harris left Japan an amateur historian named Dr. Muramatsu Shunsui moved to Shimoda. Dr. Muramatsu researched Harris and wrote a popular history, *Shimoda ni okeru yoshida shoin* (Concerning Yoshida Shoin at Shimoda, 1930), in which he argued that Harris had had a romantic affair with a Japanese woman named Okichi. Oliver Statler notes that Muramatsu's history constructs Okichi as a "national heroine," and presents a model of "Japanese womanhood sacrificed to a foreigner's lust for the sake of her country" (384–385). In other words, Muramatsu constructed an arguably orientalist history of Harris and Okichi. In his version, Harris's unreasonableness in negotiations was tempered by the ministrations of a woman willing to become his lover. Her sacrifice allowed Japan to enter the modern era.

Muramatsu's romantic fantasy served as the model for subsequent popular retellings of the Harris story. Songs, poems, and plays were written celebrating Okichi as the woman who made the Americans pliable in negotiations and Harris as the *gaijin* (foreigner) who loved her. This version of history

3. Gunboat Diplomacy on the Kabuki Stage (Wetmore)   53

even had influence in America, serving as the source for Robert Payne's novel *The Barbarian and the Geisha* and the 1958 John Wayne film of the same name based on the novel.[4] Kidō sought to counter this history with his version.

In his introduction to the English translation, Masanao Inouye states Kidō's intention in writing the play: "It is hoped that *The American Envoy* will serve as a remedy and as a corrective for the wrong impression thus being created, and that it truly represents the character of this great benefactor of Japan" (v). Kidō rejected the idea that Harris, an adamant Christian and the first American ambassador to Japan, would have an affair. Also of concern is the interracial nature of the relationship — Kidō may have been uncomfortable with the idea of a Japanese woman willingly entering into a sexual relationship with a *gaijin*. The play, therefore, offers an alternative reason for the proximity of Okichi to Harris and the events surrounding an attempted assassination of him. In fact, Harris's role as a diplomat and a negotiator are secondary in Kidō's explanation of Okichi's role in Harris's life.

The play is set at the Zen temple where Harris was accommodated while negotiating. Okichi, here called Omitsu, waits for Miura Shintaro, the son of Miura Yajuro, the Captain of the Guards at the American consulate and a guard himself. Shintaro is the one having the affair with Omitsu, and she visits the consulate to see him, not Harris. In other words, Kidō begins his play by offering an alternate explanation for the woman's constant presence at the consulate.

The leader of a group of *ronin* (masterless samurai) approaches Shintaro and asks to see Harris. Miura Yajuro orders the *ronin* to leave, affirming that "I have no intention of submitting blindly to foreigners," but if the consulate is attacked he will use his skills to defend the *gaijin* (Kidō 4). A crowd gathers to watch a flagpole erected and the American flag raised. Harris addresses the gathered Japanese, telling them, "America has no wish for war with Japan" (7). In a soliloquy after the crowd leaves, Harris's true character is revealed by his concern for Japan: "I must succeed because the whole world will benefit by this country opening her doors" (9). As in Aeschylus's *Persians*, Kidō pays his own nation a compliment by putting it in the mouth of an adversary. Kidō's nationalism allows him to show Harris having Japan's best interest at heart because of the innate value of Japan.

Shozo, the *ronin* who demanded to see Harris, reenters and attempts to assassinate him. The guards foil the plan and arrest Shozo, but Harris orders him freed as Shozo is "a noble soul" and "a misguided patriot" (Kidō 9, 10). Here we see Kidō showing Harris as recognizing that even those Japanese who oppose America are "noble" and "patriots." It is also a demonstration of how enemies can be respected and how those who threatened violence can be brought back into the social fold. We can read this as a metaphor for Japan's residual anger toward the United States over the end of the Russo-Japanese War and that despite disagreements, the two nations can work together for the betterment of both, as outlined below. The court translator enters and orders Harris to Edo (now Tokyo) Castle to see the *Tairo* (emperor).

In the next scene Omitsu, who is a servant at a nearby inn, overhears Shozo and his men planning to ambush Harris as he makes his way to the castle. She rushes to warn Shintaro, one of the guards accompanying Harris, and arrives to raise the alert just as the *ronin* attack. The guards protect Harris, who is uninjured, but Shintaro is mortally wounded defending him. Omitsu is then forbidden to attend Shintaro's funeral by Yajuro, who does not want it known that his samurai son was having an affair with a commoner. Harris praises Shintaro's bravery at the funeral and sets out immediately for the port of Kanagawa, which he has asked to be opened to American trade.

With the attack scene, Kidō not only raises the dramatic stakes, he is able to emphasize his stated goals: Shintaro's bravery and martial skills celebrate Japanese military prowess; Omitsu not being at funeral, but present during the attack also clarifies Kidō's position that Omitsu is not Harris's lover but the mistress of a guard. Kidō's narrative allows Omitsu/Okichi to remain a hero to Japan, but not for willingly submitting to a *gaijin*. Instead, her heroism consists of running to deliver the warning about the ambush, which kept Harris safe. Shintaro sacrifices his life and Omitsu loses her love so that the American may live and negotiate a treaty which will open Japan to the world. This explanation is preferable to Kidō than Muramatsu's, and serves Japan's national interests better at the time the play was written.

As the play continues, Omitsu, now mad with grief, is brought to her uncle's house in Kanagawa (again explaining her presence in the same area as Harris at the time). Hichibe, the uncle, is also the boatman responsible for ferrying people from Kanagawa to Yokohama. Higonokami Iwase, the Tairo's representative, Miura Yajuro and Harris enter the scene, looking to be transported to Yokohama. Hichibe, expressing similar anti-foreigner sentiment as the *ronin* earlier, refuses to ferry them.

To add insult to injury, Higonokami then explains to Harris that Yokohama, not Kanagawa, will be opened to America, and he is outraged. Harris demands that Kanagawa be opened. Higonokami resigns on the spot and threatens to commit *hara-kiri* for failing to convince Harris to accept Yokohama. Harris, impressed with Higonokami's fortitude and the strength of his convictions, and, by extension, the fortitude and strength of conviction of the Japanese people, immediately not only agrees to the change but promises to act as mediator should any other American object. Higonokami, thanking Harris, then rescinds his resignation and suicide threat.

Again, Kidō demonstrates that the American is impressed with Japanese martial culture. Kidō celebrates the samurai ethic, even in a period when the samurai have been outlawed, but Japanese militarism and imperialism has embraced samurai history and culture. Kidō seems to suggest that if Japan holds on to its national spirit and the character of the samurai, the United States and the west will treat it as an equal. Likewise, Kidō presents the American as a friend of Japan, not one that always understands or sees eye to eye, but one that can be convinced. Lastly, Kidō suggests that the world needs Japan and needs Japan with its martial samurai spirit intact. Harris's role was to allow Japan to assume its great role on the world stage.

Hichibe, impressed that Higonokami would commit *seppuku* in order to convince the Americans to accept Yokohama as an open port, agrees to ferry the men to Yokohama. Omitsu enters and, in her madness, recognizes Harris from the ambush and throws herself on him, crying out, "Give me back Miura-sama!" (Kidō 50). Yajuro states he was right to drive the girl from the funeral, but Harris intervenes and asks Yajuro to show sympathy to the young girl. The stage directions read: "*Omitsu clings to Harris who, unable to restrain himself any further, draws her towards him in a protecting manner*" (54). Harris's paternal concern for Omitsu is Kidō's way of explaining any physical contact between the American man and the Japanese girl. His embrace is "protective," not romantic. Harris then tells Yajuro that Omitsu is "an admirable girl and a worthy daughter-in-law" (54). Thus, Kidō refutes Muramatsu's national heroine who uses her body to help Japan in negotiations and replaces her with a heroine who sacrificed her lover and sanity to protect the life of the American envoy and, by extension, the eventual emergence of Japan on the world stage. She needed to give up everything in order to allow Japan to become an international, imperial power. Thus, Omitsu is also a model for contemporary Japanese: the national and international needs of Japan outweigh the needs of the individual. One's own desires and rights must be subsumed to those of the nation and the Emperor.

In the final scene, Harris and Higonokami arrive in Yokohama and Harris, upon viewing it, agrees it will make a fine port. Harris looks at the Pacific and closes the play with the words: "Here is the water which washes the shore of both Japan and America. May it forever preserve the peace and serve to strengthen and expand the interest of both nations as it joins them together" (Kidō 56). With these prophetic words, Kidō completes the transition of Harris as American negotiator and lover of Okichi to protective father-figure who admires and appreciates Japan and who understands the importance of opening Japan to the world and the reality of Japan's needs better than "misguided patriots" who would hold on to premodern values.

In 1909 there were still some negative feelings toward the United States about the Treaty of Portsmouth which ended the Russo-Japanese War, which the Japanese won. Forced by the American negotiators to give up most of their acquisitions obtained during the war, the Japanese felt the treaty was humiliating and displayed that the West in general and the United States in particular would not accept Japan as an equal. *Amerika no Tsukai* represented an attempt to remove lingering resentment and demonstrate not only the value of Japan's friendship with America, but that the two are equal partners in the world. Harris's willingness to back down in the face of Higonokami's threat, his protectiveness of Omitsu and even his recognition of the men who attacked him as "patriots" demonstrates a respect for Japan and the Japanese. Kidō's play, a *shin-kabuki* play performed by *kabuki* actors in a *kabuki* theatre, a blend of the traditional and modern dramas, was designed to encourage Japanese national pride, to erase lingering resentment over the Treaty of Portsmouth, to embrace the United States as (an occasionally misguided) friend of Japan, and to counter the popular history of Harris and Okichi.

The reality is that Harris most likely did have a sexual relationship with Okichi. Although no reference to her appears in his journals or letters, absence of evidence is not evidence of absence.[5] Instead, turning to the Japanese documents from the period, the Japanese negotiators discuss the affair openly. Okichi became an "attendant" in May or June of 1857 at the age of sixteen at the request of Henry Heusken, Harris's assistant (Harris was 53 at the time) (Gowon 249–255). She was responsible for teaching him Japanese manners, customs, and language in addition to serving as his "nurse." Her affair with Harris made her unpopular with her fellow Japanese and ultimately drove her to drink. She was eventually fired due to her alcoholism and sank into poverty and perhaps prostitution after Harris left Japan in 1862 (257). She committed suicide by drowning herself in 1890 at the age of 49. Harris himself died in New York City in 1878. Kidō sought to erase this history and instead create a nationalist heroine and an American envoy worthy of being an ally and friend.

Admittedly, the play is by no stretch a documentary drama. Many of the characters are entirely Kidō's creation: the Miura family, for example, is entirely fictitious. The actual captain of the guard was Ebara Soroku, whose son did not die in an ambush against the Americans. Harris did not agree to Yokohama because his Japanese counterpart offered to kill himself to atone. In fact, Harris was furious when the Japanese government refused to open Kanagawa and offered only Yokohama instead, but his protests fell on deaf ears and he eventually, after lengthy negotiations, he begrudgingly accepted the inevitable.[6]

On the other hand, some of the suppositions of the play are very historically accurate. Kidō has Harris warn Higinokami about the approach of

England, France and Russia. "The United States has no territorial ambitions," Harris cautions, "the others have. If you make a treaty with us, they can't do anything to you" (Kidō 30). While historic American territorial ambitions can be argued, Kidō emphasizes American lack of self-interest and a desire to ally itself with Japan. Peter Booth Wiley and Korogi Ichiro argue that in reality Harris frequently emphasized the threat of the arrival of the British and the French, who were already acquiring colonial territory elsewhere in Asia, which lead to the breakthrough in negotiations (476). While the specific assassination attempt depicted in the play did not occur, Harris and those who followed him as American emissaries to Japan were in constant danger of anti-foreigner violence. Harris's aforementioned assistant Henry Heusken was assassinated by *ronin* in January 1861, much like the attempt on Harris in the play. Yet, on the whole, Kidō's play, written to correct what he saw as an inaccurate history, was more inaccurate than the popular version he found so objectionable.

The Americans in Kidō's play are friends of Japan — simple, rude, and occasionally misguided, but ultimately worthwhile allies and friends. America is valuable to Japan not merely in and of itself, but as a catalyst that allowed Japan to rapidly modernize over the course of the next three decades and become the equal in every way of the western powers. Yet the Americans also needed to be shown when they were in error and Japan's samurai ethic and traditional spirit would impress those who did not understand that Japan was that equal.

Similar to Kidō, who sought to reinvigorate the theatre, critique the present and interrogate the past by writing a *kabuki* play using western-style dramatic techniques, Americans John Weidman and Stephen Sondheim sought to reinvigorate the theatre, critique the present and interrogate the past by writing a musical that incorporated *kabuki* techniques: *Pacific Overtures*. Weidman was a law student interested in playwriting whose father had previously collaborated with Sondheim. After reading Commodore Perry's journal, Weidman wrote a play about the opening of Japan and shared it with director Harold Prince. Prince suggested that Weidman rewrite the play "in Kabuki style (sic)" and that Sondheim supply the music (Gottfried 114). Jonathan Turnick, the Orchestrator, recalled that he, scene designer Boris Aronson, and Sondheim originally rejected the idea: "We didn't want to do a Japanese musical. We didn't know anything about Japanese culture" (qtd. in Gottfried 117). After much research and a trip to Japan, however, Sondheim, Weidman and Prince developed the piece into its initial form.

Pacific Overtures opened on Broadway on 11 January 1976 after previewing the previous December at the Kennedy Center Opera House in Washington, D.C., directed by Prince and running for 193 performances. The play was then revived in a much revised version in 1984 by the York Theatre Company, directed by Fran Soeder, which then transferred to off–Broadway for 106 performances. Most recently, the New National Theatre of Japan presented the play in 2000 in a production that subsequently toured New York and Washington in the summer of 2002 and revived in Tokyo in the fall of 2002. This last production was radically different than the previous ones in a number of manners, not least of which was that it was a Japanese production of an American musical about the opening of Japan by America.

Given the problem of the admitted lack of knowledge about Japan and Japanese culture by the piece's creators, a solution was suggested to shape *Pacific Overtures* that was unorthodox. Harold Prince states that the idea was "to tell the story as though it were written by a Japanese playwright in the *Kabuki* style, with the Americans as the traditional *Kabuki* villains" (qtd. in Gottfried 115). Weidman, Sondheim, and Prince "posited a hypothetical Japanese playwright who, they imagined, had visited America and then returned to his native country to write a Broadway musical," thus inverting the drama which is, in actuality, the construct of a group of American theatre artists who visited Japan and returned to their native country to write a *kabuki* play (Gordon 174).

Sondheim proudly proclaimed, "And that's how we prevented it from being 'The King and I,' because we're seeing it completely through oriental eyes" (qtd. in Gordon 174). Sondheim does not explain how it is possible for him to "see completely through oriental eyes," but one assumes that he believes he is not Othering the Japanese but making them into a Self by assuming what he believes is their viewpoint. Such naiveté is charming, but sets a dangerous mandate for the playwright attempting to view his own culture through the eyes of and give voice to a foreign Other. Despite the intentions of the creators, many initial reviews responded to the play with charges of orientalism, presenting an exotic Japan as pictured by the American imagination (Sasaguchi 27). Peter Marks called it "untrustworthy," noting that the play presented the narrative of the first official encounter between the United States and Japan "through the filter of New York writers purporting to tell the story from the Japanese perspective" (C1).

The play itself, while critical of the United States and Americans, ultimately fears what Japan will become. The main characters are all Japanese, whereas the Americans are introduced as "fairy tale ogres." The musical opens introducing Lord Abe (based on the historic Abe Masahiro), the "First Counselor to the Shogun," who makes Kayama Yaemon prefect of police in Uraga, off the coast of which American ships have spotted. Abe informs Kayama it is his job to tell the Americans to leave. The Americans instead mock Kayama and inform him that Perry will use his canon on Uraga if Japan does not open her doors to America. In addition to Kayama, Manjiro, the other protagonist, is introduced in the initial scenes.

Like Kidō, Sondheim and Weidman combine historical figures with fictional characters to create their drama. Kayama is based on the figures of Sakuma Shozan (1811–1864) and Yokoi Shonan (1809–1869) (Banfield 257). Manjiro is based on Manjiro Nakahama, also known as John Manjiro, a Japanese fisherman shipwrecked in 1841 and picked up by an American whaler. Manjiro was returned to Japan in 1851 and became a translator in the service of the *bakufu*. In 1860 he returned to America as the interpreter for the Japanese envoy to the United States. In 1864 he returned to Japan and became an English teacher in Satsuma and in 1869 he was given a post in the new Meiji government (Torao and Brown 172). Sondheim and Weidman's Manjiro believes the arrival of the Americans is a positive development: "Their coming here is the best thing that ever happened to Japan," although the other Japanese are not so certain (46). Admiral Perry, wearing *kumadori* makeup then performs an American pastiche of a *shishimai*, a lion dance.

The second act opens with the Emperor played as a *bunraku*-style puppet who proclaims Abe the new shogun, an American admiral (meant to be Townsend Harris?) enters and requests the use of a port by the Americans. Abe signs a treaty with him. A British admiral enters and demands a treaty port as well, along with a permanent ambassador. Dutch, Russian and French admirals follow and Abe is awash with treaties. Yet as more and more foreigners arrive in Japan and the interactions between the *gaijin* and the Japanese grow more complicated and dangerous, Abe plans to "appease the Westerners until we learn the secrets of their power and success. Then, when we become their equals..." (Sondheim and Weidman 99). The rest of the threat remains unspoken but it is clear that the Japanese plan to beat the foreigners at their own game.

The puppet emperor is replaced by the reciter, who becomes the emperor Meiji. He makes a number of proclamations that end the violence and embraces the barbarians, but his rise represents the manifestation of Abe's threat. Weidman and Sondheim blame Japan's subsequent militarism and imperialism on lessons learned from America:

> We will organize an army and a navy, equipped with the most modern weapons. And when the time is right, we will send forth expeditions to visit with our less enlightened neighbors. We will open up Formosa, Korea, Manchuria, and China. We will do for the rest of Asia what America has done for us [Sondheim and Weidman 102].

In this construction, America taught Japan how to be imperialistic and how to militarily, economically and culturally dominate less technologically advanced societies in the name of free trade.

This construct is borne out in the final song, "Next," which shows the rapid modernization of Japan, up to the present day, and demonstrates how Japan has become a presence in the United States and the world, citing such facts as the eight Toyota dealerships in Detroit or that Seiko is the third best selling watch in Switzerland. In other words, Sondheim and Weidman locate Japan's development after the Meiji Restoration in its economic presence in other nations.

The playwright that Sondheim, Weidman and Prince had imagined would have, out of necessity, not been a *kabuki* playwright but a *shin-kabuki* playwright. At the note at the beginning of the text, Weidman and Sondheim observe that "*Pacific Overtures* borrows liberally from the techniques of the Japanese Kabuki in every aspect of its production and performance (ix). In particular, they cite the practices of the *onna-gata* (male actors who special-ize in playing female parts), the *benshi* (a reciter), the *hanamichi* (a walkway entrance through the audience), and *kurogo* (black-clad stage assistants). In other words, Sondheim and Weidman do not appropriate the dramaturgy of the *kabuki* but rather its production apparatus and conventions. They did not imagine a *kabuki* playwright but a playwright who used *kabuki* techniques but western dramaturgy, much closer to *shin-kabuki*. Sondheim, Weidman and Prince imagined Okamoto Kidō. Even then, the writing of the play very much follows the form and structure of Broadway musicals. It is in the per-formative aspects, not the writing, that *kabuki* is appropriated.

The conventions appropriated, however, are not solely from the *kabuki*. The original musical employed a variety of traditional Japanese musical and theatre techniques. Ethnomusicologist Stephen Banfield observes that most of the music from the play comes from sources other than the *kabuki*—the *shakuhachi* flute is from "chamber music traditions," as well as the *nō* (278). Other music was appropriated from *gagaku* and *nō*. While the authors claim to be borrowing from the *kabuki*, in actuality *kabuki* is a synecdoche for all things Japanese in the production.

Even the *kabuki* elements are out of context and inaccurately interpreted. Perry is presented as "the terrifying *Kabuki* lion" (Gordon 194). Gordon asserts, "In the *Kabuki*, the lion dance is an accepted expression of victory" (194).[7] Actually, the *Shakkyo mono* (Lion pieces, but literally "stone bridge plays") are a group of dance plays based on the *nō* play *Shakkyo* ("The Stone Bridge"). Although some male lion dances exist, such as in *Kagamijishi* and *Renjishi*, typically the lion dance is a two part story danced by an *onna-gata*, telling the story of a woman who becomes possessed by the spirit of a lion (Leiter 347). While visually striking, Perry's victory dance as a lion dance is *kabuki* completely out of context. Given these facts, it might be better to categorize *Pacific Overtures* as mock *shin-kabuki* rather than mock *kabuki*.

The response of scholars and supporters of Sondheim, however, is to equate *kabuki* with Broadway: *kabuki* is to Japan what Broadway is to the United States. Stephen Banfield states:

> Underlying all this one can see how Kabuki itself runs parallel to the techniques of Broadway. It is a flamboyant form of musical theatre, roughly as old as Western opera, thriving on singing, playing, dance, spectacle, costume, star actors, titillation (the all-male cast is the outcome of a travesty role tradition) [278–279].

Ignoring the historical inaccuracies of Banfield's statement (the development of the *onna-gata* is far more socially complex than a "travesty role tradition," and is directly linked to the banning of women and young boys from the stage as a result of their links to prostitution), he engages the *kabuki* from a formal perspective, arguing that the similarities between the two allow Weidman and Sondheim to make a *kabuki* musical that is not cultural appropriation. However, the fact that *kabuki* and musicals may have some formal elements in common does not remove the orientalism inherent in *Pacific Overtures.* Joanne Gordon makes a similar argument, also seeing *kabuki* in Broadway:

> *Kabuki* is an eclectic theater of the common people, in its popularity, its emphasis on pure entertainment, its elaborate costumes, large stage, choreography, and music, it clearly has much in common with its American counterpart [178].

While there are certainly external similarities between *kabuki* and Broadway, to conflate the two as Banfield and Gordon do is to ignore the unique cultural context of both. While certainly novel, *Pacific Overtures* remains cultural appropriation by Americans to tell the story of the opening of Japan from a supposed Japanese perspective. Walter Kerr, in his review of the 1976 production, asked, "Why tell their story their way, when they'd do it better?" (qtd. in Brantley E1).

Seemingly in response to this question, Miyamoto Amon directed *Pacific Overtures* at the Tokyo New National Theatre in 2000, the first musical to be staged in that theatre. Miyamoto debuted as a director with *I Got Merman*, a three-actress musical that told the story of Ethel Merman, and since then has become one of the preeminent musical directors in Japan (Takashima 13). *Taiheyo Jokyoku*, translated into Japanese by Hashimoto Kunihiko, means literally "Pacific Overture" in the musical sense — a composition about the ocean. What is missing is the English secondary meaning of the word "pacific," meaning peaceful, and "overtures," meaning initial offers at contact. The title of the Sondheim and Weidman musical actually comes from Perry's journal in which he wrote on 16 July 1853, "I am moved to hope the Japanese will voluntarily accept the reasonable and pacific overtures embodied in our friendly letter" (105).

Taiheyo Jokyoku premiered at the New National Theatre in 2000. Remounted in Tokyo again in 2002, the production then was presented 9–13 July at the Lincoln Center Festival in New York before moving to the Sondheim Celebration at the Kennedy Center in Washington, D.C., 3–8 September and finally returning to Japan for a final run at the New National Theatre from 11 to 31 October of that year.

Sondheim and Weidman wrote conventions of *kabuki* into a Broadway musical without *kabuki* dramaturgy. As such, Miyamoto replaced Prince's pseudo-*kabuki* staging with the minimalism of *nō* techniques in order to critique Japan and the United States from a genuine Japanese perspective. The set was designed to reflect a *nō* stage, removing Prince's *hanamichi* and relying upon the *hashi-gakari* walkway used in *nō*. Whereas the American productions relied upon *kabuki*-based spectacle, Miyamoto's production emphasized performance over visuals.

Miyamoto intended the production to indict both the United States and Japan for their historical sins. In "Next," the song which ends the show designed to demonstrate how Japan has become not only the equal of the West but in many ways its primary challenger for economic supremacy, Miyamoto projected images of the bombing of Hiroshima and Japanese military aggression in Asia during the Second World War. What was initially meant to celebrate Japan's technological and social advances became undercut by imagery showing the dark side of those advances and reminding America that its use of atomic weapons against Japan are also part of the complex historic interactions between the nations on either side of the Pacific.

Miyamoto also wanted to show how "nothing has changed since the black ships came," Japan is still a corrupt nation motivated primarily by self interest as is America (qtd. in Rothstein 3). Miyamoto believes the original Sondheim and Weidman production "was a warning about materialism" (qtd. in Rothstein 3), which was borne out by Japan's bubble economy in the eighties. However, he brought the production to the United States in 2002 because he wanted "to remind Americans of what they are still doing to aggravate the world situation by creating fear, antagonism, and chaos among other nations" (qtd. in Sasaguchi 21). In post 9-11 America, that was not necessarily a message that would be well received. Yet the production was a critical and popular success (as it was in Japan) primarily because the point of view of the play (the opening of Japan from the Japanese perspective) was finally being performed by actual Japanese.[8] Yet the unique message for the summer of 2002 was to remind Americans of how their intervention in Japan in the 1850s resulted in both the positive and negative aspects that resulted, including Hiroshima and Nagasaki. Miyamoto's production did not paint Americans in black and white terms, but did, from a Japanese perspective, indicate the culpability Americans must bear for the manner in which they interact with other nations, societies and cultures.

Interestingly, *Amerika no tsukai* was performed in America by Americans a few decades after its Japanese premiere. In 1934 the Japanese Students Association at the University of Hawai'i presented an English-language production of *The American Envoy*, which had been translated by Masano Inouye in Kobe in 1931 (Blumner et al. 39).[9] It was one of a series of English language *kabuki* productions sponsored by the JSA and marked the first production of Kidō's play in English or in America.

Donald Keene observes that in plays like *Amerika no Tsukai* Kidō moved *shin-kabuki* further away from its original form by eliminating the musical accompaniment and dancing common to *kabuki* and making his dramaturgy more western and naturalistic (420). By doing so, Kidō hoped to develop a more modern drama for a modern Japan. In contrast, Sondheim and Weidman added *kabuki* elements to the music and dancing of the dramatic structure and form of the American musical in order to challenge and develop that genre in *Pacific Overtures*. Both plays use the *kabuki* to explore the moments of first contact and negotiation between Japan and the United States in order to critique elements of their own contemporary culture. Both plays engage the issues surrounding the complex negotiations (both political and cultural) between the two nations. *Shin-kabuki* never developed past the first few decades of the twentieth century, although *kabuki* as a style for adaptation (especially for Shakespeare and Greek tragedy) has grown increasingly popular in both Japan and the west in the last several decades.

That an American musical appropriates *kabuki*, misrepresents it, and contains historical inaccuracies should come as no surprise. What differentiates *Pacific Overtures* is the critique that the show aims at America for its imperialist designs, cultural insensitivity, and lack of foresight and at Japan for its loss of traditional culture and becoming as corrupt as America. *Pacific Overtures* critiques the United States for causing the loss of Japanese traditional culture, yet it exploits that culture in order to present this critique to its American audience. Martin Gottfried argues, "Ultimately the show itself would symbolize the corruption of Japanese culture: the *kabuki* theatre made into a Broadway musical" (115). An indictment of the loss of *kabuki* because of American intervention told through the appropriation of *kabuki* by Americans is indeed the height of irony. By removing the *kabuki* elements and substituting *nō*, and by performing the piece in Japan with an all Japanese cast, Miyamoto Amon and the New National Theatre Company reinscribed *Pacific Overtures* into the indictment Weidman and Sondheim intended it to be, not just of America but also of Japan. The overtures of America to Japan in the nineteenth century were not very pacific, either in intent or execution. Sondheim and Weidman thought they were critiquing America, but Miyamoto actually did. On the positive side, a century and a half after Japan opened to the west, gunboat diplomacy has been replaced with theatrical diplomacy — an exchange of performances. We must now see how the law of unintended consequences that Miyamoto highlighted in his production acts out with this exchange.

NOTES

1. For information on Townsend Harris and the early history of American/Japanese negotiations the reader is directed to Griffis, Gowon, Harris and especially Statler. For information on the Perry expedition the reader is directed to Perry and Wiley and Korogi.

2. All biographical information taken from Hisamatsu 314; Keene 420–428; and Leiter 286.

3. The original Japanese text is available in *Gendai Nihon Gikyoku Senshō* (Tokyo: Hakusuisha, 1955). Masanao Inouye's English translation has also been published (Kobe: J.L. Thompson, 1931).

4. As with the drama under consideration here, *The Barbarian and the Geisha* also was created with a political purpose. The post–Korean war film with John Wayne as Townsend Harris was made when the United States was looking for allies in Asia to fight the spread of communism. In the even of any lingering resentment toward Japan for the Second World War, *The Barbarian* was meant to show the two nations had a long history together and that the United States and Japan could get along, as long as Japan knew its place and stayed in it. With Wayne as a synecdoche for American machismo, Japan is presented in a blatantly orientalist fashion — the very title suggesting the model for the behavior of the two nations towards each other, America accepting its status as "barbarian" so long as the Japanese are demure and submissive.

5. Two different versions of the journal have been published. In 1895, William Elliot Griffis wrote *Townsend Harris: First American Envoy in Japan* which was divided into three parts. The first part was a biography of Harris before he went to Japan and the third section concerns Harris's life post–Japan, both written by Griffis. In between was Harris's journal in Japan, divided into thirteen chapters organized around key events. In 1930 Mario Emilio Cosenza edited and annotated the complete journal, released under the title *The Complete Journal of Townsend Harris*, which is more complete than Griffis's version with more accurate notes. In neither version is any reference to a relationship with Okichi.

6. For full details on this history, see Gowon, Harris and *An American Shrine in Tokyo: Memorial Meeting for Townsend Harris Held at Zempuku-ji*.

7. One of the problems with the scholarship on *Pacific Overtures* is that few of those writing on the play have accurate knowledge about *kabuki*. Even Stephen Banfield, an ethnomusicologist specializing in Japanese music, has a limited knowledge of *kabuki* as theatre, although his is demonstrably better than most. Joann Gordon, for example, insists, "[*Kabuki*] is still the popular theatre of Japan," as if life had not changed since the Meiji period, nor were there any modern theatre in Japan (177). Given the costs of tickets, the term "popular theatre" in most modern nations is a bit of a misnomer — both *kabuki* and Broadway ticket prices move them into a more elite theatre, available to those who can afford the cost of attending and live near or are able to visit the major metropolitan areas where they are produced.

8. See Brantley, Isherwood, Marks, Rothstein, and Sasaguchi for reviews of the production.

9. Technically, Hawai'i was a United States Territory in 1934, not becoming a state until 1959.

4

"Gringo" Agency and Revolutionary Disillusionment in Rodolfo Usigli's *El gesticulador*[1]

Jessica C. Locke

It took almost a decade for Mexican playwright Rodolfo Usigli's *El gesticulador* (1938) to be brought to the stage, only to run for two short weeks in May 1947[2] before being banned by the Partido Revolucionario Institucional (PRI), at that time led by President Miguel Alemán Valdés. Its allegedly distorted depiction of the post–Mexican Revolution government earned the play the reputation, though perhaps unfounded, of being the only artistic work in modern Mexico to be censored for political reasons. However, while the text certainly evidences Usigli's criticism of the shortcomings of the Mexican Revolution, particularly by means of his demythologization of the figure of the Revolutionary hero, it also enacts a more profound inquiry into the theme of Mexican national identity in the post–Revolutionary period.

Set in 1930s Mexico, *El gesticulador* tells the story of César Rubio, who, at the beginning of the play, has recently left his job as professor of history at a university in Mexico City (presumably the Universidad Nacional Autónoma de México [UNAM]) and moved back to his hometown with his wife and two children. Disillusioned with the insufficient recognition and inadequate economic compensation he believes to have received as a professor, he hopes to use his extensive knowledge and research on the Mexican Revolution in order to establish political connections within his new surroundings, and perhaps even to help found a local university where he may serve as Rector. Shortly after the beginning of the play, fortune knocks on Professor Rubio's door in the form of Oliver Bolton, a U.S. professor specializing in Latin American history at Harvard University. Bolton, whose car has broken down outside of Rubio's home, is invited to spend the night with his Mexican colleague's family, and in the ensuing conversation between the two professors, Rubio seizes the opportunity to assume the identity of his namesake, General César Rubio, the Revolutionary hero whom Bolton has been researching and who had mysteriously disappeared at the height of the Revolution. The Mexican professor's seemingly strategic impersonation of this hero will eventually result in the play's tragic denouement.

Through the characters of Rubio and Bolton, Usigli presents a frank examination of concepts such as self-interest, self-reinvention, duplicity and betrayal in relation to the post–Revolutionary crisis in Mexican national identity. In this essay, I will examine how the figure of the *"gringo"* is represented in *El gesticulador* by exploring the multiple implications of Bolton's role as the catalyst both for Professor Rubio's transformation into Revolutionary hero General Rubio and for Usigli's critique of the ineffectuality of the Mexican Revolution. By elucidating the ways in which Bolton embodies an "Other" in juxtaposition to which Professor Rubio negotiates his own identity, I will show how Bolton's intervention in the play and in the life of Professor César Rubio facilitates Usigli's criticism of the shortcomings of the Revolution.

Concepts related to otherness, duplicity and simulation are at the forefront of many of the interactions between characters in *El gesticulador* and, in my opinion, are even suggested in the work's title. Though translated as "The Great Gesture" when brought to the stage of the Hedgerow Theatre in Moylan, Pennsylvania in 1953 (Bravo-Elizando 197, n. 1), a *"gesticulador"* is actually a person, *one who gestures* or *gesticulates*. The Spanish and the English verbs —*gesticular* and *to gesticulate*, respectively— are both derived from the Latin *gesticulor, -ari,* to make mimic or pantomime gestures,[3] or, by extension, to imitate with gestures. Furthermore, *gesticulor, -ari,* is the diminutive form of *gero, -ere* which, among other things, can mean *to interpret* or *play* a role, as an actor does in drama. *Gero, -ere personam* is *to represent a(nother) person,*[4] and this is precisely what César Rubio, the professor does in deceitfully assuming the identity of César Rubio, the Revolutionary hero. The former becomes a *"gesticulador"* when he begins to "play the part" of the latter; however, his actions will soon surpass their role as mere performance, and his *gesticulación* will ultimately lead to his death.[5]

Carlos Amaya, in his article "Desdoblamiento y pérdida de identidad en *El gesticulador y A pesar del oscuro silencio,*" uses the concepts of the Other, of literary doubles and of *doppelgängers* in analyzing Professor Rubio's reinvention of himself. According to Amaya, Professor Rubio's Other is the Revolutionary hero, and the former goes through a process of transformation at the end of which his true identity is supplanted with that of the latter.

The other turns into something which is no longer "strange" to the subject, but rather, a reflection [thereof], a Double of this subject [...] the main character, who has corporeality within the context of the work, splits in two, and acquires the identity of an abstract and/or legendary character who is his double in some aspects. In this splitting, the Other turns into his Self, and snatches his identity.[6]

In order to explain the "why" of César's transformation, Amaya cites, among other studies, Ralph Tymms' *Doubles in Literary Psychology.* Following his analysis of Georg Kaiser's expressionist drama, Tymms concludes, "[...] in expressionist drama the *Doppelgänger* is separated from the idea of the evil secondary self; for Kaiser even reverses the process by showing the *Doppelgänger* as a desirable alternative to the habitual personality, and one into which the unhappy hero hopes to transfer himself" (Tymms 121). In this sense, we may understand that Professor Rubio chooses — whether consciously or subconsciously—to assume the identity of the "other" César Rubio because of his dissatisfaction with his own reality. His failure to make a professional name for himself via his professorial role is neutralized when he is presented with the opportunity to become someone who *did* in fact make a name for himself: the Revolutionary hero whose name he curiously shares.

While I concur with Amaya's analysis of Professor Rubio's transformation into the "other" César Rubio, I would like to venture the idea that the former actually has not only one, but really two "Others" into which he wishes to transform himself. If we apply Tymms' abovementioned definition of the concept of *doppelgänger* to the characters in *El gesticulador,* then Oliver Bolton — the Harvard professor whom fate brings to the doorstep of Professor Rubio's home, and who will represent the catalyst for the latter's "gesticulation" and, ultimately, his demise — might also be considered a *doppelgänger* for César Rubio. Bolton, in Professor Rubio's mind, embodies what the latter is not, what the latter has attempted and failed to become, or what he cannot be because of his condition as a university professor in Mexico.

When Bolton first appears in the play, the differences between them become immediately apparent. As Carlos Coria-Sánchez incisively observes, these differences are, in part, marked by the juxtaposition of light and dark:

From the outset, Usigli describes the protagonist in a somewhat ambiguous way, as if he wanted to make us think of two different people living in the same person: "César Rubio is dark-skinned: his figure vaguely recalls that of Emiliano Zapata" [*El gesticlador* 118]. Emiliano Zapata was, indeed, dark-skinned, but he did not have the last name *Rubio* [meaning blond-haired, and often, by extension, *light* in general], nor [did he have] characteristics that identified him as light-skinned [...] Bolton, who is interested in researching the life of the Revolutionary general, [... and] who "is of a very sun-burnt *rubio*" [124] immediately marks, with his light skin, the dichotomy light-darkness which we see throughout the work.[7]

Coria-Sánchez' text deals more broadly with Mexicans' contrary or even negative relationship with their own identity, an identity which they define in terms of other nations' peoples and their identities, including those of Spain and the United States. He cites Samuel Ramos' landmark study *El perfil del hombre y la cultura en México* and explains

> The individual vision of Professor César Rubio is the collective vision of the Mexican [...] who feels inferior [...] Usigli manifests, from the beginning, the feeling of inferiority of the Mexican, who will use a mask to hide his ambition for power. According to Ramos, as well as to Usigli and to [Octavio] Paz, the inferiority complex has its roots in the Colony and in the Spanish conquest [...] "César Rubio is dark-skinned" [...], and represents the Indian race subjugated to the white, European civilization which imposed itself on Mexico. Bolton, who is "of a very sun-burnt *rubio*" [...], represents the "superior race," that has historically controlled Mexico; and it is he [Bolton] who awakens, in César Rubio, the psychic and moral imbalance which throws him emotionally off-kilter, thus reviving his sense of inferiority.[8]

However, it is clearly not only the color of Bolton's skin and hair, and his ethnicity in general, that could potentially make him superior to Professor Rubio in the latter's own mind. In fact, as Act I of the play unfolds, we discover that Bolton also appears to represent professional superiority, though the elements upon which such superiority seem to be based are multiple, complex and, to a certain degree, disputable. For example, one could propose that Bolton's academic affiliation not only with U.S. Academia but specifically, with Harvard University, is what makes him superior to César in the Mexican professor's mind. However, in my opinion, this is not the conclusion the author intended us to reach. Even if we avoid the obvious assumption that Professor Rubio worked at the UNAM — officially the oldest university in North America with an international reputation for academic excellence and, thus, a suitable counterpart to Harvard[9] — the play certainly alludes to the potential for excellence that characterizes Mexican Academia in general. Professor César Rubio, himself a product of the Mexican academic system, had amassed great knowledge on the subject of the Mexican Revolution, at least in part via that system. It becomes clear, in his lengthy conversation with Bolton, that he is, in fact, much more knowledgeable on that subject than Bolton himself or anyone with whom Bolton has come in contact. In fact, Bolton himself explicitly recognizes the superiority of the Mexican professor's knowledge regarding General Rubio, and perhaps, regarding the Mexican Revolution in general. He asks Professor Rubio: "Why are you so intimately informed about these things? [...] you have given me unknown details of the life of César Rubio that no historian has mentioned. What have you done to know [these details]?"[10] With these words, Bolton effectively confirms César's earlier statement to his wife Elena: "But don't you realize? There is no man in the world who knows my subject as well as I do."[11]

Nevertheless, despite such allusions to the potential authority of Mexican Academia in matters related to Mexican history, we cannot deny that the play does indeed present a criticism of particular aspects of the university at which Professor Rubio worked and, by extension, of Mexican universities in general. In the opening scene, after César accuses his son Miguel of having wasted his time at the university by involving himself in student protests and strikes and by failing to graduate (we learn later that Miguel studied for six years at the university at which his father worked), Miguel retorts that the years he wasted there were less than those his father wasted there.[12] The conversation between César, Miguel and Elena continues as follows:

> CÉSAR.—[...]I wasted all of those years to keep my family alive ... and to give you [Miguel] a college education ... also, a little bit, because I believed in the university as an ideal. I don't ask you to understand it, my son, because you wouldn't be able to. For you, the university was never anything more than a permanent strike.
> MIGUEL.—And for you, eternal slavery. It was professors like you who made us desire a change.
> CÉSAR.—Of course: we wanted to teach.
> ELENA.—The university gave you nothing, César, other than a salary that has never been enough for us to live off.[13]

Moments later, César presents a frank criticism of both his university and the situation of Mexican universities in general, and implicitly blames that situation for the financial, and even perhaps behavioral, problems he and his family (particularly Miguel) suffered while residing in Mexico City:

> CÉSAR.—[...]A university professor, with four pesos a day, which they never paid on time, at a university in decay, at which no one taught and no one learned anymore ... a university without classes. A son who spent six years in strikes, setting off fireworks and shouting, without ever studying. [...][14]

With this statement, César refers to two problematic aspects of Mexican universities that could be blamed for having undermined the intellectual potential of the Mexican Academy: the inadequate remuneration received by university professors thereof, and the number, duration, and severity of student protests and their impact on university life.[15] Of course, it is precisely the arrival of Bolton on the scene that allows us to put César's criticism into perspective, for we cannot help but notice the implicit juxtaposition of the two men's situations that is reiterated throughout the first act of the play. It is clear that both Bolton and Professor Rubio recognize the superiority of the latter's knowledge regarding the Revolutionary hero César Rubio. However, it is clearly suggested that, in Professor Rubio's mind, Bolton's professional situation is undeniably more advantageous than his own —*superior to his own,* in this sense— because his university provides him with both the potential for professional development and, perhaps more importantly to Professor Rubio, the economic stability necessary to further such development. This concept is articulated by Professor Rubio himself: following his wife's expression of concern regarding her husband's interest in becoming involved in local politics, César responds, "I would not have to do that if I were a university professor in the United States, if I earned as much as that *gringo,* who is fairly young."[16]

Professor César Rubio's allusion to the financial superiority of U.S. university professors is almost immediately followed by the first implicit reference to the Mexican professor's desire to transform himself into what the Other— Bolton —represents. César explains to his wife:

> I was thinking that perhaps ... you already know how interested Americans are in Mexican things [...] I was thinking that perhaps this man can get me something there [in the U.S.] ... a History class on the Mexican Revolution. It would be magnificent.[17]

In my opinion, this moment may be considered to be Professor Rubio's first step toward his future decision to take on the role of an Other. Although, ultimately, the Other into which the Mexican professor will transform himself will not be Bolton, but rather General César Rubio, the Revolutionary hero Bolton is researching, Professor Rubio's comparison of his own situation with that of his U.S. Other— his "double" who lives on the other side of the U.S.–Mexico border and who is interested in the same academic subject matter as he is— is what drives him to consider the possibility of self-transformation as a solution to his own troubled financial and personal situation. In toying with the idea of going to the United States to teach Mexican History, he alludes to his desire to become, in his professional life, *what Bolton is*: a Latin American History professor in the United States.

In this sense, I propose that Bolton acts as a catalyst for Professor Rubio's *"gesticulación"* and self-transformation prior to the moment other critics view as Bolton's catalytic contribution to that transformation, i.e., the conversation between the two men later that same evening. During that conversation, Professor Rubio, upon being promised a monetary reward for divulging what he knows about the subject of Bolton's research, gives Bolton highly detailed information about the Revolutionary hero César Rubio, information that the Mexican professor has acquired through years of research on the Mexican Revolution. But Bolton refuses to believe that César could possess such knowledge merely because of his research. He alludes to his skepticism by asking his Mexican colleague, "Why haven't you put all of this into a book?" Despite César's presumably ingenuous response —"I don't know ... inertia; the idea that there are too many books has prevented me [from doing so], perhaps ... or simply [because] I am not fecund" — Bolton simply responds, "It is not likely [...] I am sorry, but I do not believe it."[18]

Prompted by Bolton's repeated expressions of disbelief, Professor Rubio continues to modify the story of his knowledge on the hero, as well as the story of General Rubio itself, until finally uttering the words which will ultimately seal his fate: he claims that César Rubio, the Revolutionary, could be, "in appearance, any man ... a man like yourself ... *or like me ... a professor of the history of the Revolution,* for example."[19] The dialogue that follows seems to be designed to present Bolton as the true catalyst for Professor Rubio's transformation, and Professor Rubio, as a man who simply seizes the opportunity presented by the immediate confusion:

> BOLTON. — (*Almost falling backwards*) You?
> CÉSAR. — (*After a pause*) Have I stated it that way?
> BOLTON. — No ... but (*Reacting brusquely, he stands up*) I understand. That's why you have not wanted to publish the truth! (*César looks at him without answering*) That explains everything, right?
> CÉSAR. — (*He nods his head. With a concentrated voice, with his gaze fixed in space, without noticing Elena, who watches him intensely from the dining room*) Yes, it explains everything. The forgotten, betrayed man, who sees that the Revolution has turned into a lie, a business, could decide to teach history ... the truth of the history of the Revolution, couldn't he?
> [...]
> BOLTON. — Yes. It's ... marvelous! But you...
> CÉSAR. — (*With his strange smile*) Doesn't this seem incredible, absurd to you?[20]

I believe it is important to note that neither here nor in any other part of that evening's conversation with Bolton does Professor Rubio openly claim to be the Revolutionary hero about whom he and Bolton have been speaking. In fact, he does not even offer an explicitly affirmative response to Bolton's direct question: "You?" Rubio's ambiguous responses thus allow Bolton to interpret them as he pleases, and, as is logical given his professional aspirations, the U.S. professor chooses to believe that he has singlehandedly found the missing Revolutionary General César Rubio. For this reason, whereas Laura Rosana Scarano defines Bolton as "the active recipient of th[e] fiction that, successively, is going to be modified in its ending in accordance with the interests of its creator and the demands of its recipient,"[21] I consider Bolton's role to be much more complicit than that of a mere, albeit "active," recipient. I believe that Bolton, by interpreting Rubio's ambiguous remarks in such a way so as to fit his own professional (and ultimately, financial) agenda, actually acts as co-creator of the fiction that, as of the beginning of Act II of the play, will be perpetuated by Professor-turned-General Rubio's subsequent actions.

In this sense, I agree that the conditions necessary for the professor's self-transformation and subsequent demise do, in fact, most concretely come into being during, and as a result of, the fateful conversation between Rubio and Bolton. However, in returning to my idea that the first true moment of Bolton's role as catalyst for Professor Rubio's transformation occurs *prior* to that conversation, I believe that this initial moment of catalysis also provides the grounds upon which the concept of revolutionary disillusionment will be developed throughout the rest of the play. Implicit in Professor Rubio's discourse, after Bolton's arrival but before their fateful conversation, is the idea that *in Mexico*, the history of the Revolution — and the Revolution itself— was considered to be of little value, unworthy of consideration, given its failure to bring about positive change. The fact that Professor Rubio was unable to achieve success in his academic career despite the depth and breadth of his knowledge on the Revolution is reiterated by his acknowledgement that only *outside of Mexico* would he be able to put that knowledge to good use. This idea is echoed by Bolton himself:

> I am especially interested in the history of Mexico. An incredible country, full of marvelous things and monsters. If you knew how little is known about the things of Mexico in my homeland, above all in the East. That is why I have come here [...] my university sends me in search of information, and, moreover, I have a grant to write a book.[22]

First of all, this statement serves to highlight the contrast between Rubio's and Bolton's respective possibilities for professional advancement in the area of Latin American History. This contrast, in turn, helps to reiterate that *within* Mexico, being an expert on the Mexican Revolution is useless, perhaps even ridiculous, given the ineffectuality of that Revolution as it is presented in *El gesticulador*: in the end, the Revolution did nothing more than create an equally or perhaps more disadvantageous situation for Mexicans like Professor Rubio than the situation they experienced before its occurrence. In this sense, I concur with critic Pedro Bravo Elizondo's reading of one of the messages implicit in the play: "what I deduce from my reading of *El gesticulador*, more than the [fact of] the gesticulation in itself, as a defensive weapon of the Mexican — or of the Latin American — is the lack of opportunities for people like César Rubio."[23] The lack of opportunities to which Bravo Elizondo alludes may be — and oftentimes has been — blamed on the shortcomings of the Mexican Revolution.

Likewise, Bolton's statement also evidences the fact that the Mexican Revolution not only created an unfavorable professional and economic situation for Mexicans like Professor Rubio, but also, paradoxically, served as a source of profit and gain for foreigners — ultimately, for the Other. Professor Rubio cannot do anything *in Mexico* with his knowledge of the Revolution, but Bolton, in the United States, can symbolically turn the Other's story into gold: upon his return to the United States, he publishes a series of articles in the *New York Times*, detailing his interview with the "Revolutionary hero César Rubio"; we may assume that these publications subsequently brought him both fame and fortune, as the saying goes. Professor Rubio's transformation into his Mexican Other (General Rubio) has two clear consequences, both of which serve only to reiterate the no-win situation of the middle-class Mexican after the Revolution. By means of his transformation, Professor Rubio not only inadvertently allows another — his U.S. Other — to reap the benefits of his own research and knowledge on the Revolution; he also unwittingly sets the stage for his own death at the hands of General Navarro, the same man who, years before, had also killed the "real" General César Rubio.

For its part, General Navarro's intervention in the life and lies of Professor-turned-General Rubio may raise questions regarding the PRI's decision to ban public performances of the play, given that Rubio's assassination at the hands of Navarro actually seems to suggest that the professor deserved to be punished for betraying the truth of the Revolution. As Peter Beardsell explains,

> In his own defence [to the accusations made by the PRI regarding the play's anti-revolutionary nature], Usigli always argued the opposite: that *El gesticulador* is "una obra revolucionaria" ["a revolutionary work"...] since it favors the truth of the original Revolution and *attacks the falsehood into which corrupt individuals had led the country* [Beardsell 252].[24]

Beardsell also highlights the "apparent contradiction" that characterized the government's charges against the play by alluding to the implication, found among those charges, "that Usigli was attacking previous regimes (or Mexico at large) *on behalf of the present regime*" (Beardsell 252). Why, then, would the play have been banned by that "present regime"? Of course, in order to answer this question, we must take into account the implications of Navarro's role not only in the death of Professor-turned-General Rubio, but also, in that of the "real" General Rubio, who had been Navarro's commander. While Navarro may have put an end to the distortion of Revolutionary truth by killing the professor-turned-General Rubio, in having killed the "real" General Rubio, he had ultimately betrayed the Revolutionary ideals embodied by that "sincere revolutionary," as he is referred to by Octavio Paz.[25] In this way, Navarro's implicit role in the promotion of revolutionary values and in the denouncement of revolutionary betrayal is undermined, in retrospect, by his previous actions.

Though it may be believed that the multiple characterization of Navarro as hero and villain, and the apparently contradictory nature of his behavior, confuses the play's message regarding post–Revolutionary Mexico, I believe that it may actually be yet another way in which Usigli endeavored to convey the reasons for his own disillusionment with the Mexican Revolution in general. By insinuating that Navarro — in murdering both the "real" and the "false" General Rubios — acted neither in favor of nor against the ideals of the Revolution, but rather, out of sheer self-interest, Navarro is no more and no less guilty than Professor Rubio of allowing a lust for personal power to motivate his betrayal of the Revolution *as an idea* — an idea in which Usigli himself proclaimed his belief, and the failure of which Usigli never ceased to lament:

> My personal childhood memories authorize me to denounce, in the most emphatic way, this vertiginous struggle — which still reflects on us — in which, with all norms lost, the revolution was transformed into the wolf of the revolution. [...] A child of a generation that saw human beings dying and bodies burning in the city streets; who ate the unleavened bread and drank the vinegar of the revolution; who had no diversion or romantic escape other than the first World War, and who, because of this, believes in *the need for the revolution as an idea*, has, at least, the right to an opinion.[26]

It becomes clear from this quote that Usigli, like a large part of the Mexican population who had lived through the Revolution, was not against the Revolution *in and of itself*, nor was he against the original principles embodied by that Revolution. He was, however, critical of the Revolution's betrayal of itself; that is to say, the general betrayal of Revolutionary values by those Revolutionaries who acted primarily in the name of self-interest and the desire for personal power. As Gordon Ragle notes,

> Usigli (and many other writers in the thirties) sees the central fact not as the revolution, but as the revolution betrayed. Betrayal here is not only political but social. It is the failure of the Mexican people to discover in the revolution that which it never had, a clear set of principles upon which to base their regeneration — in so many words, a failure to justify the blood bath ["Rodolfo Usigli and His Mexican Scene" 307].

It is difficult, if not impossible, to deny that the topic of Revolutionary betrayal is clearly linked to that of self-interest in *El gesticulador*. I have already alluded to Navarro's betrayal both of his commander, General Rubio, and of Revolutionary values in general, as well as to Professor Rubio's betrayal of himself and of his family, of his passion and reverence for the subject of the Mexican Revolution, and of the concept of Revolutionary "truth." However, Navarro and Professor Rubio are not the only characters in the play who exhibit such forms of betrayal. Professor Rubio's son Miguel, for example, betrays his father at the end of the play, though he returns to his own ideals and his own initial rejection of his father's betrayal in doing so: near the end of the play, Miguel decides to take no further part in his father's charades and, thus, refuses to intervene in the imminent assassination of the latter. Furthermore, throughout the play, César's wife Elena and their daughter Julia betray their own values and beliefs in their willingness to carry on with César's lie. Finally, Bolton, who — we must note — had promised Professor Rubio that he would not divulge to his U.S. colleagues the "truth" (in fact, the *lie*) about what he learned from his interview with his Mexican colleague, soon betrays the Mexican professor out of sheer lust for personal recognition and economic compensation. It becomes very clear that both the Mexican and the U.S. characters of the play are not only capable but also guilty of such betrayal. In fact, betrayal is the one common factor which defines both the Self and the Other; it is, as presented in *El gesticulador*, a component of both Mexican and U.S. behavior in general. We may see, then, that though Usigli presents multiple critiques of what both the Mexican and U.S. characters represent, stand for or embody — though the Mexican characters may choose to "gesticulate," to imitate or mimic others, or to attempt to *become* another in order to further their personal or professional interests, and though the U.S. citizen may commit acts of personal or even cultural betrayal in the name of his own professional and pecuniary advancement (Professor Rubio says to Bolton, "You [in the U.S.] buy everything [...] codices, manuscripts, incunables, the archeological treasures of Mexico; you would buy Taxco, if you could take it home with you"[27]) — there seems to be a more broad criticism of twentieth century American society — "American" meaning *in all of the Americas* — implicit in *El gesticulador*. This criticism illustrates the egocentric priorities that motivate disloyal and deceitful behavior, and it serves, in my opinion, as one of the reasons for which this work, seventy years after it was written and sixty years after it was first staged, continues to arouse profound critical interest and inquiry within the Americas.

In the conclusion of his article "El concepto de la revolución y de lo mexicano en *El gesticulador*," Pedro Bravo Elizondo affords two different — though interrelated — messages we may potentially extract from Usigli's play:

> The transformations in our America [i.e., the Americas] are not brought about by individual heroes, but rather, by the will of the people. The dramatic quality of *El gesticulador* is undeniable. The re-reading of it leaves us with another impression regarding its message or its contents. But that is our fault, as we read history from different angles [Bravo Elizondo 205].[28]

First of all, this passage refers to a concept expressed throughout the play regarding the possible reasons for the failure of the Mexican Revolution. As many Revolutionaries ultimately abandoned the principles of the Revolution in order to achieve or attain personal recognition and power, thus neglecting "the will of the people," the Revolution in itself was unable to bring about positive, tangible and collective forms of change. In this way, the Revolution — precisely because it was dominated by people aspiring to become "individual heroes"—came to represent a failure in the eyes of many Revolutionary-era Mexicans like Usigli. Second of all, this quote, in alluding to "our America" as the collective entity of the Americas, evidences a reason for which Usigli may have used Bolton—ultimately a fellow "American" to Professor Rubio—to highlight not only the differences, but also, the similarities, that exist among us as *Americans*. In this way, pre-existing notions about what is foreign and what is familiar within the Americas are called into question and ultimately challenged. Certainly, *El gesticulador* forces both its Mexican and its U.S. audiences to reevaluate the "angle" from which we define ourselves and Others—the Other—in contemporary society. Herein lies the complexity, and the power, of *El gesticulador*.

NOTES

1. To facilitate the reading of this essay, I have translated all quotes originally in Spanish, both those from Usigli's *El gesticulador* (Ed. Daniel Meyran, Madrid: Cátedra, 2004) and those from Spanish-language secondary sources. The only exceptions are the quotes taken from Octavio Paz's *El laberinto de la soledad*, the English translations of which I have taken from *The Labyrinth of Solitude and Other Writings (The Other Mexico, Return to the Labyrinth of Solitude, Mexico and the United States, The Philanthropic Ogre)*, trans. L. Kemp, Y. Milos and R. Phillips Belash (New York: Grove, 1985). The original Spanish version of each translated quote can be found in the corresponding endnote thereto.

2. As Peter Beardsell explains, upon the first staging of the play in 1947, "President Miguel Alemán quickly directed that [*El gesticulador*'s] run should be limited to the theatre's typical length: two weeks." Furthermore, he adds that "when it was staged again a few months later the Federación Teatral effectively sabotaged its chances." "Usigli's Political Drama in Perspective," *Bulletin of Hispanic Studies* 66.3 (1989): 252–253.

3. Please see the definitions for "Gesticulor, -ari" in *Cassell's New Latin Dictionary (Latin-English/English-Latin)* (Ed. D. P. Simpson. New York: Funk and Wagnalls, 1959), and for "Gesticulate" in *Webster's New World Dictionary: Second College Edition* (New York: Simon and Schuster, 1984).

4. Please see the definition for "Gero" in the *VOX Diccionario Ilustrado (Latino-Español/Español-Latino)* (Barcelona: Bibliograf, 1999).

5. In his essay "Máscaras mexicanas," Octavio Paz alludes to Professor Rubio's gesticulation in order to make a broader statement regarding Mexican identity and behavior in general: "Through dissimulation we [as Mexicans] come closer to our model, and sometimes the gesticulator, as Usigli saw so profoundly, becomes one with his gestures and thus makes them authentic. The death of Professor Rubio changed him into what he wanted to be: General Rubio, a sincere revolutionary and a man capable of giving the stagnating Revolution a fresh impetus and purity. In the Usigli play Professor Rubio invents a new self and becomes a general, and his lie is so truthlike that the corrupt Navarro [the general who killed the "real" César Rubio and who will kill Professor-turned-General Rubio as well] has no other course than to murder him, as if he were murdering his old commander, General Rubio, all over again" (Octavio Paz, "Mexican Masks," in *The Labyrinth of Solitude* 41). The original Spanish quote reads as follows: "Simulando, nos acercamos a nuestro modelo y a veces el gesticulador, como ha visto

con hondura Usigli, se funde con sus gestos, los hace auténticos. La muerte del profesor Rubio lo convierte en lo que deseaba ser: el general Rubio, un revolucionario sincero y un hombre capaz de impulsar y purificar a la Revolución estancada. En la obra de Usigli el profesor Rubio se inventa a sí mismo y se transforma en general; su mentira es tan verdadera que Navarro, el corrompido, no tiene más remedio que volver a matar en él a su antiguo jefe, el general Rubio." Octavio Paz, "Máscaras mexicanas," in *El laberinto de la soledad. Postdata. Vuelta al Laberinto de la soledad* (Mexico City: Fondo de Cultura Económica, 3rd ed., 1999): 44–45.

    6. Carlos Amaya, "Desdoblamiento y pérdida de identidad en *El gesticulador y A pesar del oscuro silencio,*" *Revista de humanidades* 2 (1997): 12–13. The original Spanish quote reads as follows: "El otro se vuelve ya no algo 'extraño' al sujeto sino más bien un reflejo, un Doble de éste [...] el personaje principal que tiene corporeidad dentro del contexto de la obra se desdobla y adquiere la identidad de un personaje abstracto y/o legendario que es su doble en algunos aspectos. En el desdoblamiento, el Otro se vuelve su yo, y le arrebata su identidad."

    7. Carlos Coria-Sánchez, "El gesticulador: contextualización del 'yo' mexicano," *Cuadernos Americanos* 75 (1999): 211. The original Spanish quote reads as follows: "Desde el comienzo, Usigli describe al protagonista de una forma un tanto ambigua, como si quisiera hacernos pensar en dos personas diferentes habitando en una sola: 'César Rubio es moreno: su figura recuerda vagamente la de Emiliano Zapata' [...]. Emiliano Zapata era moreno, efectivamente, pero no tenía ni el apellido Rubio ni características que lo identificaran como rubio de piel [...] Bolton, quien está interesado en investigar la vida del general revolucionario, [... y] quien 'es de un rubio muy quemado' [...], marca inmediatamente con su piel blanca la dicotomía luz-oscuridad que vemos a través de la obra."

    8. Coria-Sánchez 213–214. In my translation of this quote, the page numbers I give for the citations from *El gesticulador* have been taken from the Cátedra edition cited throughout this essay. The original Spanish quote by Coria-Sánchez reads as follows: "La visión individual del profesor César Rubio es la visión colectiva del mexicano [...] que se siente inferior [...] Usigli manifiesta desde el inicio el sentimiento de inferioridad del mexicano que usará una máscara para cubrir su ambición de poder. Tanto para Ramos como para Usigli y [Octavio] Paz, el complejo de inferioridad tiene sus raíces en la Colonia y la conquista española [...] 'César Rubio es moreno' (p. 10), y representa la raza india sometida a la civilización blanca europea que se impuso en México. Bolton, quien 'es de un rubio quemado' (p. 30), representa a la 'raza superior,' los que históricamente han controlado México, y es él quien despierta en César Rubio el desajuste psíquico-mental que lo desequilibra emocionalmente reavivando su sentimiento de inferioridad."

    9. C. E. Castañeda's 1930 article "The Oldest University in America" reminds us that for centuries, the UNAM has represented a symbol of national pride and academic excellence: "By royal decree of Charles V given in 1551 the necessary authorization was secured for the establishment of a Royal and Pontifical University in Mexico. Two years later the university was officially opened with a regular faculty and a small group of students [...] some of the most illustrious men of Mexico and many who shed glory on Spanish literature, arts and sciences passed through the halls of this venerable university. By 1775, the time of the American Revolution, the University of Mexico had granted 29,882 Bachelor's degrees and over 1,162 Doctor's and Master's. It is worthy of note that at this time the thirteen American colonies could point to only two really old institutions of learning: Harvard and the College of William and Mary." *Hispania* 13.3 (1930): 247–249.

10. *El gesticulador* 140. The original Spanish quote reads as follows: "¿Por qué está usted tan íntimamente enterado de estas cosas? [...] antes me ha dicho usted detalles desconocidos de la vida de César Rubio que ningún historiador menciona. ¿Cómo ha hecho usted para saber?"

11. *El gesticulador* 129. The Spanish quote reads: "¿Pero no te das cuenta? No hay un hombre en el mundo que conozca mi materia como yo."

12. *El gesticulador* 120. The italics are Usigli's; the original Spanish quote reads as follows: "Miguel.—(*Mirándolo*) Son menos que los que *tú* has perdido en ella."

13. Usigli, *El gesticulador* 120. The original Spanish quote reads as follows:

César.—[...]Yo perdí todos esos años por mantener viva a mi familia ... y por darte a ti una carrera ... también un poco porque creía en la universidad como un ideal. No te pido que lo comprendas, hijo mío, porque no podrías. Para ti la universidad no fue nunca más que una huelga permanente.

Miguel.—Y para ti una esclavitud eterna. Fueron los profesores como tú que nos hicieron desear un cambio.

César.—Claro, queríamos enseñar.

Elena.—Nada te dio a ti la universidad, César, más que un sueldo que nunca nos ha alcanzado para vivir.

14. *El gesticulador* 121–122. The original Spanish quote reads as follows:

César.—[...]Un profesor de universidad, con cuatro pesos diarios, que nunca pagaba a tiempo, en una universidad en descomposición, en la que nadie enseñaba ni nadie aprendía ya ... una universidad sin clases. Un hijo que pasó seis años en huelgas, quemando cohetes y gritando, sin estudiar nunca. [...]."

15. The long tradition of student protests at public Mexican universities, and at the UNAM in particular, is one that has been carried into the twenty-first century: as we may recall, the protest of a tuition increase kept the UNAM closed for 292 days from April 1999 to February 2000 (see Marny Requa's article on Adolfo Gilly's lecture "The Long Strike at UNAM: Higher Education and the Restructuring of the Mexican State," which Gilly gave at the Universidad Nacional Autónoma de México on March 20, 2000 [<http://socrates.berkeley.edu:7001/Events/spring2000/03-22-00gilly/index.html#re sources>. Accessed Oct. 15, 2007]).

16. *El gesticulador* 129. The original Spanish quote reads as follows: "No tendría yo que hacerlo si fuera profesor universitario en los Estados Unidos, si ganara lo que ese gringo, que es bastante joven."

17. *El gesticulador* 129. The original Spanish quote reads as follows: "Estaba yo pensando que quizás.... Ya sabes cuánto se interesan los americanos por las cosas de México.... [...] Estaba yo pensando que quizás este hombre pueda conseguirme algo allá ... una clase de historia de la revolución mexicana. Sería magnífico."

18. *El gesticulador* 141. The original Spanish dialogue reads as follows:

Bolton.—[...]¿Por qué no ha puesto usted todo esto en un libro?"

César.—No lo sé ... inercia; la idea de que hay demasiados libros me lo impide quizás ... o soy infecundo, simplemente.

Bolton—"No es verosímil [...] Perdóneme, pero no lo creo."

19. *El gesticulador* 144. The italics are mine; the Spanish quote reads as follows: "[...] en apariencia, un hombre cualquiera ... un hombre como usted ... *o como yo ... un profesor de historia de la revolución*, por ejemplo."

20. *El gesticulador* 144–145. The Spanish quote reads as follows:

Bolton.—(*Cayendo casi de espaldas*) ¿Usted?
César.—(*Después de una pausa*) ¿Lo he afirmado así?
Bolton.— No ... pero (*Reaccionando bruscamente, se levanta*) Comprendo. ¡Por eso es por lo que no ha querido usted publicar la verdad! (*César lo mira sin contestar*) Eso lo explica todo, ¿verdad?
César.—(*Mueve afirmativamente la cabeza. Con voz concentrada, con la vista fija en el espacio, sin ocuparse en Elena, que lo mira intensamente desde el comedor*) Sí, lo explica todo. El hombre olvidado, traicionado, que ve que la revolución se ha vuelto una mentira, un negocio, pudo decidirse a enseñar historia ... la verdad de la historia de la revolución, ¿no?

21. "Metateatro e identitdad en 'Saverio El Cruel' de Roberto Arlt y 'El gesticulador' de Rodolfo Usigli," *Alba de América* 6.10-11 (July 1988): 204–205. The italics are mine. In the original Spanish version of the article, Rosana Scarano refers to Bolton as "el activo receptor de esta ficción que sucesivamente, va a ser modificada en su desenlace de acuerdo con los intereses de su creador y las exigencias del receptor."

22. *El gesticulador* 131–132. "Es mi pasión; pero me interesa especialmente la historia de México. Un país increíble, lleno de maravillas y de monstruos. Si usted supiera qué poco se conocen las cosas de México en mi tierra [...], sobre todo en el Este. Por eso he venido aquí [...] Entonces, mi universidad me manda en busca de datos, y, además, tengo una beca para hacer un libro."

23. Bravo Elizondo 204. The Spanish reads as follows: "Lo que deduzco de la mi [*sic*] lectura de *El gesticulador*, más que la gesticulación en sí, como arma defensiva del mexicano — o del latinoamericano — es la falta de oportunidades para seres como César Rubio[...]."

24. The italics are mine. Beardsell cites vol. III, p. 532, of Usigli's *Teatro Completo* (Mexico City: Fondo de Cultura Económica, 1979) as the source for Usigli's self-defense.

25. "Mexican Masks" 41. See note 6 for the full quote in Spanish and in English.

26. Rodolfo Usigli, "Ensayo sobre la actualidad de la poesía dramática," Mexico City: Editorial Sytlo, 1947, pp. 259–260; cited in Bravo Elizondo 199. The italics are mine. The original Spanish quote reads as follows: "Mis recuerdos personales de infancia me autorizan a denunciar del modo más enfático esta pugna vertiginosa — que se refleja aún sobre nosotros — en la que perdida de toda norma, la revolución se convirtió en el lobo de la revolución. [...] Un niño de una generación que vio morir seres humanos y arder cadáveres en las calles de la ciudad; que comió el pan ázimo y bebió el vinagre de la revolución; que no tuvo otra diversión ni escape romántico que la primera guerra mundial, y que por eso, cree en *la necesidad de la revolución como idea*, tiene, cuando menos, derecho a opinar."

27. *El gesticulador* 137–138. The Spanish reads: "Ustedes lo compran todo [...] los códices, los manuscritos, los incunables, las joyas arqueológicas de México; comprarían Taxco, si pudieran llevárselo a su casa."

28. The original quote reads as follows: "Las transformaciones en nuestra América no se efectúan por héroes individuales, sino por la voluntad de los pueblos. La teatralidad de *El gesticulador* es innegable. La relectura de ella nos deja otra impresión, en cuanto a su mensaje o contenido. Pero la culpa es nuestra, pues leemos la historia desde ángulos distintos."

PART II: CONTEMPORARY AMERICA AND AMERICANS IN WORLD THEATRE

5

Srbljanović's Ugly American: Simultaneously Constructing Serbian and American Identities

Melissa Rynn Porterfield

As the Balkan Wars of the 1990s drew to a close, the citizens of the former Yugoslavia were faced with the challenge of trying to construct for themselves a new national identity capable of containing both the country's rich cultural traditions and its nuanced history of inclusion and exclusion of its culturally diverse inhabitants, while still honoring the memory of the hundreds of thousands of its inhabitants who perished in one of the bloodiest civil wars in history. Like so much of the country's civilian infrastructure, its theatres and their artists had been all but decimated in the aftermath of the wars. As conflict in the region began to heat up again in the early 1990s, hundreds of defiant artists who had formerly fought to define Yugoslavia's national identity as the cold war ground to a halt were encouraged to flee the region and practice their theatre of dissent in exile abroad (Panovski 5). Disillusioned by the failure of their own society and the lingering effects of decades of war, a new group of young playwrights emerged in the mid-nineties who have since been referred to as the country's "lost generation" (7). Most of these writers were born under the rule of the former Yugoslavia but had spent the majority of their lives living in isolated pockets of ethnically cohesive regions. Unlike their predecessors whose works harkened back to the country's long and culturally rich past in order to find a cohesive national identity against which to hold the disintegrating nation up against, this new generation of playwrights, influenced by the hyper-violence of Western artists such as Sarah Kane and Quentin Tarantino (9), began to look to America and Western Europe for clues as to how to model their new nationalism.

One of the strongest and most public of those new voices was that of Serbian playwright Biljana Srbljanović. In 1999, in her acceptance speech for the prestigious Ernst Toller award, she expressed the identity crisis faced by so many of her contemporaries.

> Ladies and Gentleman, it is difficult for me to thank you for awarding me this prestigious award. For, who am I? My identity is stolen by world politics, national politics. It is definitely lost somewhere during the last war. I can't find it, no matter how hard I try. I can't find it at any "lost and found" office at the airports I have been to. I can't find it in any language, in any culture [qtd. in Panovski 10].

Srbljanović and the rest of the "lost generation" were awash is the wake of a tempest of shifting identities, and their solution was to retreat within. The works of this group of authors were characteristically darkly xenophobic, and post-modern to the point of nihilism. Critic Naum Panovski notes that their works had an almost obsessive focus on the "other," which is "mostly seen as an enemy, appearing as destroyers and conquerors. They are responsible for the disaster, for suffering... [Their work] is a bitter and shocking picture of a claustrophobic, desperate, and devastated environment offering no exit ... and one that seems willfully ignorant about others" (Panovski 9).

While playwrights from more stable countries are able to hold up their own national identities as a standard against which their creation of the American can be formed, Srbljanović's work is much more complicated. She is faced with the daunting task of constructing a stable identity for herself and the other citizens of the former Yugoslavia, while simultaneously constructing a depiction of the foreign forces that left the citizens of her country to perish in the wake of their own violent identity crisis. Because of this, her depiction of Americans is inherently wrapped up in her perception of the West as a whole; a fact that is due in no small part to NATO's failure to intervene during the early years of the wars and its final devastating decision to engage in the air strikes which crippled civilian services in already war torn areas.[1]

Resentment towards the NATO and the rest of the West, was at a highpoint in the former Yugoslavia during the 1990s.[2] Taking on the fictional voice of a kind of Yugoslavian Everyman—of Bosnians, Serbs and Croats alike—Srbljanović's "Diary of a Defiant Serb" reveals the growing xenophobic sentiments felt in the region.

> I hate Albanians because they are Albanians, Croats because they're not Serbs. I despise Bosnians because they don't exist, I can't stand the English because I don't speak their language. I curse the Americans because they're nasty to the Native Americans, I can't forgive the Germans their unification. I spit on Italians because they have better-looking ruins, the French really get up my nose with their French. Serbia makes me angry because it's small, extremely small, so very small for my incredibly big ideas.

Within this rant of pervasive hate for the foreign lies evidence of an element of self-loathing at the region's own failure to sustain a stable identity, and its failure to provide a cultural and academic life for herself as an artist and an intellectual. It is under this larger umbrella of hate for the "other" that Srbljanović constructs her version of the "ugly American,"[3] against which she creates a new identity for her own people.

Born in Stockholm, Sweden, in 1970 to a Montenegrin father and a Serbian mother, Biljana Srbljanović was raised in Belgrade and self-identifies as a Serb (Munk, "Beginning" 32). She is considered one of the finest Serbian playwrights, and is the author of *The Belgrade Trilogy, Family Stories, The Fall, The Supermarket* and *America: Part Two*.[4] In 1995, she completed her degree in dramaturgy from the Academy of Dramatic Arts in Belgrade where she is now a faculty member. Her first produced play, *The Belgrade Trilogy*, was written as her final project towards her degree and was produced at the Sterijino theatre festival and symposium, in Novi Sad, a city in the Vojvodina district (32). While the play was originally poorly received by the older, more conservative theatre audience there, it found its audience once the production moved to Srbljanović's hometown of Belgrade. Like many of her subsequent plays, *The Belgrade Trilogy* held tremendous appeal for the youth of the city who easily identified with the characters of the play (Munk, "Interview" 32). Erika Munk, an American theatre scholar and artist who visited the region several times during the 1990s, noted that Yugoslav[5] theatre of the early years of the decade was conspicuously silent on the issue of the war and its effects on its citizens. Their sense of identity remained largely intact, but cracks in their stoic façade were beginning to show. "Young men who fought in Croatia and Bosnia from 1991 to 1995 returned as victimizers claiming victimhood [sic]. An enormous silence, unbroken by artists, intellectuals, or the political opposition, hung over the repression in ... [the region] and fed its racism and viciousness. Then NATO brought the war home" (Munk, "Before" 1).

In the early years of the conflict, Belgrade had managed to escape the majority of the destruction experienced by the surrounding provinces as a result of the wars, but as the fighting moved closer to the city, its inhabitants, who had previously been able to hold the war at a kind of "safe" distance, were no longer able to separate the horrors of war and genocide from their daily lives. But by 1995, the year that *The Belgrade Trilogy* premiered, the citizens of Belgrade had begun to become more vocal about the war — in the streets and in the theatres. Citizens were forced, like the characters in Srbljanović's play, to choose sides in the deadly battle for life and national identity, or to make the choice to flee their homes and become one that the thousands of refugees who found themselves adrift within the borders of their own country or unwelcome guests in other countries. The segments of the population hardest hit by this mass exodus included the elite, young adults, artists, and intellectuals. Srbljanović's work came from her own experience of watching so many of her peers turn their back on their own country in order to survive. "There was this period when people were leaving all the time. I spent two or three years at the airport, at the bus station, saying good-bye to people, making farewell parties" (Munk, "Interview" 32). *The Belgrade Trilogy* couldn't have been more timely.

Set on New Year's Eve in three different cities around the world, Prague, Sydney and Los Angeles, with a final, short epilogue scene which takes place in Belgrade, the play shows us a glimpse of the life of three groups of Serbian refugees as they struggle to survive in their new worlds. The opening scene deals primarily with the difficulties faced by two Croatian brothers who, in order to make a living, have taken jobs as Latin dancers at a disco in Prague. The two argue repeatedly over their decision to immigrate and over the fate of those they have left behind. One brother in particular, Mica, struggles to assimilate into Czech society while maintaining his own, original identity as a Croat. While he is adamant that the two remain true to their roots, it is clear that he has become unsure as to what those roots really are. Referring to a man he met selling Christmas trees on the street, Mica excitedly tells his brother that the man was "one of ours. I mean, a Croat... One of us... I think he spoke Serbian, I mean Croatian. Whatever. The main thing was I could understand him" (Srbljanović, *Belgrade* 267). Srbljanović points out that the ethnic hatred which once ripped Yugoslavia apart at the seams must now be sacrificed in order to retain solidarity against foreign influences. In her vision of the world, it is only possible to locate one's own national identity when faced with the external pressures that threaten to subsume it. It is easier to be Yugoslavian abroad than in the remains of the former nation.

This theme of creating national identity against the threat of foreign intervention repeats itself in the second scene of the play, which is set in Sydney. The scene concerns itself with two young immigrant couples, one of which has a newborn baby. Each of the adults takes a different stance on their willingness to embrace the customs of a new country. Sanja, the mother of the child, is unwilling to embrace even the material conveniences of their new life and is resentful of having to leave her parents and grandparents behind. The child's father, Milos, chides his wife over and over again for her refusal to try to see the benefits of the capitalistic system in which they find themselves. The two even disagree over the name of their child. Milos wants him to have the name Johnny, while Sanja calls him Nikolas. Milos sees capitalism as their way to a better life and conflates the identity of Australia and all Western countries under the general umbrella of that economic system.

Though he seems relatively eager to assimilate to his new identity as an Australian, Milos recognizes the cache that an American sounding name might afford their child in the future, and insists, much to his wife's chagrin, that the child be called Johnny. As a refugee Milos's own ethnic heritage affords him no real benefit and because of this he is anxious to raise his son with the identity that will afford him with the most privileges; and in the domain of capitalism that identity is unquestionably that of the American.

It is in the third scene of the play, set in Los Angeles that we finally get a taste of Srbljanović's picture of the American, but its face is worn by two of her country's own people. The two immigrants in this scene, unlike their counterparts in the first two scenes, no longer self-identify as Slavs. In fact, in the opening moment of the play, Jovan and Mara recognize their common bond as pot-smokers before they realize that they are both former citizens of Belgrade. As the two share a bowl in the backyard of a house party they begin more formal introductions.

> JOVAN. Hi Mara. I'm Jovan.
> MARA. Jovan? You're one of us?
> JOVAN. [as he takes a hit from the pipe] Looks like it. Where are you from?
> MARA. New York. From Belgrade really. But I live here now. And you?
> JOVAN. I'm from here. I mean, I come from Belgrade, but I live here now. In Hollywood.

In contrast their fellow countrymen the first two scenes, Mara and Jovan do not reminisce about life in Belgrade. They barely acknowledge that it is their homeland, preferring to focus on their new and superior identities as Americans. The powerful pervasiveness of American culture is hinted at as the same discussions of differences between Croats, Bosnians and Serbs that have been heard in the first two scenes are replaced in this one with an argument over which American temperament is better: New York or L.A. even the music of the scene bears the undeniable mark of Western consumer culture. In contrast to the traditional folk and dance music found in the two previous scenes, the music of the third scene is a Beatles song. The two Slavs hazily recall the song of another "refugee" of sorts, Jo-Jo, from the hit "Get Back." As the two break into full voice for the amusingly appropriate chorus,[6] they are both are seemingly unaware of how the pervasiveness of American commercial culture has erased their own history, making it almost impossible for the two to truly "get back" to where they belong.

In contrast to the first two scenes, the Los Angeles scene seems to have the most in common with Srbljanović's own account of the mass exodus of her friends who abandoned their own artistic work in order to pursue opportunities in America. Sadly, as characters Mara and Jovan soon discover, in the country where capitalism is king, artistic jobs are even harder to find than they were in their war-torn homeland. Jovan is an actor and, like Srbljanović herself, a recent graduate from Belgrade's Academy of Dramatic Art. After some prodding on behalf of Mara, he reveals that only a few months after graduation he had already been cast in a commercial for Belgrade television. When he sings the jingle, Mara remembers having seen the ad for a garlic vitamin supplement on television there. He was also an active critic of the government there, participating in rallies and protest theatre. But ultimately it was his art that provides Jovan with the reason to leave his own country. He tells Mara the story of how, during a performance of a *commedia dell'arte* play funded by the country's Ministry of Culture which toured through out schools in Serbia, his cast was attacked by a student in the audience. Hurling racial epithets at them from the house, the student stormed the stage and the theatre narrowly avoided erupting into a brawl. After the performance the cast expected to receive an apology from the teachers for the behavior of their students, but instead they received a lecture. "She said we shouldn't have put on anything from Croatian literature. 'The kids hate Croats, you have to understand.' ... I should understand why kids want to lynch me — nationalism isn't forbidden in law.... I was fed up with everything. I was ashamed. Ashamed of my own people" (Srbljanović, *Belgrade* 302).

Jovan believed that America would provide the artistic opportunity and freedom that his own country could not. But this too proves disappointing, as America's art world was not as welcoming as he had hoped: Jovan has yet to act in America and finds little time to audition while keeping up with his money-job of moving furniture. Mara too has been disappointed by the lack of success in America's art world. Though she was a successful concert pianist before immigrating, she has not even seen a piano since leaving Belgrade, and, instead, waits tables at a local café. Unlike the characters in the first two scenes, who, despite other adversities, have at least managed to find more financial and material success than they had in Belgrade, the new Americans have not found the freedom of expression they have been searching for, nor the secure lifestyle that they believed that America would provide. And while they have found it easy to slip mindlessly into the comforting miasma of American pop culture, they are unable to forget that their own art has been paralyzed in this process of submersion. Both characters discuss the possibility of returning to Belgrade but quickly dismiss the notion, as the visas required for the visit would prevent them from being allowed to return to America. Unlike the immigrants in Prague and Sydney who are able to maintain their native identities in the hope of one day returning to their homeland, in Srbljanović's America the price of entry is a case of forcible cultural amnesia and the reward is artistic paralysis and minimum wage labor.

As midnight approaches in Los Angeles, we get our first glimpse of the "ugly American" of the play, whose identity is tellingly intermingled with that of the natives of Belgrade. A very drunk, very loud and very belligerent man stumbles outside onto the patio from the raging party within the house. Daca, who in the vivid physical description provided by Srbljanović looks more like an example of "euro-trash" than most Americans are capable of conjuring in their own imaginations, is a proud, 18-year-old American. But Jovan and Mara flatly refuse to accept the validity of that identity. To them, his name and his bad English (infinitely poorer than their own as immigrants) mark him immediately as being one of their native people. Even when he tells them he is from Tucson, they continue to question him about how he got to America. As they trade stories about their own long and arduous flights from Eastern Europe to the West coast of America, they turn to Daca, inviting him to join in their community of complaint, he responds,

DACA. What flight? I came here by car.
MARA. What kind of car?
DACA. (*proudly*) My old Man bought me a Cadillac for my birthday and sent me to my auntie in L.A. to see how it runs.
(*Jovan and Mara look at him in disbelief.*)
JOVAN. Hey, Mara, we must be really high.
DACA. (*very suspicious.*) Something not clear here?
JOVAN. (*sincerely*) Excuse me, but I really don't understand. How could you come to America by car?
DACA. Stupid question. What do you mean come here? I was born here.
JOVAN. Where?
DACA. In Tucson of course, idiot ... Arizona, yes? My old man emigrated twenty years ago. He knocked up my mother here, so I was born here, logic [Srbljanović, *Belgrade* 306].

Daca's identity as an American is troubling to the other two in a number of ways, the most aggravating of which is that he has made seemingly no effort to assimilate into the culture into which they have fought so hard to blend. His ability to claim American status has not been attained by his embrace of culture, as Mara and Jovan's own pseudo–American identities have been, but has instead been achieved by the simple fact of his having been conceived at the right place, at the right time. Despite the fact that, outwardly, he resembles the stereotype of the European more than they do, he has lead the charmed life of an American youth, which has long been the focus of hate and envy abroad. In contrast to Jovan and Mara, who recount the hardships that they have endured along their journey towards becoming American citizens, all that was required of Daca, other than the fortuitous location of his birth, was that he turn 18 — and drive the American car bought by his daddy.

But Srbljanović's condemnation of the American national identity does not stop with the assertion that it is a privilege too easily won and too ambivalently maintained. She is interested in critiquing the power that it affords those who wield it. When Mara makes the mistake of giggling at Daca's inaptitude with English, he violently turns on the two, calling her a cunt. Jovan admirably sticks up for her and demands that Daca leave her alone, but the damage has been done. The American has been insulted — and retaliation, in American terms, requires force. Daca issues an ultimatum to Jovan: either defend what is his (in this case "his" woman) or stand aside and let someone else have it.

> DACA. Shut your face, cunt ... [to Jovan] If you want to give the girl one, all you have to say to me is: "Piss off, dude, I want a fuck..." (*Jovan and Mara are shocked. Daca becomes more and more aggressive*) But if you don't intend to fuck her, and it's my presence that bothers you, then we have a problem.
> JOVAN. Oh really? What happens then?
> DACA. (*smiling as he pulls out a huge pistol*) Then I'll blow you away [Srbljanović, Belgrade 308–309].

At the top of his lungs Daca chastises Jovan for his failure to be a man and for his choice to forsake his Slavic identity; an identity which Daca feels that he, despite his American citizenship, is more knowledgeable of than the former Slavs themselves. Screaming, Daca asserts his own cultural authority, to the confused and frightened pair that he holds within his sights.

> DACA. I'm one of the Zemun mob, you know. Know what that is, you ape? I'm not like these American fuckers. I know who I am and where I come from. I visit my grandparents every summer and meet up with the gang. So that my roots don't wither and so I don't forget what seed I come from [Srbljanović, Belgrade 309].

Yet when he demands to know where exactly Jovan is from, Daca is forced to admit that he has never heard of that area of Belgrade. This incongruity between the native, cultural identity encouraged in Daca and the cultural amnesia required of Jovan and Mara, parallels the precarious position of immigrants in our nation. As is so often the case in America, we encourage our own citizens to be proud of their national and ethnic heritages in order to support the fallacious image of our country as a welcoming melting pot of varied cultures, yet simultaneously we require those that we allow onto our welcoming shores to discard as much of their native culture as is possible in order to prove their willingness to be truly American.

The violence of the scene elevates from there as Daca threatens and terrorizes the two at gunpoint until the terrified Jovan urinates in his pants. That, it appears, is enough for Daca. He quickly dismisses the notion of raping Mara as he had previously threatened, because, as he maintains, she's a slut and not really his type anyway. Humiliating Jovan by asserting his own hyper-violent masculinity and his rock solid cultural identity seems to have been his goal all along, and once the terrified Croat has been threatened into submission by the dominant American, the cultural hierarchy has been rightly re-ordered to reflect American superiority.

But, as is the case with so many of Srbljanović's characters, Daca's identity is a complicated one. Just as Jovan and Mara's Slavic identities are, in part, defined by their relative comparison against those of the West, Daca's American identity is defined in part by his Eastern roots. His cultural position as playground bully affords him the kind of unwarranted superiority which is achieved through threats of violence without having to take any significant action. His character is symbolic of the widespread international view of America in the 1990s, as being a nation who was[7] willing to hold weaker nations under the threatening thumb of our perceived, superior military prowess while simultaneously drowning them in a wave of our own consumer-based culture of capitalism.[8] Daca, who was not born in Yugoslavia, purports to instruct the foreigners on how the correct way to embody their own national identity, while failing to note the incongruities of his own identity as an American who is more proud of his ethnic heritage than his actual citizenship. For Srbljanović he is the personification of the popular view of America as the policeman of the world: a powerful martial entity, whose threats are intended only to shore up its own national identity — not to protect and serve. For the audience, Daca's American identity is formed in direct opposition to the weaker foreigners whom he both instructs and terrorizes.

The end of the scene bears an eerie resemblance of the American-led NATO bombings of Belgrade and other Slavic cities in an attempt to end the war and genocide that had raged unchecked in the region for so long. While Jovan and Mara cower in a pool of their own urine on the patio, Daca turns his back on them and begins to walk away, bragging of his own skills as a marksman. As he sets his gun down on a nearby table, it accidentally goes off, shooting Jovan in the head. When Mara wails that he has killed Jovan, Daca callously responds that it was an accident. The scene ends with Mara crying over the body of her dead countryman, and Daca coolly returning to the party inside. Srbljanović parallels Daca's cruel indifference to the result of his fatal action with America's lack of concern for the "collateral damage" inflicted during the devastating NATO bombings of the region during 1994 and 1995. The air strikes approved by President Clinton and were allegedly intended to strategically take out Serbian military targets while avoiding heavily populated civilian area. Instead they succeeded in decimating civilian and humanitarian services in Belgrade, Sarajevo and other metropolitan areas, and were responsible for the deaths of thousands of innocent men, women and children. Despite that, American military leaders characterized the bombings as a successful and necessary step in securing the safety of the region.[9]

The success of *The Belgrade Trilogy* assured Srbljanović a career as a playwright in her own country, but her success abroad was built on more than simply the strength of her writing. Her renown on the international stage was due, in part, to her own identity as a Serbian artist who did not flee the country during the wars. The sheer lack of playwrights who remained in the region alone afforded her an advantage in the battle for recognition. But beyond that, Srbljanović gained additional international attention for her first hand account of the siege in Belgrade, which was published in English in *The Guardian* under the title "Diary of a Defiant Serb." During the third Balkan war, the American media was eager to secure first hand accounts of life in the war-torn region. As the siege wore on, American newspapers, magazines and journals clamored for stories of civilians struggling to survive in the most deplorable of circumstances, and during the sieges in Sarajevo and Belgrade their frenzy intensified.[10] The most prized of these accounts were those that came from children and young adults. Long after the Dayton Accord issued in a period of relative peace in the region, American publishers continued to solicit for translations of journals kept by those who were behind the lines of the sieges. Despite her own protestations of embarrassment over the work for its overly emotional content (Munk, "Beginning" 30), "Diary of a Defiant Serb," brought Srbljanović a new level of international recognition, and her work as a playwright was offered more significant consideration abroad by virtue of her identity as a siege survivor. This new level of international attention sparked enough interest in her work to support German, Swedish and English translations of *The Belgrade Trilogy*.

Soon after the fighting in the region came to a halt, Srbljanović's second play, *Family Stories*, opened in April of 1998 at a Belgrade theatre called Atelier 212. Like *The Belgrade Trilogy*, this new work experienced instant success with the youth of the former Yugoslavia. The play garnered a wider following after it was produced at a series of international theatre festivals in Eastern Europe. The play was presented at the Sterijino Pozorje, the Belgrade International Experimental Theater Festival and as part of the protest efforts of the Otpor movement (Munk, "Before" 5–7). After the play won the award for the best new play at the Festival of Novi Sad, it quickly attracted international attention and was subsequently translated into several new languages and produced in Germany, Poland, Romania, Slovenia, Switzerland, the Netherlands, France and the United States (Munk, "Beginning" 32). Her reputation as a significant, authentic Serbian playwright was enhanced by her identity as a survivor of the siege, and the combination of the two allowed her to find fans among some of the same people that she condemns in her plays. Despite her utterly unflattering depictions of Americans and her virulent condemnation of America and the West's role in the Balkan Wars, Srbljanović's works have often been produced in the United States — more so than any of the works of the other members of her lost generation — and has regularly received critical praise.[11] Her identity as a political playwright and her often violent opposition to both the American government and her own allows her to occupy a unique space in which she remains credible, if not heroically revolutionary, to the majority of audiences in both countries.

In *Family Stories*, Srbljanović takes critical aim at a more than a few political targets. The play follows a group of children in Belgrade who play house with one another. In a series of short, episodic scenes the children take on different familial roles (with one Croatian child consistently occupying the role of the family dog) and act out a series of domestic scenes. Darkly humorous and disturbingly violent, the children cast themselves as the perpetrators and victims of domestic and sexual abuse, racial hate crimes, xenophobia, paranoid rants and repeated murder in order to work through their own reactions to living in society ravaged by decades of violence. The play received particularly increased attention because of its focus on the children of the region. Humanitarian organizations used the alarmingly frequent choice of women and children as the intended, not accidental, targets of military violence in the country. The Red Cross and UNICEF published a series of findings studies which highlighted the particularly brutal treatment inflicted on children in the Balkan Wars, in the hopes that it would create a swell of international outrage at the situation that would prompt the American-led NATO forces and other foreign military and humanitarian forces to intervene in the fighting.[12] Srbljanović's depiction of the grim reality of these children's lives is heartbreaking and though the majority of her condemnation of America's role in the events of the wars takes the form of veiled implications it is clear that she blames the reluctant superpower for its unwillingness to engage in the region in a timely and thorough matter. For the better part of the play "America" is constructed as the invisible oppressor in the room — able to bring the characters to their knees, all the while remaining conspicuously absent. America is at once abusive and neglectful: a force to be feared and a saving grace that promises hope and never delivers.

In the third scene the children play out a scene in which the family is better off financially and more well educated than their neighbors. The parents in this scene, who are intended to be parodies of the Miloševićs,[13] spend their time teaching their son English. Unlike the other parents in the play, this couple does more than merely struggle to survive — they are the oppressors. Like the former president and his wife, who were widely criticized for their racist and elitist views, the parents of this scene are depicted as traitors for their over familiarity with American NGO's and corporate heads. They degrade the population at large for their stupidity and teach their child that learning English and being able to effectively blend into Western culture are his only hope of surviving in the devastated country. Srbljanović condemns the couple because they, like many citizens at the time, believed of the Miloševićs, have given up on the country and are merely biding time and making preparations for what they believed was the inevitable occupation of the country by the American armed forces. Their association with the English speaking West marks them as traitors to their country and unfit to rule over the country or their household. But the joke is on them. Their son, who has no desire to learn English, even though it is "for his own good," murders his parents when their callous neglect of him finally becomes unbearable. In this analogy the parents, the Miloševićs and America are all conflated as elitist power mongers who are more interested in their own public image than actually aiding the people who are tragically at their mercy.

Scene seven is comprised of a series of monologues in which the children relay nightmarish versions of their daily life. At the end of each of the monologues the children pass around a bottle of anti-depressants which they pop like candy while bemoaning their fates. After the final monologue in the series, Andrija, the child who most often takes on the role of the murderer in their games, innocently announces,

ANDRIJA. Have you heard that over-the-counter sale of sedatives has been banned? (...[the others] *comprehend in surprise, dismay. They touch their chests, necks and heads in exaggerated shock ... and completely unexpectedly, they die. They simultaneously collapse lifelessly.*) [Srbljanović, *Family Stories* 37].

Srbljanović includes this event in order to evoke cases in which tainted or expired medical supplies were delivered to the country, often under the pretense of being part of humanitarian aid packages. Specifically, anti-depressants were donated by pharmaceutical companies in order to combat the overwhelming cases of Post-traumatic Stress Disorder experienced by the citizens of the war torn areas.[14] The pills in the scene, like the countries they are from, promise to bring an end to the intense suffering experienced by the people, but in their efforts to "help" they inadvertently cause the death of the very people they intended to protect. The parallel extends beyond the case of the anti-depressants and recalls the mass civilian casualties which occurred as a result of the NATO air strikes intended to bring about a cease-fire in the region.

In scene eight, Andrija, as a teenage boy, returns home after having participated in a demonstration against the Bosnian police which has turned violent. The march-turned-riot was led by mercenaries from the Dominican Republic hired by Western forces to combat the state-sanctioned efforts of genocide perpetrated on the people of the region. In reality, the use of mercenaries allowed Western military leaders to assuage themselves of any guilt they may have felt over their failure to engage overtly in the region's civil war, without officially committing any their troops to fight in a war that many Americans saw as another Vietnam. Andrija, representative of the youth of the country, is happy to take any help he can find to exercise his revolution against the official government forces. His parents, however, are depicted as rabid racists who are staunchly opposed to American interference in their country's troubles. His mother, Milena spends the better part of the scene, when she is not being hit by her abusive husband, accusing her son of being a junkie and of dealing drugs brought into the country by Germans. His father, Vojin, is furious at his son's actions and accuses him of being a traitor. Vojin nearly beats his son to death after accusing him of collaborating with the Americans against the country's police and armed forces.

ANDRIJA. But Papa, I didn't fight, I only yelled...

VOJIN. Who did you yell at, you American piece of shit? Who did YOU shout at? At OUR police? At OUR people? In whose name did you shout?

(VOJIN *suddenly speaks with Milosević's voice.*)

Did you do something for the fascists? For Hitler and Kohl? For the motherfucker Clinton who's divided our people?

ANDRIJA. Papa ... Mama, tell him....

MILENA. (*beginning timidly*) I heard it on the radio, it wasn't Clinton...

VOJIN. (*yelling, storming around the room*) What did it report! Which radio, what bullshit!

(VOJIN *rips the plug of the old-fashioned radio out of the wall. Grabs the appliance.*) They think they can come in and order me around in my own country! ... You sold yourself to their flag. In the middle of Serbia, the cradle of the myth of Kosovo, Czar Lasar and Dusan the Great! ... I shit on their history, may President Clinton rule their country, then maybe he'll leave us alone! [Srbljanović, *Family Stories* 38–39].

In this passage, as Vojin recalls the names of his country's most famous heroes and forefathers in the same breath as he rails against American interference in the region, two things become clear. First, despite civilian outrage at America's failure to intervene in the conflict in the region during the early years of the wars, there appears to have been equal outrage over the audacity of American interference in the final years of the war. Second, the passage reveals how Srbljanović depicts one version of her own country's national pride as hinging on the construction of America as an unwanted force of foreign intervention. While it important to note that Vojin's view of America is not intended by Srbljanović to be representative of the sentiments of all of her fellow citizens — he is after all depicted a stubborn and paranoid member of the country's old guard — it clear that he is meant to be the mouthpiece for the xenophobic sentiments of a significant and vocal section of the population.

Srbljanović's ability to appeal to an international audience lies, in part, in her willingness to remain critical of both her own government and those of its friends and enemies. Citizens of former Yugoslavia can identify with the plights of their compatriots who, against all odds, struggle to survive and maintain a stable sense of their own collective identity. European nations can find comfort in her depictions of the "ugly American" who bullies less powerful nations. And the American theatre audience, despite being faced with often virulent reflections of themselves, is able to identify with Srbljanović herself: a brilliant artist who is critical of the specifics of her country's governing policies but who is nonetheless defiantly proud of her own national heritage. Her ability to navigate the complicated terrain of national identity in the wake of the Balkan wars marks her as being both an authentic voice of her own nation and an admirable and approachable ambassador to foreigners interested in trying to find a way into the complex landscape in which she dwells.

NOTES

1. For a more in-depth discussion of the role of America and the West in the Balkan wars see James Gow, *Triumph of the Lack of Will: International Diplomacy and the Yugoslav War* (New York: Columbia University Press, 1997). See also Wayne Bert, *The Reluctant Superpower: United States' Policy in Bosnia, 1991–1995* (New York: St. Martin's Press, 1997).

2. For a survey of Yugoslav sentiments towards the West see the discussions in Stjepan G. Mestrovic, *The Conceit of Innocence: Losing the Conscience of the West in the War against Bosnia* (College Station: Texas A&M University Press, 1997). For a closer examination of how the West was depicted in the later years of the conflict see Calin Hentea, *Balkan Propaganda Wars*, trans. Cristina Bordianu (Lanham, MD: Scarecrow, 2006).

3. I have used the term "ugly American" in reference to the original call for papers at the 2007 ASTR conference which prompted the writing of this piece.

4. Though I had hoped to include a critique of Srbljanović's most recent work, *America: Part Two*, in this work, it has not yet been translated into English or French (my language proficiencies).

5. I will take this opportunity to admit I have had great difficulty in trying to settle on an appropriate and historically correct means of referring to the country and people of the former Yugoslavia during this tumultuous and transitional time. As often as possible I have tried not to make distinctions between the citizens of that region in terms of religious or ethnic divides, nor have I employed any of the names of the short-lived republics that came and went during the last half of the twentieth century. As often as it has been possible I refer to the "region" as Yugoslavia and to the series of conflicts and wars as the Balkan wars.

6. Srbljanović, *The Belgrade Trilogy* 297.

7. I use the past tense here because I believe that since 9/11 the international perception of the United States as a superpower who is unwilling to engage in military action abroad has significantly changed.

8. See Bert and Henetea for more on the perception of Americans during the 1990s.

9. For more on the American role in the NATO bombing see Heneta and Gow.

10. See Mestrovic's work in chapters 4, 6 and 9.

11. See Caroline Burlingham Ellis, "*Family Stories*: A Slapstick Tragedy," rev. of *Family Stories* by Biljana Srbljanović <http://www.theatermania.com/content/news.cfm/story> 26 April 2002. See also Carolyn Clay, "Babes in Belgrade," rev. of *Family Stories* by Biljana Srbljanović, *The Boston Phoenix*, 1 February 2008 <http://www.bostonphoenix.com/boston/arts/theater/documents/02249642.html>; Aleksandar Lukac, "Invitation to an Exorcism," rev. of *Family Stories*, by Biljana Srbljanović, *Toronto Slavic Quarterly* 9 (Summer 2004): <http://www.nowtoronto.com/issues/2005-09-29/stage_theatrereviews7.php>; Will Stackman, "Aisle Say" <http://www.aislesay.com/MA-FAMILYSTORIES.html>, 26 April 2002; and Ed Siegel, "An Effective and Affecting *Family Stories* at the Market," *The Boston Globe*, 26 April 2002, C15.

12. For a more thorough look at UNICEF's findings and an overview of the statistics on violence against children see David M. Berman, "In the City of Lost Souls," *Social Studies* 86.5 (1995): 197–205.

13. Srbljanović makes this clear when the paper that the mother in the scene has been working on has direct quotations from the well-known diaries of President Milošević's wife.

14. See Berman.

6

The American Hyphen in Modern Irish Theatre: Irish-, Academic-, and American-Americans in the Plays of Brian Friel and Beyond

Thomas B. Costello

The latter half of the twentieth century has seen countless foreigners written onto the stage by Irish playwrights. While these characters are frequently born of nationalistic stereotypes, more often than not the foreigners that take to the Irish stage are American. Although the waves of Irish emigration flooded the shores of both Britain and the United States, emigrating to England simply isn't as dramatic as emigrating to America, and returning from the U.K. would pale in comparison to a homecoming from the United States. Thus, in Irish theatre of the past fifty years, America has become a primary "Other" to Ireland. "The simplistic nineteenth century view of America as the land of wealth and opportunity is regularly invoked, but only to be discredited" (Carlson 10). As the facts of Irish life have changed radically within the past decades, so too have the roles that Americans play in Irish drama.

Although these American foreigners crop up in any number of modern Irish playwrights' work, Brian Friel has likely written more Americans onto the Irish stage than any other playwright. Over the years Friel's Americans have taken many shapes; his returned, now hyphenated, emigrants first appeared in 1964 as the Sweeneys in *Philadelphia, Here I Come!* Just two years later Ireland's "domestic atmosphere is suddenly and violently shattered" in

Friel's 1966 *The Loves of Cass Maguire*. This "domestic atmosphere" is both the interior of the box set and Ireland itself, as the rogue Irish-American returned-emigrant Cass truly shatters both. With antics such as these, Friel's returning Irish-Americans rarely go unnoticed.

Friel also leads the next wave of Americans across the sea, this time with credentials: These Academic-Americans come to study Ireland with a view to possess. Academia is their microscope as they uproot family, history and art, all in the hope of bringing it back to America with them. In plays such as *Aristocrats, Give Me Your Answer, Do!* and *The Freedom of the City* it is the Academic-American credentials that allow these characters access to the center of the Irish panopticon, where they try to take what can during their brief visits. Functioning primarily as objective foreigners and outsiders to the Irish situation, these Americans unwittingly become the vehicles for change within plays where the action is stuck without them.

Finally, in recent years the Celtic-Tiger has instigated a shift towards capturing American-Americans, as more particular hyphens have become hollow and unnecessary. These "American" glimpses of otherness range from Billy's failed emigration in Martin McDonagh's *The Cripple of Inishmaan* to Frank McGuinness's doomed American captive in *Someone Who'll Watch Over Me*. Occasionally portrayed as a type of Stage-American, these American-Americans often are born of stereotypes and nationalistic "otherness" on the Irish stage. The notable exception is McGuinness's *Dolly West's Kitchen*, where colorful American characters are brought beyond simple stereotype, and their foreign perspective ultimately helps troubled Irish characters out of closeted homosexuality and loveless marriage.

The concept of "American" and "America" as distinctly foreign within the plays discussed here is significant. In the vast majority of plays I will be examining, American roles are just that; construed as broadly American and contrasted against specific Irish ones. On the contemporary Irish stage Americans have become the foreign character of choice for many playwrights. Whether through emigration, academia or just plain Americanness, American characters have helped to shape Irish drama just as America and the idea of "America" have had a profound influence on Ireland over the years.

The Returned Irish-American: From Ballybeg to Philadelphia and Back Again

> "...a disturbing mixture of Same and Other, impossible to fully place on either side and serving to expose the tensions and inadequacies of both."
> — Marvin Carlson, on the returned-emigrant [Carlson 2].

The most easily recognizable Americans who appear in Irish drama are the returned emigrants. Whether on a short holiday or moving back "home" in a more permanent way, they are drawn in stark contrast to the Irish who have stayed, and these returned emigrants typically dominate the stage. Brian Friel essentially defined the role of the Irish-American returned emigrant for Irish theatre with *Philadelphia, Here I Come!* (1964) and two years later he would feature her almost exclusively in *The Loves of Cass Maguire* (1966). Friel's contemporary, Tom Murphy would also follow on, integrating returned emigrants into much of his later work.

Philadelphia, Here I Come! chronicles Gareth O'Donnell's final day in Ireland before emigrating to America. Gar, his father "Screwballs" and their housekeeper Madge all live behind the family shop, where their routine has become painfully mundane and the future holds little promise for Gar. The play opens with Gar singing, "Philadelphia, here I come, right back where I started from...." His emigration to Philadelphia is imminent, he has just enough time left to gather his things together and ruminate on the situation.

Half way into the play we meet Con and Lizzy Sweeney, an Irish-American couple who are visiting Ireland. They are in their late 50s and have been drinking, and Lizzy is "more than usually garrulous" (Friel, *Selected* 60). She is the sister of Gar's late mother and dominates the scene in their country kitchen; she goes on and on about all the things they have to offer Gar in America. It quickly becomes clear that the childless Sweeneys desperately want Gar to fill in the void in their lives. While Gar ponders how much of a sacrifice it would be to live with the Sweeneys and if he could ever get used to Lizzy, we meet "the lads," Gar's mates. They're a wily bunch, and despite their joviality they collectively personify just how little there really is to look forward to for Gar in Ballybeg. It is the same story every night; they buzz around the kitchen talking about revelry and girls, yet end up doing nothing at all.

The play's treatment of emigration is of major relevance. Gar is captured as a pre-emigrant, a snapshot of how emigration comes to be. *Philadelphia* makes it clear that the material gains won from emigrating to America, however slight they may be, come at a significant spiritual and emotional cost, as evidenced by Lizzy. However, the situation in Ballybeg is no better and Gar's outlook for staying in Ireland may be different, but it is equally grim. Thus Gar is on the brink of the single greatest decision of his life: In choosing to leave Ireland Gar not only gives up his home, but he also must forfeit his Irishness and adopt the American hyphen. The rules are clear; once an emigrant leaves Ireland they will only be "Irish" while abroad, upon returning home to Ireland they will be "Irish-American" forevermore.

After the critical and commercial success of *Philadelphia, Here I Come!*

Friel recognized the potential for a character like Lizzy Sweeney to expand and fill the stage on her own. Just two years later Friel would bring the Irish-American back and place her center stage in *The Loves of Cass Maguire*. If the Sweeneys escaped judgment in *Philadelphia*, there was no such chance for Cass:

> *The subdued domestic atmosphere is suddenly and violently shattered by CASS's shouts. She charges on stage [...] shouting in her raucous Irish-American voice. Everyone on stage freezes* [Friel, *Loves* 9].

The Loves of Cass Maguire depicts a single woman's return to her native Ireland after forty years in America, during which time she has become a foreigner. She emigrated during hard times and has spent the years struggling to earn a living in New York while sending money home to Ireland to support the family that she left behind. When Cass returns, she learns that her brother has been relatively successful in Ireland and all the money she had been sending home over the previous forty years was unnecessary. In no time Cass's disposition has alienated her family and she is kicked out of their house, sent to live in the "Eden House," an old folks home that she refers to as the "workhouse." Ironically, it is the money that she sent home which goes towards funding her final days in captivity. Cass regularly breaks the fourth wall and addresses the audience directly, defying theatrical convention much like *Philadelphia* did. In doing this, Friel depicts Cass as a crass foreigner both within the narrative's framework and within the theatre's; she doesn't play by the rules in either place.

This framework of desolation and otherness can also be seen in the later works of another Irish playwright, Tom Murphy. In *Conversations on Homecoming* (1985) Michael returns to Ireland from the States only to be caught telling the same lies that he told on his last visit some ten years ago, much like Gar's mates' recurring stories in Ballybeg. Despite Michael's emigration his life States-side remains stagnant and impotent, and his finances seem to have only slightly benefited. Set in the 1960s, *Conversations* takes place in a floundering Co. Galway pub called "The White House," a sardonic snapshot of the entrails of the American Dream: Neither Michael nor the "White House" have found success in their American recastings.

The desolation continues in Murphy's *The Wake* (1998) when Vera returns from her questionable profession in New York to bury her grandmother who, it turns out, actually died months earlier. Like Cass, Vera is wildly out of touch with her family and is left to stay with an old friend-cum-lover while pondering what to do with the old hotel that she has inherited. Meanwhile the family regards her Americanism and unspoken profession with much skepticism, while they bicker over who should get the hotel. The same holds true for *The House* (2000) as we see characters return to Ireland after a period of employment abroad. Most have been in the UK, with the lone exception of "Goldfish" who has just returned from America, where nobody knows precisely what he does: They simply understand that it is very unbecoming of a person, likely illegal, and most importantly it doesn't pay nearly as well as it should. The themes are consistent; emigrants return as impotent Irish-Americans without significant material rewards.

In Helen Lojek's examination of Friel's "Stage Irish-Americans" she concludes that these characters all seem to have lost something considerable in their move across the sea:

> Their divorce from Irish soil allows the lilt to fall from their language, blarney to degenerate into braggadocio, and spirituality to dry into materialism. The end result is a stereotype which affirms the native Irishman's decision NOT to emigrate, for to do so is to trade things of real value — family and land and the music of the language — for the shallow materialism and vulgarity of the Stage Irish-American [Lojek, "Stage Irish-Americans" 84].

Lojek details that Friel's characters do not epitomize the stage Irish-American, but rather they are related to it. However there is a crucial difference between the situations created in *Philadelphia* and *Cass Maguire*. Gar's situation is genuinely desperate, and his options were he to stay home are so few that his ultimate decision is made out of necessity. Friel repeals this condition in his next play, even though Cass likely faced a similar dilemma when emigrating, she is far less successful than her brother who stayed in Ireland. This contradicts the economic expectation, which in turn causes Cass's breakdown. Apparently over just two years, Friel's outlook on emigration changed significantly, as did his impression of America.

The dual nature of Friel's relation to Ireland and America comes through in both these plays, and Ireland certainly isn't safe from Friel's criticism. Although Friel's treatment of Lizzy is far from kind or sympathetic, it is certainly no more cruel than his treatment of the larger situation in Ireland. The dramatic tension of *Philadelphia* rests on whether or not Gar will emigrate, and Friel cuts Ireland no slack with Gar still choosing to emigrate despite seeing the state of his Aunt Lizzy. The hyphen is worth the risk for Gar, as the consequences of staying are even more dire. Likewise, when Cass raises a toast *as Gaeilge* upon her return, her "Irish" sister-in-law mistakes it for German (Friel, *Loves* 34) a subtle dig at the modern condition of Ireland, where the indigenous language and culture was being eroded (Lojek, "Stage Irish-Americans" 82).[1]

The "domestic atmosphere" that Cass and the others shatter is not simply the interior of the box set, but the larger domesticity of Ireland itself. *Philadelphia* was written on the heels of Friel's first escape from what he called "inbred and claustrophobic Ireland" and his American sojourn provided him a "sense of liberation" (Roche 78). However, within a few years this sense of liberation was creeping into the rest of Ireland in the form of middle-class materialism, and it concerned Friel immensely. In 1970 he remarked that "the turn the Republic has taken over the past nine or ten years has been distressing, very disquieting. We have become a tenth rate image of America — a disaster for any country" (Murray, *Friel* 27). Indeed, as the years passed, despite both popular and financial success from the States, Friel would come full circle, saying that "I don't like America at all. It still has some virtues, and it's a very generous country. I loved it when I went there first and I was very enamored of it, but this left me very rapidly. Now I dislike it very much" (34). As Friel's outspoken interest in America changed, so did the place of Irish-Americans in his plays, leaving the reins of the Stage Irish-American to Tom Murphy who has charted the emigrants decline through the present.

The Academic-American: Catalysts with Credentials

> *"He is a quiet, calm, measured American academic in his mid fifties."*
>
> — Brian Friel's notes for *Aristocrats* [*Selected* 253].

Brian Friel creates a very distinct picture as he sets the stage for *Aristocrats*, his 1980 history play focusing around the decline of the Catholic big house. Friel explicitly notes that the historian in the play is American, earning Tom Hoffnung the distinction of being the only character whose nationality is explicitly laid out in the introductory stage directions. So too, a very similar Academic-American plays a pivotal role in Friel's earlier play *The Freedom of the City* (1973), where Dr. Philip Alexander Dodds is an American sociologist who pinpoints the "culture of poverty" as a fundamental problem in the North. More recently the Friel's Academic-American returned to stage as David Knight, the purchaser for "that university in Texas" who seeks to assess an Irish writer's worth in *Give Me Your Answer, Do!* (1997).

The Academic-Americans created by Friel are written into Irish drama as separate and distinct from their typical American counterparts, the returned emigrant. Where Irish-Americans are scrutinized by the "real" Irish, Friel's Academic-Americans invade and scrutinize Ireland. They are in Ireland to study, however their objective is not to discover facts or trends, but to find the specifics that they seek. The result of their detailed study is a sort of intellectual dissection, where Academic-American characters destine to usurp traditional notions of history and import them to the States for private use.

Despite what might be seen as their ill intentions, Friel uses the American-Academic as a means of escape from the otherwise torpid homegrown circumstances. An audience can then relate to the foreigner via the combination of otherness and credentials, so that a "qualified" American can shed light on the troubled situations presented on stage.

Written in 1973, set in 1970 and ostensibly about 1972, *The Freedom of the City* is Brian Friel's homage to Bloody Sunday; the day that thirteen unarmed Civil Rights protesters were killed by British military forces in Derry, Northern Ireland.[2] The event was real, but the plot of Friel's play is fictional: In episodic fashion it follows a Civil Rights march getting broken up by the authorities, during which time three marchers, Michael, Lily and Skinner, seek refuge from the CS gas in the first open door they find. It so happens that the door they choose is Derry's Guildhall, and without knowing it they have stumbled into the Mayor's Parlor. In the end, all three are gunned down by a formidable array of military forces who have gathered outside. In interweaving episodes, we also follow the resulting tribunal of inquiry, its testimonies, and ultimately its verdict, taken verbatim from the actual findings of Lord Widgery regarding Bloody Sunday. Also interspersed are speeches by a priest (representing Catholicism), a television reporter (representing the media), and an Irish balladeer (representing revolutionary mythmaking); each plays a significant role in escalating, magnifying and perpetuating the violence of the situation. Finally, there is the American sociologist, Philip Alexander Dodds, who is a foreigner in every way, shape and form. Dodds never interacts with anyone on stage; he simply lectures directly to the audience on the "culture of poverty."

The Freedom of the City begins with a Brechtian tableau as the lights come up on the bodies of the three main characters, dead and strewn about the stage. They are introduced by name as soldiers drag their bodies off stage and the Judge explains how the tribunal will run. With a shift in lighting and the crescendo of a civil rights march offstage, an Academic-American enters:

> Good evening. My name is Philip Alexander Dodds. I'm a sociologist and my field of study is inherited poverty or the culture of poverty or more accurately the subculture of poverty [Friel, *Selected* 110].

Described as an "elderly American professor with an informal manner" (Friel, *Selected* 110), Dodds is discordant with the faux historical box that is Friel's *The Freedom of the City*. His relaxed entrance as the audience hears a civil rights protest turn to violence offstage places him distinctly outside of the action. He addresses the audience directly, cracking the fourth wall and setting himself apart from the theatrical set and narrative. He is neither immediately condescending nor sympathetic; his discourse is academic and involved. The play progresses as if Dodds was giving a lecture and the dramatic action was his PowerPoint presentation. He speaks about poverty and the impoverished, and the action of the play gently follows his lead.

> People with a culture of poverty suffer much less from repression than we of the middle class suffer, and indeed, if I may make the suggestion with due qualification, they often have a hell of a lot more fun than we have.
> (DODDS *goes off left. The dressing-room door is flung open.* SKINNER *is dressed in splendid mayoral robe and chain and wears an enormous ceremonial hat jauntily on his head...*) [Friel, *Selected* 135].

Here Dodds engages with the audience directly. Although he has addressed the audience before, this time it carries a certain poignancy, as he begins this lecture with: "middle class people — with deference, people like you and me — we..." (Friel, *Selected* 135). This doesn't just crack the fourth wall, it obliterates it. As a foreigner Dodds implicates the Irish audiences at the Abbey Theatre, directly addressing their demographic and economic place in society,[3] forbidding them from regarding the play as distinctly "other." The audience is middle-class and guilty: it would be highly unlikely that anyone seeing the play could relate to the abject poverty of Skinner who has no job and no home, much less Lily, who has eleven kids and a sick husband all living in a two room flat with no running water "except what's running down the walls. Haaaaa!" (137).

The character of Philip Alexander Dodds is Friel's most creative dramatic device within *The Freedom of the City*. The role is paramount to shifting the focus away from Bloody Sunday and towards the very real underlying social problem of poverty. Although *Freedom* could never escape the Bloody Sunday parallels, Dodds' foreign perspective provides an authoritative voice pointing to poverty as the fundamental problem at hand. His Academic-American credentials allow him to scrutinize the poverty that allowed for such a state of affairs to come to fruition in Derry, and in Northern Ireland as a whole. However it is exactly this distance that juxtaposes Dodds against the main characters in *Freedom*. While he can speak eloquently about poverty, what it is and how it works, it is only through the actions of Michael, Lily and Skinner that an audience can truly appreciate that poverty. Thus Friel uses the Academic-American to create a dialectic examination of poverty that both demonstrates and educates about the real troubles underlying the Troubles.

Brian Friel's *Aristocrats* premiered in the Abbey Theatre, Dublin, in 1979. The play takes place on the terrace and in the sitting room of Ballybeg Hall and is set, like most of Friel's work, across several sunny afternoons in Donegal. Also a fictional framing of a real situation, the play chronicles the decline of the Catholic big house in Ireland. The physical house is literally in shambles and the O'Donnell patriarch lies on his deathbed upstairs while his children listen in on his senility via a "baby alarm." Although all the Irish characters in *Aristocrats* are "native Ballybeggians," the aristocratic O'Donnells are defined sharply in contrast to the "peasant" locals. Finally, sitting center-stage as the lights come up is Tom Hoffnung, the "quiet, calm, measured American academic in his mid fifties" (Friel, *Aristocrats* 253). He soon reveals that he has been there for the better part of a week, researching the "life and lifestyle of the Roman Catholic big house [... and] its political, cultural and economic influence both on the ascendancy ruling class and on the native peasant tradition" (281).

While Tom Hoffnung is researching "what we might call a Roman Catholic aristocracy" he, like the Judge in *The Freedom of the City* claims to be on a fact-finding mission. The youngest son, Casimir, proves to be his veritable gold-mine of family stories and lore. Casimir has a name for just about every furnishing in the house; a chaise longue called Daniel O'Connell, a Bible called Hilaire Belloc, a footstool called GK Chesterton, even a cushion called Yeats; and each name corresponds to an anecdote relating to the person who once sat, fell on or tripped over the item in question. Casimir seems to remember each person and event vividly, and as the play progresses Casimir's stories become more and more colorful, yet less likely to have ever occurred.

Eventually as Hoffnung is "checking, rechecking, cross checking and double checking" his facts, he asks Casimir about a simple "question mark" he had in his notes. Despite Casimir's vivid recollections of Yeats visiting the Hall to investigate ghosts, it seems as though he died two months prior to Casimir being born. When confronted with this conflicting information, Casimir simply pauses and then moves on to something completely unrelated. Despite his eagerness to help, his stories simply don't mesh well with the apparent realities of time and history as presented by Hoffnung.

Just as in *Freedom*, Friel uses history as the foundation for a play dealing with issues more deeply seeded. In *Aristocrats* the underlying focus is on memory, mythology and the constructs of both. The stories that Casimir tells Tom Hoffnung do not withstand the scrutiny of science, as induced by the Academic-American. The theme is one that Friel has visited before; in *Philadelphia, Here I Come!* Gar's father fails to validate Gar's remembrance of a childhood fishing trip. Likewise, fact and memory feature in Friel's "Self-Portrait" of 1972:

> The facts. What is a fact in the context of autobiography? A fact is something that happened to me or something I experienced. It can also be something I thought happened to me, something I thought I experienced. Or indeed an autobiographical fact can be pure fiction and no less true or reliable than that [Murray, *Brian Friel* 38].

Here Friel makes a clear distinction between the stoicism of scientific history, represented by Tom Hoffnung, and the more romantic notions of memory, such as those painted by Casimir. Eamon, who is married to Casimir's sister, vocalizes Friel's sentiment when he tells his brother-in-law "there are certain things, certain truths, Casimir, that are beyond Tom's kind of scrutiny" (Friel, *Selected* 309–310). And when the family discusses abandoning Ballybeg Hall, it is Eamon, a local who grew up in the shadow of the big house, who cannot stand the thought of the Hall being deserted. Regarding Casimir's sister's discussion of the building, Eamon blurts out: "Judith's just like her American friend: the Hall can be assessed in terms of roofs and floors and overdrafts" (318). To Eamon, the Hall is far more than a simple physical structure. Thus Friel's romantic notions of history are confounded by the very real economic dilemma facing the family, as maintaining the house has fallen beyond impractical, it is impossible; even the bank considers the building a liability. It seems as though Academic-American reason and Irish sentimentality have come to an impasse.

It is here that Tom Hoffnung, as an Academic-American, provides a sort of hope for the family and their small town. In fact, quite literally "Hoffnung" is the German word for "hope," a fact that Casimir points out enthusiastically during the play, and "Ballybeg" is the Anglicized translation of "small town" in Irish/Gaeilge. Despite the death of the aristocracy, the impending desertion of the house and the dwindling influence in their "small town," the family may yet escape being written out of history. Tom Hoffnung's book could extend the influence of the O'Donnell family in perpetuity and perhaps preserve the dignity of the place, even if the Hall itself is destined to fall into the hands of looters.[4] That said, the cost of immortality is profound, as Hoffnung is looking to control as well as chronicle the family's colorful history: Ultimately it is Hoffnung who will write the book, and it will be *his* history of *their* rise and fall.

Much more recently, *Give Me Your Answer, Do!* also enjoyed its premiere at the Abbey, this time in 1997. It is a semi-autobiographical fiction much in the same vein as Friel's *American Welcome*, both feature Irish writers contrasted against American foreigners who seek absolute control over the Irishman's creations. In short, *Give Me Your Answer, Do!* brings to the stage Friel's latest Academic-American, David Knight, who has come from a university in America to purchase an Irish writer's collection. It is a thinly veiled snapshot of American universities attempting to purchase Friel's life work, before he bestowed it to the National Library of Ireland.

In all of these works, Friel's Academic-Americans are simply American, in contrast to his Irish characters who are, say grocers from Ballybeg or a mother of eleven from Derry. Friel's attention to biographical detail is lost on "others," his Academic-Americans are sufficiently foreign in name and rank. The anonymity is intentional; they are abstractly American, just like the Dream. Academia is the microscope that they use as a tool to analyze all things Irish. In making notes, speeches and purchases, the Academics are gradually collecting bits of Ireland. Just as emigrants were lured by materialism, the Academic-Americans are drawn in the opposite direction, hoping to commodify, control or explain their Irish subjects.

In particular, the characters of Tom Hoffnung and David Knight are explicitly looking to usurp and own pieces of Ireland to which they have no clear relation. Just as the Irish-Americans came back "home" looking to add meaning to their lives, the Academic-Americans have crossed the sea in the hope of adding some meaning to their work. Materialism looms large, and Friel leaves us to assume that the American institutions behind the academics are fueling such intellectual imperialism. The contrast of an Academic-American against the literal Irish "small town" of Ballybeg creates a very interesting dramatic imbalance: the tiny fictional town of Ballybeg versus the real omnipresent idea of America.

The fact that *The Freedom of the City, Aristocrats* and *Give Me Your Answer, Do!* all found their premieres at the Abbey Theatre in Dublin is worthy of attention. No longer is the question simply about Friel creating these Academic-Americans, rather it is the National Theatre of Ireland that is producing them; one nation framing another. Incidentally, both *Freedom* and *Aristocrats* have been brought back to the national stage within the past decade at the Abbey, making it possible to move from text to production.

In the Abbey's 1999 production of *The Freedom of the City*, Professor Dodds is every bit as much an Academic-American as an audience could hope, he is even dressed in the stereotypical patched-elbow jacket. His initial presence on stage is relaxed, although virtually motionless as his hand movements are kept to a minimum. His accent is straightforward upper mid–Atlantic without any hint of drawl; the typical American media accent. He delivers his lectures from the apron, right or left, and never crosses the boundary of the proscenium into the three-wall box set. He is literally as far outside the action as possible without leaving the stage. Therefore his lectures come across clean, and as the play progresses he warms and becomes more animated, moving slightly on his feet and gesturing with his hands. Although his speeches cannot compete with the graphic action onstage, his influence does; significant lighting shifts concentrate all attention on him when he speaks. Indeed, he could almost be lecturing at a sociology conference.

Aristocrats was remounted at the Abbey in 2003. This time the Academic-American Tom Hoffnung is costumed in a light colored suit, generally with his jacket off as he works. When he appears on the terrace, he wears a wide brimmed white hat, presumably to protect his head from the devastating Donegal sunshine (Friel, *Selected* 300).[5] His accent is sharper and more pronounced and there is a certain nasal twang that resonates throughout the production. His demeanor is quiet, as Friel noted, and he is generally observing. This is amplified during the play-within-a-play: while Claire, Casimir and Willie pretend to play croquet, Hoffnung stalks around the stage, silently taking pictures of their behavior. This is not part of the script, and colors Hoffnung as somewhat more invasive than Friel's text makes him out to be. However, when Hoffnung confronts Casimir about the "facts" he appears to do so with genuine curiosity and he softly retreats when he realizes that he has crossed a line.

Perhaps more interesting than the individual productions is that the Abbey chose to cast the same actor, Bosco Hogan, as both Dodds and Hoffnung. The similarity in character between these two plays had already planted the seed for a stock character, and this casting decision gives the argument even more weight. That said, given the actual production values, the roles were not presented as readily interchangeable, and Bosco Hogan did an admirable job handling the characters differently. Even if Hogan was the Abbey's current "American-accent man,"[6] such a casting decision blurs the line here between characterization and stereotype. Fortunately the Academic-American patched-elbow jacket didn't follow Hogan to *Aristocrats*.

The American-American: From Stereotype to Savior-type

> "An American is, I repeat, a valuable asset. A prize possession.
> Prized, yes, but not loved. There is a price permanently placed on
> the American's head."
>
> —Adam in *Someone Who'll Watch Over Me*

As the framework surrounding America has shifted from a place of refuge to a place of influence, so too have the characters that embody America in Irish drama. Emigration from Ireland has not only sharply declined in recent years, it has been overshadowed by immigration; a trend previously unknown in Ireland. Tourism has exploded as well, and with these changes have come a great number of new characters and themes that revolve around America. Where earlier American characters were typically qualified in terms of their hyphens, this later wave of Americans is most importantly American. As American-Americans, their primary function is to embody a sense of America, whether as a cultural, political, or philosophical other. Although some of these characters still cling to sentimental hyphens of heredity, they are no longer meaningful qualifiers: Americanness has trumped previous hyphens, and in the course of Irish drama, the American-Americans' insistent claims of various ethnic ancestry is simply indicative of the average American, who claims to be anything but.

These American-Americans at times hit the stage as animated stereotypes, placed within the frame of Irish drama to highlight alleged cultural differences. Brian Friel's *American Welcome* (1980) is a superb example in which a grotesque American director is created as a caricature born of stereotype. Marie Jones's *Stones in His Pockets* (1996) and Martin McDonagh's *The Cripple of Inishmaan* (1996) both stage American stereotypes that are inexorably related to Hollywood, an obvious cliché used to great comic and satirical end. McDonagh's title character vies for an Irish role in an American film, while Jones features American-Americans in the forms of a Hollywood cast and crew who have come to capture Ireland on film. In both instances the hyper–American film industry is portrayed as at odds with the reality of Ireland and her people as depicted on the stage.

Among contemporary Irish dramatists, Frank McGuinness has introduced several remarkable American-American characters into his later work. In *Someone Who'll Watch Over Me* (1992) Adam is the American among stereotypes; his obsession is with fitness while he is held captive as a hostage along with an Irishman and a Brit. *Dolly West's Kitchen* (1999) provides the most interesting juxtaposition of characters, with two American soldiers surreptitiously crossing the border into Donegal during the heat of World War II. Marco and Jamie, a flamboyantly camp Italian-American and a reserved Irish-American hardly personify the average American hero-types, yet they have a profound effect on those around them as the war comes and goes in *Dolly West's Kitchen*.

These American-Americans are generally indebted to traditional American stereotypes enough to perpetuate the framework of America as distinctly other, however their dramatic function is much more than that of comical or mocking stereotype. Drawn in contrast to versions of Ireland on the stage, the American-American is manifestly qualified as a stand-in for America. No longer unsuccessful emigrants or specialized appropriators, this distinctly American wave of Americans has been washed upon Irish stages to highlight attitudinal differences, for better or for worse.

Brian Friel's *American Welcome* is a short play consisting of one monologue, spoken by an American theatre director to a visiting Irish playwright. The director is greeting the playwright as through it is their first meeting before a première, and the playwright never sets foot on the stage. The director's blinding enthusiasm and chatty manner leave no room for the playwright; this is a one-man show. In the course of this extended greeting, the director admits that he has had to make some slight changes to the script to make it suitable for an American audience. He then reveals that he has brought in outside help to rewrite what is essentially the entire play, for purely linguistic reasons. Ironically Friel wrote *American Welcome* for an American company, the Actors Theatre of Louisville. This tiny play undoubtedly reveals a significant autobiographical glimpse of Friel's regard for American directors, just as *Give Me Your Answer, Do!* unabashedly stages Friel's impression of large Academic-American libraries.

Marie Jones's *Stones in His Pockets* and Martin McDonagh's *The Cripple of Inishmaan* both rest largely on Hollywood iconography and make use of actual milestones in Irish-American filmmaking history. Framed around American film companies shooting on location in Ireland, both plays capture the extent to which communities are affected and obsessed with the American filmmakers. *Stones in His Pockets* is unique in that it features just two actors sharing the responsibility of playing a number of various male and female roles. The action centers around Jake and Charlie, two local lads who have been hired as extras for the filming of *The Quiet Valley*, which will be another major motion picture sentimentally looking back at Ireland. The American production company also hired Mickey, another local whose claim to fame is having been an extra in *The Quiet Man* (1952) with John Wayne. The company brought their star American actress with them, Caroline Giovanni, who is desperately trying to patch up her sorry imitation of the Irish dialect called for in the film. A fourth local, Sean, was turned down for extra work due to a fondness for drugs and drink, and a bitter run-in with Caroline in the local pub ends with him being thrown out. As the drama unfolds, Sean is devastated at being thrown out of his own local pub on account of Caroline, and he thus fills his pockets with stones and drowns himself. The American film director and his production assistants fear the Irish weather and desperately push forward with filming, refusing to grant the local extras a day off to mourn. Fed up with the situation and woefully aware that Hollywood will only allow the Irish to play extra roles in "Irish" films, Jake and Charlie decide to write their own screenplay. The play ends with them discussing the true story of a lad who killed himself because of a film being shot in Ireland; they're calling it *Stones in His Pockets* and the American-American film director doesn't think it will work.

The Cripple of Inishmaan is set in 1934 with the filming of Robbie Flaherty's *The Man of Aran*.[7] When the small community on Inishmaan hears about the filming, everybody wants to be involved somehow. Billy, the crippled title character, is endlessly ridiculed for his disability and ultimately decides to leave Inishmaan for America. An American film company invites Billy to Hollywood for a screen test because they have an upcoming film featuring a young crippled Irishman, a description Billy fits perfectly. Knowing that he is a shoe-in for the role, he severs all ties with his family and goes to Hollywood where he lands in a squalid hotel room. Ultimately the film company casts a young healthy boy from Florida to play the Irish Cripple, and Billy is consequently crushed and dismayed. He returns to Ireland, only to announce that he turned down the role after it was offered to him. Despite having been gone for just four months Billy is branded "Irish-American" upon his return and his aunts constantly scrutinize his changed vocabulary. In typical McDonagh fashion *The Cripple of Inishmaan* blends absurdity with violence and tragicomedy throughout. Although no American characters appear on stage per se, their actions offstage drive the action of the play. In rejecting Billy for the role of the Irish cripple, it is the American-Americans who crush Billy's one chance at success. Likewise the play is rife with references back and forth across the sea, and Billy's American experience is captured with a scene set in America, embodied by his sordid Hollywood hotel room. Thus, in less than half a year *The Cripple of Inishmaan* depicts a complete failed emigration cycle, where Billy not only is forced to retreat to his place in Ireland, but in doing so he brings home the added burden of his newly hyphenated branding.

Frank McGuinness's *Someone Who'll Watch Over Me* is the story of three hostages in Lebanon, one American, one Irish and one British. They share a cell and their lives, laughing together, crying together and pretending together, because while in captivity they are all each other has. They compare notes on their own nationalities while their captors remain generically "Arab" just as they are primarily white[8] or western hostages. At times the trio tries to rationalize what is happening off stage, or what their "Arab" captors are going to accomplish, yet their conversations always come back to their nationalities:

> MICHAEL: You both scare the shit out of me.
> EDWARD: English people always scare the shit out of me as well. As for fucking Americans —
> MICHAEL: Yes, they are all quite mad —
> EDWARD: Can you imagine what it was like to land in here with that Yankee —
> MICHAEL: Yes, it must have been worrying —
> ADAM: What the fuck is this? [McGuinness 113].

Despite their differences, they take a great amount of solace in simply having each other as they tread on the brink of madness. Eventually Adam, the lone American is taken away and killed, leaving Michael and Edward to speculate why. Ultimately Edward is allowed to go free and the play finishes with Michael alone in the cell, still in chains. Although first performed in 1992, the play retains a considerable resonance with ongoing conflict in the Middle East, particularly with respect to the role of America in the region.

The simple fact that Adam is the lone casualty of a play so driven by nationalistic types decidedly places him as the representative American-American, who bears the brunt of international tensions both within and without the safety of cell.

Dolly West's Kitchen provides a remarkably fresh depiction of the American-American in Irish drama. The play focuses on the West family who live in a remote house in Donegal during and after the second World War. Dolly West lives in the house along with her mother Rima, her younger brother Justin, her older sister Esther with husband Ned, and the young housekeeper Anna. Before long Rima, the matriarch of the house, has brought home two Americans that she spied while she was in town, instinctively knowing that they would play a significant role in the household.

> MARCO: I am Marco Delaviccario. This is my Irish-American cousin, Jamie O'Brien. We signed up together. Jamie brought the clothes he was standing in and a change of underwear. I brought one taffeta dress and a change of high heels. Who knows what might happen in the heat of battle? [McGuinness, *Dolly West* 203].

Jamie is as quiet and reserved as Marco is flamboyant and camp. As time goes by the guests couple-off with the Wests; most notably Marco brings the Irish Justin out of the closet, and Jamie decides to forge a life with the housekeeper Anna. Jamie also fathers a child with Esther, who had previously been unsuccessful in conception with her husband. Thus the Americans, though very different, have managed to bring about significant change in the West household. Having seen the family taken care of, Rima passes away peacefully in her chair, glass of whiskey in hand.

These plays tend to capture American-American characters in situations characteristic of their time. An explicit example of Friel's dedication to and concern with the constructs of language, *American Welcome* was written on the heels of *Translations* and offers a strikingly explicit and sardonic view of the American bastardization of his work and language. In many ways *American Welcome* is a ten-minute manifestation of Friel's worst nightmare; an American director butchering one of his plays. That there was no apparent malice behind this fictional destruction of an Irish writer's work is both funny and a bit disarming. America is framed in all its glory, passively destructing culture in the name of accessibility. This absurd rendering allows audiences on both sides of the sea to laugh at the situation, as the American Director is distinctly "other" through his fiction, as if he were a cartoon character parading around a real theatre demanding respect. However at the roots of this rampant stereotype caricature are real deep-seeded issues, specifically Friel's love and respect for language. Language has always been a significant concern for Friel, and *Translations* is continually cited as such. Friel chooses to use an ignorant director for *American Welcome* to highlight his immediate concern regarding the production of his work in general, and he specifically chooses an American-American as the focal point of this exercise.

In fact, a great number of Friel's plays have been translated into countless languages. However, Friel's imaginary director translating the play *within* English is framed with absolute absurdity. It is not the American director who needs the play translated, rather it is the audience, the collective notion of America in general. The director is merely the messenger and the stand-in for the audience, the American-American as it were. This grotesque framework is particularly important, as the play was written for and premièred in America, and in the heartland no less.[9] The irony of the production and locale's framework is very significant to Friel, as his work is never far from American stages. He has enjoyed considerable success abroad, and several of his plays have premièred in America before moving to Ireland. Despite this commercial success, *American Welcome* is a comic backlash at the hand that feeds him, framing the absurdity of commercial American theatre in a format that is anything but. This explosion of stereotype pulsing through Friel's over-zealous director in *American Welcome* works precisely because it is so farcical. The usual dangers associated with stereotype are here overcome using the framework of absurdity; the grain of salt that turns scandal into comedy. American audiences, after all, do tend to enjoy laughing at "crazy Americans."

Like *American Welcome*, the framework of *Someone Who'll Watch Over Me* is deeply connected to stereotype. Throughout the play the characters trade mild digs such as: "sarcastic Yankee," "very profitable. Very American," "why are the Irish so religious?," "don't the Irish like foreplay?," "...you're an Englishman. How dreadfully unfair" (McGuinness 90, 95, 98, 100, 102). The hostages wear their nationalities on their cuffs and are framed to personify those nationalities through stereotype. Adam is athletic, materialistic and an easy target for the Europeans. Although Edward and Michael don't blame Adam for their imprisonment outright, they repeatedly imply that being held hostage with an American is bound to make their situation worse or get them killed.

This political framework of *Someone Who'll Watch Over Me* is accentuated by its conclusion, with each nationality on very different paths. Although foreign policy is well in the background of the play, the ultimate destination for the characters is framed parallel to their country's international activity. Adam is killed for America's aggressive tactics, Michael remains imprisoned for Britain's complicity, and Edward walks free thanks to Ireland's neutrality.

These political frameworks were radically different thirty years prior, when Brian Friel framed Ben Burton as the lone American-American in *Philadelphia, Here I Come!* As a "regular" American he is framed as a quiet enough man who seems to be nothing but helpful. It is the Irish-Americans who appear the most lost through their displacement. Although Mr. Burton lacks any known family, the Sweeney's praise him for his kindness and willingness to help, as if he himself personified America. Indeed, when Lizzy loses control of herself and breaks down, it is Ben who is the first to offer help, stepping in to bring the car round. Just a few years later, the Americans that we hear about through *Cass Maguire* are depicted as anything but philanthropic. In fact it is Cass who has been supporting her American friend Jeff while in New York. The one time she legitimately thought he was going to propose to her, the tiny gift box contained a tri-color shamrock broach that he had traded an Irish bum a sandwich for. Thus two failed Irish emigrants are captured in varying states of disrepair; the promise of a tiny jewelry box embodied their American dream, only to yield a pathetic cluster of fake diamonds arranged in a tacky Irish-American piece of kitsch.

These romanticized notions of Ireland take centre stage in the Hollywood-obsessed plays of Marie Jones and Martin McDonagh. Although no actual American appears in *The Cripple of Inishmaan*, America itself is framed on the stage in a scene set in Billy's Hollywood hotel room. This, the only scene that actually takes place in America is itself a fiction, Billy's apparent death is in fact just him rehearsing for the screen test. This representation removes America one step further from reality and tricks the audience into believing that the fictional Billy is dead, when in reality his fictional death was itself fiction, thus confounding their suspension of disbelief. Not only is Billy in a squalid hotel room, but his entire experience there is based around falsehood, just as the mass export of American entertainment is based around fiction.

As McDonagh frames the fiction of Hollywood his reference point is the landmark film *The Man of Aran*. This film is a perfectly apt starting point, as it is a prime example of American filmmaking in Ireland; the quest to create an authentic fiction. The now infamous shark-hunting scene from the film is brought to back to life in *The Cripple of Inishmaan* so the townspeople can scoff and throw eggs at it. With a bit of tongue-in-cheek humor, McDonagh is able to frame the influential film against another rendition of those same Aran islanders, highlighting the wild discrepancy between the real and the fictional, all within the world of his play, of course.

Marie Jones' *Stones in His Pockets* uses the same tactics, recalling John Ford's *The Quiet Man*. Micky's one claim to fame in life is that he was an extra in *The Quiet Man*, and the new film that is being filmed on location is titled *The Quiet Valley*, obviously looking to bank on the relation. This repetition in title and location demonstrate the stagnant framework of Hollywood mythmaking, implying that not only are producers looking to make those stereotypical films, but that audiences want to see them. The crowning moment in the play is the conclusion that Jake and Charlie are committed to writing their script, while the American director insists that it won't work. As audiences on either side of the pond experience the production, they are left with the thought that they have just been watching Jake and Charlie's play, and the know-it-all American producers are proven wrong.[10]

Both Jones and McDonagh use the framework of Hollywood to debunk the stereotypes perpetuated by it. Instead of the glitz and glamour normally associated with major motion pictures, these plays depict angst and desolation surrounding the filming. A deromanticized version of Hollywood framed within an Irish play is precisely the opposite of what the American producers set out to capture by shooting on location. In both plays the townspeople adamantly disagree with the content of the films, citing gross errors in both the actions and attitudes represented. Yet despite their disagreement or disapproval of the films, the native Irish characters in the plays still yearn to be near the films, if only to mock them.

In many ways, *Dolly West's Kitchen* reverses the trend in bringing American characters of any type to the stage. It was written and produced in the height of the Celtic Tiger in 1999, yet it is set during World War II, making it, like *The Cripple of Inishmaan*, another period-play. McGuinness has the luxury of writing with perfect hindsight, placing into a historical context the seeds for the future relations between America and Ireland. Quite the opposite of the returned emigrants who preceded them, Marco and Jamie show the capacity to love and produce offspring, yet not in any traditional sense; Justin and Marco live together in the family house while Jamie has sired a child with Esther who is married to another man.

Both of McGuinness's Americans play very special roles within the West household. Marco's campy confidence secures his place as an outsider, and these qualities help bring the tough young Justin out of the closet. Marco and Justin ultimately move forward with the support of the West family within their isolated world, where they have all that they need. Jamie is framed as an outsider who is caught between two women, and ultimately it is the Irish women who have control of his future, as Esther denies him and Anna accepts him. It is significant that Rima, the West matriarch, brings Marco and Jamie to Dolly West's kitchen on that fateful day, they didn't just show up. Although she doesn't survive the production, Rima is the main agent for change within the household. McGuinness makes clear that Rima's instincts brought this motley crew together, maintaining the tradition that it is the Irish who chose to transform themselves, using the American-Americans as catalysts.

These recent American characters and themes exist by virtue of their American iconography, typically without credentials or meaningful hyphens. Although both Marco and Jamie refer to their hyphenated nationalities, the others around them do not. Their hyphens are intra–American identifiers, monikers they choose to imbibe, as opposed to the "Irish-American" label imposed upon all who emigrate, however brief their stay abroad might have been. All of these American-Americans are framed in distinct contrast to the otherwise Irish plays they populate. Even though *American Welcome* is set in America, the Director defines himself and his American audiences as patently different than the Irish, so far as to require a rewrite of the play. The playwright never appears, and may very well have long since turned his back on the director.

In both the *Cripple of Inishmaan* and *Stones in His Pockets* the Irish artists turn their backs on America as well, Charlie and Jake move on with their film script and Billy leaves America all together. This framework of Ireland standing strong independently is exemplary of the early days of the Celtic Tiger when these plays were written. With the need to emigrate firmly in the past, Ireland's fortitude provided a fertile ground for these representations of the American-American to develop. As McGuinness demonstrates with *Someone Who'll Watch Over Me*, in an age of increasing globalization nationalities can still play a profound role in personal interactions. In the cell in Beirut, these nationalities ultimately define who will walk free, who will remain imprisoned and who will die.

Finally, *Dolly West's Kitchen* stands alone in its framing of Americans. When Marco and Jamie are brought to rural Donegal, they bring with them liberation and escape. They break through stereotypes and are well-rounded characters who help the West family move on with their lives. As Americans, national otherness is one facet of their character, and they each in their own way make connections with the Wests on a personal level. They remain outsiders, but are outsiders who are let in, rather than turned away from. Indeed, Jamie serves as the first "Irish-American" on the Irish stage who is capable of having children, even if it is out of wedlock, and with a married Irish woman. Against a backdrop of war these American-Americans bring a forward momentum without the usual strings of materialism attached.

When any Americans hit the stage, cultural differences define their characterization and create the framework of otherness crucial to the dramatic action. American characters are framed as so "different" than their Irish counterparts that they shake things up to the extent as to affect a real change on those around them. Whether as a monologue in a ten-minute play festival or as part of an epic tale of imprisonment, these American-Americans are used within recent Irish theatre in order to magnify cultural differences that help to drive the drama.

Conclusions

As the relationship of America with Ireland has changed radically over the past fifty years, so too have the American foreigners who populate the Irish stage. Beginning with *Philadelphia, Here I Come!* in 1964, Friel makes clear that emigration will attach a weighty hyphen to an individual's nationality: These Irish-American characters are loud, brash, and impotent, but perhaps worst of all, they have failed to find the material success that lies at the center of the emigration/American dream.

The Academic-Americans that follow the emigrants home bring qualifications, however their success in helping unpack Irish troubles is confounded by their imperialist motivations. While they offer a different kind of refuge for those struggling in Ireland, they remain tied to material gains, much like those Irish-Americans that they followed. Lastly, the American-Americans of contemporary Irish drama bring a diverse character set to the stage. Although stereotype is still at play in some works, it is denied in others, and ultimately, finally, the Irish-American has gained the ability to reproduce, if only in conjunction with the Irish-Irish.

NOTES

1. Gaeilge has since become much more popular in Ireland, thanks to an ongoing initiative to bring the country towards bilingualcy.

2. The current consensus is that those who were killed were unarmed.

3. Although somewhat of a generalization, it is widely understood that the bulk of the Abbey Theatre's typical patronage was then, and remains, upper-middle class. This is a fair enough estimate for our purposes here, as endeavoring to explore the minutia of the Abbey's patronage at great length is a task for another volume — and perhaps a worthy one at that.

4. Which is what Eamon insists will happen immediately after they leave.

5. Indeed, in the text Hoffnung warns Judith that she should have her head covered as well.

6. As was mentioned to me casually while I was doing research in the Abbey's archives.

7. Robbie Flaherty's *The Man of Aran* (1934) is one of Flaherty's "man vs. nature" docudramas, filmed at a great risk — both financial and physical; it was one of the most expensive films made at the time. It features a family on Inishmore and their hardships as they battle the elements in the west of Ireland. Much acclaimed at the time, it would later come under significant scrutiny for its romanticism and historical inaccuracy.

8. The original production featured an all white cast, however later productions would often opt for a black actor to play the role of the American, Adam.

9. *American Welcome* was written for and first produced by the Actors Theatre of Louisville, Kentucky.

10. The ironic conclusion of the play is accentuated by the fact that audiences have just watched a *play* called "Stones in His Pockets," not a *film*, which is what the boys say that they are going to write.

7

Of Human Rights and Playwriting Against Empire

Neilesh Bose

Orientalized appearances of South Asia are no stranger to modern Western theatre. From Peter Brook's 1985 stage production of and 1989 film of the *Mahabharata*, to Jerzy Grotowski's 1960 *Sakuntala*, and Ariane Mnouchkine's 1986 *The Indiade or India of their Dreams*, the Orientalist eye has gazed upon South Asia more than a few notable times in the contemporary theatre.[1] Though understudied in comparison to other genres of artistic and cultural production, such as the novel or the visual arts, Indian theatre's place in the European and American Orientalist imaginations has received a smattering of academic attention.[2] However, the theatrical gazes that South Asians have placed on the West have been almost completely ignored in contemporary criticism.[3] *Maanusher Adhikare*, translated as *The Rights of Man* in English, a 1969 examination of the Alabama Scottsboro trials of the 1930s, arose from the pen of Utpal Dutt, one of the twentieth century India's leading playwrights, actors, directors, and theater theorists. This essay examines the aesthetic and political parameters of Dutt's landmark text and its early production history. *Maanusher Adhikare* functions as one of the few twentieth century plays to appropriate and interrogate the United States of America and its socio-historical landscape in a South Asian language.

A Revolutionary Theatre: The Life and Work of Utpal Dutt

Utpal Dutt voluminous *oeuvre* has indisputably marked him as one of the major players of twentieth-century Indian theatre. His life in the theatre as playwright, actor, director, and theorist spanned five decades, beginning at the tail end of British colonial rule and continuing until his death in 1993. In 1947, the year of Indian independence, Dutt joined his first theatre group — Shakespereana — and trained in the most colonial of all traditions, the theatre of Shakespeare. Dutt quickly transformed into a Marxist theatre artist, as he later argued "[t]hose were years wasted performing Shakespeare before an intellectual audience" (qtd. in Chatterjee, "Utpal Dutt" 1). Soon he turned Shakespearana into the Little Theatre Group (LTG) in 1952. This group began Dutt's multi-faceted career with political theatre in West Bengal. The LTG produced Bangla-language originals as well as plays adapted from Western authors like Brecht to propagate for social change.

Dutt was also actively involved with the Indian People's Theatre Association (IPTA), a theatrical wing of the Communist Party of India. Through travelactive in anti-imperialist and anti-capitalist politics in the 1940s. Dutt joined the group in 1951, but soon felt stifled by the group's lack of sensitivity toward political aesthetics, as he lamented that "In [the IPTA] plays ... whenever the proletarian hero walked on stage, conflict and drama disappeared — an oversimplified, anemic, spiritless Symbol of Revolution gesticulated and spoke dull sermons" (qtd. in Chatterjee, "Utpal Dutt" 2).[4]

In the 1950s and 1960s, Dutt wrote many politically leftist plays, some for institutions like the IPTA, such as the 1951 *Chargesheet*, a play about imprisoned communist activists. In 1959, Dutt wrote and directed *Angaar* (Charred Coal), about coal-mine workers, before he split formally with the Communist Party of India. In the 1960s, Dutt's *Kallol* (The Wave), *Ajeya Vietnam* (Invincible Vietnam), and *Teer* (Arrow) developed Dutt's dramaturgy as a revolutionary Marxist theatre practitioner. By the late 1960s, the Naxalite movement, a visible, Mao-ist inspired guerilla movement in West Bengal had emerged as a vital part of leftist politics and meshed with Dutt's Marxist theatre practice.

In 1968, Dutt wrote *Maanusher Adhikare/ The Rights of Man*, which played to packed houses in Calcutta and elsewhere in India in 1968 and 1969. During the turbulent 1970s, Dutt contributed many more plays in a Brechtian mode, such as *Tiner Talowar* (The Tin Sword), *Tota* (later named the Great Rebellion, about the 1857 Indian mutiny-revolt), and *Dushwapner Nagori* (The Nightmare City), about Calcutta in crisis. From the 1970s onward, Dutt became consumed with the dramaturgy of *jatra*, in its declamation, incorporation of song, dance, and drama together, and its conception of "total performance." This idea informed Dutt's understanding of a Marxist revolutionary aesthetic that could engage with and mobilize masses of people.

In addition to his many plays and memorable productions, Dutt contributed a great deal to theatre history and theory to the Bangla and English languages. His 1972 *Shakespearer Samajchetana* (Shakespeare's Social Consciousness) marks possibly the most searching analysis of Shakespeare and Elizabethan theatre, in the Bangla language. In English he is best known for his work on theatre aesthetics, *Towards a Revolutionary Theatre*.

Dutt's career as a theorist and practitioner emphasized the burden of creating a form that would incorporate a politics of revolution. In *Maanusher Adhikare*, not only did Dutt stick to his own long-standing politicization of form, but he also incorporated his own appropriations of a foreign, distant people. The Scottsboro affair, particularly when seen from a non–American vantage point, undoubtedly provided a fabulous set of conditions for dramatization. After even the most powerful evidence substantiating the innocence of the defendants appeared, racism and classism of a vicious sort, directed the outcomes. Whereas the racism and indignities of colonial and postcolonial South Asia have been represented in South Asian theatrical traditions at least since Dinabandhu Mitra's 1860 *Nil Darpan* (The Indigo Mirror), the idea of America has rarely been apparent in modern South Asian theatre. Dutt's entry into this topic was colored heavily by his own Communist politics and therefore much of his presentation of the facts distorts the historical record. The details of this historical record, though, must be examined at length for an assessment of Dutt's interventions.

The Story of Scottsboro

The facts of the Scottsboro case and the tribulations of the boys involved are now beyond dispute. Nine black boys were framed for the rape of a white woman in 1931 in Alabama. A protracted battle between the state, the regional legal apparatuses in Alabama, and the defendants then ensued. Even though none of the defendants were executed, each one of them languished in jail for several years. Though four of them had charges against them dropped in 1937 (after spending 6 years in various jails), the remaining five lived haunted lives after being granted parole in the 1940s. Haywood Patterson lived as a fugitive until he was caught in Detroit. Only one, Clarence Norris, lived to receive a pardon and to experience the 1980s. Well after Reconstruction, life for black men in the South wasn't much better than a life condemned to slavery. Being framed for raping a white woman, for stealing from a white man, in short, for disrupting the power structure of the American South was not a strange thing in 1930s Alabama. Lynchings were on the rise in the South in the 1930s and the vigilante "justice" that whites pursued was common knowledge to most.

The Scottsboro narrative began on March 25, 1931, when a train from Chattanooga to Memphis stopped at the Paint Rock station in Alabama. At this stop, a group of nine black boys were apprehended by the local police. From Georgia came Charlie Weems, Ozie Powell, Clarence Norris, Olen Montgomery, and Willie Roberson. All were in their teens except for 20-year-old Weems. From Chattanooga, Haywood Patterson, Eugene Williams, and Andy and Roy Wright appeared. Patterson at age 20 was the oldest and most articulate of this group. From an adjacent gondola[5] appeared two white women, Ruby Bates and Victoria Price, who after being accosted by the local sheriff accused the black boys of rape. The details of Bates and Price's allegations varied but essentially they claimed that the boys jumped onto their gondola from an adjacent boxcar and brutally gang-raped them. This was allegedly done after the black boys had fought and thrown a group of white boys off the train. The Paint Rock Station Master received a call from the Stevenson station master who reported that he saw a disturbance between white boys and black boys. By the time the train pulled into Paint Rock, a mob assembled, looking for the black boys already accused of a crime. Within a matter of minutes, the police found the nine boys, quickly arrested them, and took them to the Scottsboro jail. In 1931, all of the boys, save Roy Wright because of his juvenile status, were easily tried and convicted of rape and sentenced to death.

Because of the tireless work of the American Communist Party, this 1931 Alabama rape trial of nine black boys accused of raping white women made international headlines. Subscribers of the *Daily Worker* read editorials urging "Negro and white workers ... [to] smash this murderous frame-up. Hold protest meetings. Wire protests to the governor of Alabama. Demonstrate May Day against lynching whether by a boss mob or by the bosses' state" (qtd. in Goodman 27). Through the efforts of the International Labor Defense (ILD), the legal wing of the Communist Party, after the Alabama Supreme Court upheld the convictions, the U.S. Supreme Court reviewed the case in appeals and reversed Alabama's decisions and a re-trial was ordered. The first re-trial, set for the spring of 1933, was shifted to Decatur, Alabama and was presided over by Judge James E. Horton. This trial marks the entry of the famous New York criminal lawyer Samuel Leibowitz, hired by the ILD. Destined to become the next Clarence Darrow, Leibowitz had an impeccable record and was notorious for defending gangsters and criminals. Leibowitz's appearance catapulted the NAACP—long competing with the ILD for the boys' attention—and the ILD into a conflict between the Communist Party and race-based activists. As both vied for the control of the Scottsboro boys, the ILD finally took over in 1932.[6]

During the little publicized second trial in Decatur, Samuel Leibowitz and his ILD associate Joseph Brodsky battled against the prosecution team of Thomas Knight, Jr. At this trial, Leibowitz demonstrated to the jury that both Ruby Bates and Victoria Price had reputations of being prostitutes and vagabonds. He also proved that they had sexual intercourse with men soon before the infamous train ride. Doctors' testimony contradicted the charges of rape by the black boys as not nearly enough semen had been found to warrant the charge of rape. Moreover, the condition of the girls when the charge was laid hardly qualified as traumatic. Additionally, one of the witnesses for the prosecution, Orey Dobbins, who testified to seeing the girls on the train on March 25, 1931, mistakenly said they were wearing dresses, when nearly every other party in the investigation agreed that they were wearing overalls as opposed to dresses. Finally, the girls claim that the boys entered onto their gondola from an adjacent box-car was disproven. The train in question only had consecutive gondolas and so the boys could not have jumped on from an adjacent box-car. To make the case air-tight, Leibowitz ended his arguments by calling Ruby Bates, who recanted her accusations at the end of the trail, citing that she had been coerced by Price to give a fake accusation. Even with all of these points in the defense's favor, the jury found Patterson and all the other defendants guilty as charged.

Soon after the case, Judge James E. Horton, a liberal Southerner, published an opinion listing all the reasons why a retrial must take place. In addition to all the aforementioned problems that Leibowitz presented, Judge Horton also remarked at the absurdity of the girls' claim: a group of boys raped two white women in broad daylight and passed through several train stations while doing so! After Judge Horton's opinion, a new trial was set for November 1933.

Dutt's Intervention

This is where Dutt's text enters, punctuated as it was by a prologue, a short scene of Black Power militants catching a white Marine who raped and attacked women in Vietnam. In this prologue, as the black activists decide what to do with the white Marine, they reminisce about a time in America when the entire political system militated against black power or dignity. This time was the time of Scottsboro. The play within the play (of the trials) then begins as a flashback to the 1930s. Dutt starts at the beginning of the November 1933 trial, taking place soon after Judge Horton's opinion. At this point in the Scottsboro narrative, two trials have already taken place rendering guilty verdicts, the Communist Party is publicizing and politicizing the trials across the world, and the world is also coming to terms with growing fascism in

Europe. Progressive German forces responded actively to the Scottsboro crisis and a New York–based German political theater group, the German Proletariat Theatre, wrote and performed an agitprop piece in 1931 entitled *Scottsboro.*

One significant portion of the Scottsboro narrative left out of the Dutt text is the landmark shift of judges. After the second trial, Judge Horton, a liberal, progressive Southern Democrat was removed from the case and Alabama appointed Judge William Callahan, a right-wing populist not formally educated in the law. Callahan appears in Dutt's play from the start of Act II and his impetuous interruptions of Leibowitz imply that the entire Scottsboro affair was characterized by such behavior. In fact, the previous trial of March–April 1933 presided over by Judge Horton showed a far different legal context. Here Judge Horton ended his trial encouraging the jurors to exhibit fairness, tolerance, and a respect for justice.[7]

In Dutt's play, Act II covers the trial in which Thomas Knight, Jr., the Attorney General of Alabama, led a prosecution against Haywood Patterson, defended by Samuel Leibowitz, with Judge William Callahan presiding. This trial occurred in November 1933, though Dutt's text lists an incorrect date — November 20, 1931 — at the top of Act II. A whole range of history that took place before and after this particular trial informs the events Dutt portrays in his story.

This history includes the massive press build-up of the Communist Party and the trial in which Leibowitz and Knight fought under Judge Horton, a far different experience than a trial under Judge Callahan. Dutt even alludes to this history on page 28, when Joseph Brodsky objects to the composition of the jury and Callahan responds by assuring Brodsky that the "first jury would be retained for this trial as well."[8] By point of historical fact, the trial in Dutt's play is the third trial and Judge Callahan is referring to the jury used in the second trial completed in Decatur earlier that year. This demonstrates, however, that Dutt was aware of the multiple trials the Scottsboro defendants endured. Also, on page 84, during Attorney General Knight's interrogation of Haywood Patterson, Knight asks him if he was tried before, in Scottsboro. Haywood responds by saying "the trial there was a farce." These two references clarify that Dutt was aware of the plurality of trials the Scottsboro defendants had to experience.

Even though he incorrectly lists 1931 at the top of Act II instead of 1933, the events portrayed in Act II conform to the historical record. True to transcripts of the trials and coverage of the trials by scholars and journalists,[9] Callahan behaved callously and spared no attempt at interrupting and manipulating Leibowitz's legal strategies. Additionally, Leibowitz's courtroom antics in Dutt's text find confirmation in most accounts of the trial. After the trial ends with a guilty verdict, the play then includes an epilogue with the same black power activists implementing their own execution upon a white rapist Marine. Right before they execute him, they declare Haywood Patterson, the most articulate defendant in the Scottsboro trials and the semi-protagonist of Act II of *Maanusher Adhikare*, an "unarmed martyr ... [whose last words were] the day when my brothers rise up with guns, I will live again" (92).

The actual Haywood Patterson never uttered those words and was never executed by the state. After being denied pardons and parole, Haywood Patterson was incarcerated for the 1930s and most of the 1940s in various jails in Alabama. He was moved from death row in Kilby Prison to other jails in Birmingham and Etowah, depending on his legal situation regarding death sentencing. In 1948, he fled Kilby Prison and made it to Detroit where the FBI captured him in 1950. Michigan authorities, however, refused to extradite him. While in Detroit, he was able to collaborate with Earl Conrad to write the historical account, *Scottsboro Boy*, in 1950. In the meantime, he was arrested and convicted on other charges in Michigan. In 1952, while in jail, he died of cancer. Although the events in Act II are historically accurate, the martyrdom attributed to him by Dutt's prologue black power activists is completely fictional.

Another aspect of the Scottsboro narrative that escapes inclusion into *Maanusher Adhikare* is the maelstrom of political activity that occurred after the 1933 Decatur trial chronicled in Act II. In 1935, the Scottsboro Defense Committee (SDC) was formed with the help of the ILD and sympathetic activists and politicians all over the country. The young New York preacher Allan Knight Chalmers, made extraordinary strides toward helping the Scottsboro defendants and formed an Alabama chapter. Most of the defendants' lives were spent in jail waiting on appeal after appeal. In 1937, four of the nine boys, Roberson, Montgomery, Williams, and Roy Wright had the charges against them dropped. After this development Chalmers and the SDC pushed to receive pardons for the remaining five. Only one, Clarence Norris, finally received a pardon in 1976 whereas three others were paroled in the 1940s.[10]

Other areas in Dutt's text would rankle an historian of early twentieth-century America. Regarding the status of Ruby Bates and Victoria Price as prostitutes, white men refer to these women, in Dutt's play, as "whores," on page 18 and 21, before the trial began. White men, regardless of economic class, would probably never have referred to any white woman in such a manner. These occurrences appear in Dutt's text at points in the narrative where it is even unlikely that anyone would have known about Bates' and Price's reputation as prostitutes. Nobody would have known about Bates and Price because Leibowitz's courtroom corroboration of their prostitution and reputations hadn't yet happened.

Dutt also takes license with the historical pattern of events at Paint Rock station in 1931. During their infamous capture, the boys were rounded up and sent to the Jackson County jail in Scottsboro. As the boys were being loaded into a truck to be taken to the jail, Ruby Bates approached the Deputy Sheriff of Jackson County, Charlie Latham, and then accused the boys of raping her and Victoria Price. This occurred approximately twenty minutes after the train had stopped at Paint Rock. Having arrived at the Scottsboro jail, Jackson County Sheriff M.L. Wann sent Bates and Price for medical examinations. At the jail, a large mob had gathered in front of the jail yelling: "Give 'em to us!" and "Let those niggers out!" With the help of plainclothes civilians he just deputized, he guarded the jail and prevented a lynching from taking place. Believing that the mob may overtake the jail, with the help of recently deputized assistants, Sheriff Wann transferred the boys to another jail in nearby Etowah, to await trial.[11]

In *Maanusher Adhikare*, a confrontation occurs between the boys and the local deputies assigned to arraigning and transporting them to jail. In this confrontation, locals accuse the boys of rape based on a quick off-stage testimony by Bates and Price. Here the local deputies violently question the boys, especially Haywood Patterson. The deputies and the boys have a protracted argument in which the deputies demand that they boys confess to their crime and boys respond. Haywood even goes so far as to say on page 20 that "I couldn't do something as heinous as this to a woman, black or white." Also on page 20, after being punched by the local deputies, Haywood says, "My father and mother are honest working folk. They taught me that the human body — human beings — are to be honored. These two women — white, pink, whatever — they are liars! Haywood Patterson has never put his hands on a woman who is not willing!"

Though Haywood was undoubtedly the most articulate of the group, this type of language probably never arose. For much of the play, Haywood acts as a rising protagonist who represents the entire group, who fights back, and who always responds to white racism. In this respect as well, Dutt takes license with history, as both the type of language he would have spoken as well as his actions were not nearly as magnificent as Dutt makes them out to be. Dutt also embellishes the events at Paint Rock before the trials occurred. Though a large crowd had gathered due to quickly spreading rumors, the attacks on the boys portrayed in the play simply did not take place.

Another point of historical accuracy is worthy of mention. During the start of the trial, on pages 24 and 25, reporters goad Attorney General Knight and his team to mention the many people around the world who supported the defendants. A rising litany of names and then corresponding and increasingly vulgar responses by court spectators to the names then appears, such as

Romain Rolland — a frog-eating Frenchman, Madame Sun Yat-Sen — chink, Thomas Mann, Einstein — Jew bastards, Theodore Dreiser — Judas. Not only is this occurrence unlikely, but also the probability that spectators in the courtroom would know of these people and respond to their names being uttered is as unlikely.

The characterization of Samuel Leibowitz by Dutt warrants similar scrutiny. Leibowitz appears as a radical activist committed to the International Labor Defense and to the Communist Party. Although Leibowitz fought tirelessly for the defendants through several trials and appeals, he was hardly a Communist, by affiliation or by ideology. He was a Democrat and a believer in the American system of politics, justice, and capitalism. Leibowitz became wealthy as a criminal lawyer defending anyone who claimed innocence through expert research and interrogation of witnesses who often were lying. The ILD approached Leibowitz because of his impeccable record and attention to justice, even though he wasn't a Communist. When William Patterson, then national secretary of the ILD, asked Leibowitz to head the defense team, he assured Leibowitz that he would not be expected to espouse Communism or give up any of his own views.

It is rumored that Leibowitz seized upon the opportunity to increase his own fame by winning a landmark case that was already making international headlines. Whatever the case may have been, Leibowitz was not a political crusader nor was he a radical social activist. He was an expert lawyer who was eager to win and prove that the justice system could work all in the South as well as the North. He went so far as to say that "if it is justice that these black men be adjudged innocent... I cannot believe that the people of Alabama will be false to their great heritage of honor, and to those brave and chivalrous generations of the past, in whose blood the history of their state is written."[12] These are not the words of a radical Communist, but of a Northern liberal out to prove that justice does get served. Many times during the entire Scottsboro affair, headstrong Leibowitz butted heads with Communist Joseph Brodsky, also assigned to the case. However, in Dutt's text, Leibowitz and Brodsky seem both to be ardently in support of Communist Party directives and of the agenda of radical social change. In Leibowitz's closing statements on page 88 and 89, he delivers an ornate critique of the racism that he witnessed in Alabama and the outrage he has over the American racialized legal system. He actually paraphrases Martin Luther King's "I Have a Dream" speech from the 1963 March on Washington. During the final portion of his closing arguments on page 89, he includes a long call to radical arms:

> We are not protestors, nor are we acting out in self defense. We are defendants and we are accusers. Our charge is *against the millionaires who run the United States*, who divide us to kill our brothers for mere political gains. Against those

who are smearing the great reputation of America before all people of color of the world and making us hang our heads in shame. Against those who are opposing our government and keeping racism alive, stirring it up. The decision is yours, but don't deny human beings their human rights [italics mine].

After this, Leibowitz holds a quick conference with Attorney General Knight and then does not utter another word in the play. Such a speech would be likely to come from a Communist like Joseph Brodsky, not Samuel Leibowitz. Whereas Dutt acquired a steady stream of information about activities of the Communist Party in America and throughout the world, it is likely the Party newspapers had colored Leibowitz a little bit redder than he really was.

Though Dutt's literary characterization bears out this interpretation, his reflections on his own performance as Leibowitz in the 1968–69 Calcutta production signal political self-awareness and audience participation in the creation of character:

> I was engrossed in the ideals of the man, his unrelenting fight for the rights of his black client, Haywood Patterson, defying the hysterical white mob. Right through rehearsals I was trying to build up this idealistic lawyer, refusing to compromise in any way whatsoever. But that was not the part I had written, and it needed the first-night audience to break down this one-sided and false picture of an airy idealist, and bring out a shrewd, earthy professional lawyer, who knew every dirty trick the prosecution was likely to play and played it better. The way the audience greeted the first cross-examination of a false witness — a roguish, sympathetic laugh, that seemed to wink and say: we know you are tricking the man into perjury, but well done, only crooks can fight crooks.... In my struggle with the part of Liebowitz, almost unknown to me, I had sought a mechanical solution to the problem of Good and Bad, and had thought of Leibowitz as a Messiah. The constant factor — audience — rectified this process, and I was forced into the negative features of the man.... All the elements of Leibowitz's cunning and even brutality were there in the play all the time, staring at me. And yet in rehearsals I had moderated them to the kind pronouncements of a latter-day sermon on the mount [qtd. in Ghosh 53–54].

In Dutt's analysis of his own performance and relationship to the audience, he anticipated critical problems identified thirty-seven years later!

Dutt's awareness of the tension between melodrama and realism in his play functions as more than simply an interesting endnote. Indeed, Dutt's entire theatrical manifesto was marked by a commitment to form. Form was at least as important as content to Dutt.[13] In Dutt's particular context — that of a postcolonial playwright critiquing empire — melodrama occupies a particularly vexing position. Dutt's sensitivity toward the melodramatic component in politically-inspired theater, and for a postcolonial audience, touches upon a broader issue in postcolonial dramatic aesthetics. Unlike the role of melodrama in the West, such as the well-known nineteenth-century melodramas of England and the United States, realism and modernism in post-colonial theatre do not neatly arrive in a package that has evolved out of its formative, melodramatic stages.[14] Though the notion of melodrama evolving into realism has been critiqued,[15] Dutt worked in a vastly different political, cultural, and dramaturgical universe than any dramatist in the West using melodrama, or confronting melodrama, in their politics. Unlike a Brecht, who certainly advocated the use of song, dance, and spectacle, Dutt's aesthetics were informed by a colonial theatre history in which dramatic performance and dramaturgical development were colored by Orientalism, racism, and colonial modernity.[16] For a playwright whose history is shaped by the dislocations of a rising fascism, like Brecht, but also by an altogether colonially-inflected experience of the theatre, melodrama and realism do not oppose each other in stark evolutionary terms.

Indeed, melodrama may even be essential to the politicization of theatre. Melodrama's potential purchase with radical politics certainly enjoys a precedent in the West, as in the plays of famous melodramatists like Boucicault and Stowe.[17] Critics all commented on the heavy-handed nature of the melodramatic dialogues and characterizations, to the degree that they exceeded their own staying power. For Dutt, though, we also see a remarkable awareness of the written text's relationship with the performance text. From reading *Maanusher Adhikare*, a picture of Leibowitz as tireless social crusader is easily drawn. But Dutt admits that the audience had a major role to play in shaping how Leibowitz would eventually work. Not only a peripheral role but a major part was played by the audience in making sure that this production's politics were not simply a company of leftists speaking to other leftists, but also included the agency of Leibowitz's other sides, like his cunning and his will to win. This in turn sharpens Dutt's piece as historical drama, as propaganda piece, and as experiment in political aesthetics.

From Decatur to Dutt

Writing in 1961, Dutt took merely three days to create a play out of only the court transcripts in front of him. From 1961, when Dutt began writing the play, Vietnam splashed onto the world's newspapers and civil rights workers had started freedom rides into the South. By the time the play was produced in Calcutta in late 1968 and continued to run in repertory through 1969, the American civil rights movement and the chaos of the 1960s had taken full force. The Naxalbari uprising, a Maoist movement in the Bengal countryside, had also begun in 1967. The famous year of 1968 is usually marked by the assassination of Martin Luther King and Bobby Kennedy, the student revolutions in France, the Cultural Revolution in China, the chaotic and violent Democratic National Convention in Chicago, and the Soviet invasion of Czechoslovakia and the end of the Prague Spring. Most of these events are understood as landmark moments in modern history.

In its Indian context, the 1968–69 production of *Maanusher Adhikare* drew a variety of responses from the Calcutta press. Writing for *Frontier*, a primary vehicle for commentary and critique in post-independence Calcutta, Sumanta Banerjee commented on how powerfully the play confronts the futility of liberal and non-violent politics in a racialized society, as he argued that "the entire burden of the play indicates the futility of the liberals' struggle for justice in a race-ridden society" (qtd. in Chattopadhyay 255). While Banerjee appreciated Dutt's political dramaturgy the *Amrita Bazar Patrika*'s review thought that the "dramatist could be a little more forgiving [in its propaganda]: he could add some more good fellows to diversify the crowd of rabid Whites [in the trial scenes]" (qtd. in Chattopadhyay 160). Overall, however, this critic found a Brechtian satisfaction in the way Dutt forced the audience to "forget their positions on this side of the footlights and behave at times like persons identified with the force of the cause, presented in the other side ... in their willing suspension of the observer's role" (qtd. in Chattopadhyay 161).

On the issue of the Black Power prologue and epilogue, most critics agreed with *The Statesman*—one of India's oldest English-language newspapers — and its reviewer who wished to be "spared these lectures, which do little to reinforce the moral; in fact the, the contrivance by which the bitter legacy of the American south is linked to the present Negro militancy could altogether been avoided" (qtd. in Chattopadhyay 156). All recognized the technical splendor, the use of Black American spirituals and folksongs, and the quality of acting, but though almost all supported the theme, few supported the heavy-handed propaganda. Dutt had no problems admitting that the play directly propagandized his politics, as he said in 1968 — being influenced by Piscator — that "the most effective political propaganda is propaganda that places facts and truths at the disposal of the audience" (qtd. in Ghosh 54). For the critics, the political propaganda didn't ring truly enough.

Maanusher Adhikare as Postcolonial Praxis

Errors in historical accuracy abound in Dutt's text: the date at the top of Act II, the use of flowery, standard English for characters such as Haywood Patterson, the presentation of Leibowitz as a social radical,[18] and discrepancies in historical chronology. Though Dutt based the play entirely on library research, he certainly integrated a detailed understanding of American history into the details of the story he wished to tell. Leibowitz has been recorded as saying that he chose to represent the boys to defend "the basic rights of man," the phrase that served as the title of the play (qtd. in Goodman 104). Dutt also incorporated into his text Langston Hughes' poem "The Negro Speaks of Rivers" by including a paraphrase of it in the lines of a black power activist in the epilogue. He was evidently aware of Martin Luther King, Jr.'s, "I Have a Dream" speech on the 1963 March on Washington as elements of it appear in Leibowitz's lines near the end of the play. Names like Paul Robeson, Malcolm X, Abraham Lincoln — essential figures in African American history — also appear in appropriate settings in his epilogue. This demonstrates Dutt's facility with his chosen topic, even with the occasional mishaps in historical chronology.

As Dutt pained to create a theater style whose dramaturgy as well as politics preached revolution, he destabilized the hackneyed notion that the "West" over-determined and Orientalized the "non–West." Two issues often overlooked in contemporary postcolonial discourse emerge from a reading of Dutt's important text. First, America — with all of its internal tensions and contradictions — is constructed as the "West," as opposed to imperial Britain or France, the usual targets of non-metropolitan writers. Secondly, the theatre becomes a site of critical engagement. Understandings of colonial encounters, debates, and aesthetics, in the South Asian context, have long been focused on the novel and other forms of written literature at the expense of theater, performance, and non-literary forms of communication.[19] Academic and popular appreciation of South Asia's aesthetic contributions to the world has been dominated by English-language prose, the Bollywood film industry, and emergent English-language diasporic cinema. Theater in South Asian languages, a lively site for critique, engagement, and encounter rarely makes academic or popular headlines. With Dutt's *Maanusher Adhikare*, we find a glimpse into how the formerly colonized may have understood the West in ways not captured in novels or films. Dutt offers a sophisticated commentary on what is at stake and how his fight — an international, Marxist fight — shall take place. The time for putting theater in its postcolonial place is long overdue.[20]

NOTES

1. The most recent work on French theatrical appropriations of India is Binita Metha, *Widows, Pariahs, and Bayederes: India as Spectacle* (Lewisburg, PA: Bucknell University Press, 2002). Though a full-scale historical investigation of how India has been represented across various European and American stages awaits its researcher, a sizable literature has analyzed the ways in which Peter Brook's interests in India manifested in his

theatrical and cinematic work. A collection of works that engages the debates about the Orientalizing impulses in Brook's *Mahabharata* appears in David Williams (ed.), *Peter Brook and the Mahabharata: Critical Perspectives* (New York: Routledge, 1991).

2. For the visual arts, see Hermione De Almedia and George H. Gilpin, *Indian Renaissance: British Romantic Art and the Prospect of India* (London: Ashgate, 2005) for a recent appraisal. The scholarly literature on the representations of India in British novels is vast; M. Keith Booker, *Colonial Power, Colonial Texts: India in the Modern British Novel* (Ann Arbor: University of Michigan Press, 1997) contains a useful overview of the major debates in the field. Jyotsna Singh's *Colonial Narratives/Cultural Dialogues: "Discoveries" of India in the Language of Colonialism* (London: Routledge, 1996) contains a useful chapter "The English Nabobs: Eighteenth-Century Orientalism," which offers insightful analysis of Samuel Foote's 1778 play *The Nabob*. Another excellent analysis of this play occurs in Stephen Gregg, "Representing the Nabob: India, Stereotypes, and Eighteenth Century Theatre" in Tasleem Shakur and Karen D'Souza (eds.), *Picturing South Asian Culture in English: Textual and Visual Representations* (Liverpool, UK: Open House Press, 2003). Mita Choudhury in *Interculturalism and Resistance in the London Theatre, 1660–1800: Identity, Performance, and Empire* (Lewisburg, PA: Bucknell University Press, 2000) also includes a useful approach to how British playwrights, producers, and actors often depended on the "foreign" for creating a British theatre culture. Chatterjee, *The Colonial Staged*, argues that Orientalist ideas of Indian theatre infected the growing numbers of South Asian (for Chatterjee, Bengali) playwrights of the nineteenth century.

3. A growing literature on South Asian American studies, including Prasad and Bhatia has begun to create an analytical foundation for the study of cross-cultural traffic in the arts and culture between South Asia and America. However, theatre as a political and aesthetic corridor between the two areas, has received almost no scholarly attention. A small but fledgling number of works confront the South Asian diaspora and its theatre traditions, such as Chatterjee, "South Asian American Theatre" and Bose, ed., but the representation of America in South Asian–language theatre is nearly absent from contemporary criticism.

4. Dutt has encountered such a conflict in the creation of *Maanusher Adhikare* as well — see the section below on this subject.

5. Gondolas were cars with sides extending upward five feet from the floor. In the train in question, the gondolas were half-filled with ballast, a gravel called "chert." See Carter 4–10.

6. The NAACP backed away from the case in 1932 and the ILD seized the case for its purpose of protesting capitalist-backed oppression worldwide.

7. See Goodman 173–82.

8. All references to the play refer to Neilesh Bose and Sudipto Chatterjee, eds., *The Rights of Man* (Kolkata: Seagull India, 2009).

9. The main accounts of the Scottsboro narrative, Carter's *Scottsboro: A Tragedy of the American South* and Goodman's *Stories of Scottsboro*, confirm Dutt's representation of this trial, especially Callahan's behavior and Leibowitz's energetic performances.

10. See Goodman 278–318 and Carter 369–98, *passim*.

11. This account is taken from Patterson and Conrad and the description in Carter 4–10.

12. Leibowitz 189–90, quoted in Goodman 104.

13. See Chatterjee, "Utpal Dutt," and Gunawardana for analyses of Dutt's political aesthetics.

14. See Hays and Nikolopoulou for a collection of essays on this theme and Gerould for a discussion of melodrama's relation to realism.

15. See Postlewait for a critique of how melodrama is often relegated to realism's precursor in an evolutionary, linear sense.

16. See Chatterjee, *The Colonial Staged,* for an analysis of this process in the 19th century Bengali context.

17. See Chatterjee, "From 'Vanguard,'" for a recent take on the avant-garde theatre in the Bengali context, including the Indian People's Theatre Association and the aesthetic politics Dutt strongly advocated.

18. Dutt himself was aware of this one-sidedness in his analysis of his own performance (noted in this essay).

19. See Bhatia for an argument that stresses the importance of theater in colonial and postcolonial South Asia. Other relevant analyses of contemporary Indian theatre include Dalmia, Dharwadker, and Chatterjee, *Theatre Beyond the Threshold.*

20. I wish to thank Sudipto Chatterjee for his range of talents that resulted in our joint translation of *Maanusher Adhikare.* Thanks also to Kevin J. Wetmore, Jr., the editor of this volume, for his vision and patience.

8

KATHY's Parody of *Singin' in the Rain*

Nobuko Anan

On a green lawn under the bright sunshine, three blond-wigged Japanese women in American dresses from the fifties and sixties dance around, fall over, and have a tea party to the accompaniment of Gene Kelly, Debbie Reynolds, and Donald O'Connor singing "Good Morning" from classic film *Singin' in the Rain* (1952). In the film, a "good" girl Kathy played by Debbie Reynolds dubs the blond bombshell star, but in this dance of the performance troupe also named KATHY, the members are dubbed by these Americans — with their faces obscured by black tights, these performers have no mouths. What can such a performance tell us about contemporary Japan's national self-image? Do the antics of these performance artists reveal gender conflicts within Japan?

This paper examines the performance troupe KATHY's parody of *Singin' in the Rain* in light of the issue of postwar Japan's national identity crisis and the stereotypical gender identity that continues to be faced by contemporary Japanese women. The key metaphor of the film I will focus on is the change from silent film to talking pictures that is shown by the split between body and voice and the dubbing of the female voice. I will scrutinize how the troupe KATHY appropriates such split in their parody of the film in their video work *Mission/K* (2002)[1] in order to resignify the Japanese women's bodies constructed as the byproduct of postwar, U.S.–defined modernity.

KATHY is an all-female Japanese dance/performance troupe formed in 2002. With a name evoking the image of generic American white women, three members usually wear blond, bobbed wigs and 1950s/1960s-style pastel-colored dresses. This nostalgic, lovely image of good girls is mixed with grotesqueness since they cover their faces with black tights and their arms and legs with white tights, thus obscuring their racial and personal identities. They de-personalize themselves, claiming to be under surveillance and controlled by an invisible, powerful, god-like entity called Kathy. Thus, the group name is also the name of this entity that urges them to dance/perform. Henceforth, following Carol Martin's article, which includes a brief analysis of the group, I use "KATHY" to refer to the group name and "Kathy" to refer to the god-like entity.[2]

Coming from a background of classical ballet, the members of KATHY often parody Western dance. In their parody of *Singin' in the Rain*, they are seen performing in a Broadway manner as though through a fish-eye lens, thus giving viewers the impression that they are watching KATHY's performance through Kathy's surveillance camera. Typical of their performances, the members occasionally perform "failure" in a very humorous way; for example, they might fall down or dance a misstep. I would argue that these failures performatively suggest that they cannot/do not live up to Americanization (as "demanded" by Kathy). Before interrogating the performance, I will present some historical and theoretical background to ground this discussion. Note: I follow Japanese name order in this essay, family name precedes given name.

Postwar Japan: "Little Boy" and Invisible Women's Bodies

JAPANESE WOMEN'S BODIES— NATIONALISM AS AESTHETICS

Japan's modernization project began in the late nineteenth century. After the early phase of the project, which was based on an imitation and adaptation of Western modernity, what emerged is, according to Yumiko Iida, "nationalism as aesthetics" or the "anti-modern revolt" which is "expressed in calls for Japanese identity in which the aesthetic desire cultivated by the inscriptional violence of the modern is confused with the desire for national identity" (6). In Western-defined modernization/rationalization, things Japanese could only be expressed by aesthetic terms, since the realm of Japanese aesthetics was "discovered" and valued by the West, and hence not abolished in the national pursuit of Western-defined modernity (Iida 14). *Kokutai*, which arose as a corporeal regime in the 1890s (Oguma 50) and most strictly regulated the people's physical bodies in the 1930s as a wartime ideology (Iida 19; Igarashi 48–52), is a manifestation of nationalism as aesthetics. Translated as national body or polity, *kokutai* defines the Japanese as the members of the extended Imperial Family sharing "a timeless Japanese cultural essence" embodied by the Emperor (Iida 5). In *kokutai*, Japanese women's bodies were assigned the role of "good wives, wise mothers," who reproduce culturally pure Japanese males who can fight to extend the Emperor's territory. Thus, while men were associated with the progressive power to transform Japan into a modern nation-state, women were fixed in traditional roles as the core of the national essence.

After the defeat in World War II, Japan was forced to transform into a democratic nation by the U.S. Occupation (1945–1952). While Japan's prewar modernization was modeled on European nation-states such as Britain and France, its postwar modernization looked solely to the U.S., with democracy as a symbol of modernity. In this period, women's status seemed to have been drastically changed. For instance, they were given suffrage in 1945 (Iida 69).

In these circumstances, however, "nationalism as aesthetics" arose again as a manifestation of the masculinist desire to return Japanese women's bodies to their "proper" role. In mainstream, postwar *shingeki*,[3] male theatrical authorities seemed not only to have cast a nostalgic gaze on Japan's "glorious" past but also to have attempted to suppress their fear of Americanized Japanese women. Carol Fisher Sorgenfrei suggests in her analysis of *Bungaku-za*'s (The Literary Theater) productions of *A Streetcar Named Desire* (beginning in 1953) that Blanche Du Bois's nostalgia for Belle Reve signified Japanese nationalists' longing for the prewar period. However, at the same time, Blanche, who molested a teenage boy, resembled *pan pan* (prostitutes for American soldiers) and threatened Japanese men's masculinity. Thus, by having a Japanese actress perform such an American woman who is destroyed by excessive or aggressive characteristics of modernity, argues Sorgenfrei, these males could both express their nostalgia for prewar Japan and warn Japanese female audience members not to be like American women ("Victory in Defeat; Mimetic Transformation and the Performance of National Identity in Postwar Japan," paper presented at American Society for Theatre Research in 2006).

Male literary figures in the 1950s and the 1960s also reacted to the symbolic castration by the U.S. and attempted to bring back the lost Japanese "strong" male bodies. Novelist/playwright Mishima Yukio, who often narcissistically staged his homoerotic, bodybuilder-like body, committed ritual disembowelment in 1970 after his paramilitary group failed to convince postwar Japan to bring back Emperor worship as the national essence (Sorgenfrei 165; Iida 147–150). Moreover, literary critic Etō Jun mourned the loss of what he believed to be the traditional Japanese family, in which father as the patriarch represents ethics while mother always sacrifices herself for her male child(ren) (Iida 133–137). He considered that the emergence of Americanized mothers brought about by the U.S. "reinstallation of the modern" (Iida 5) had displaced fathers from the divine patriarchy and claimed that, in such an inverted "fatherless" Japanese society, children would remain "immature," lacking an ethical foundation (Iida 136–137).

POSTWAR JAPAN AS "LITTLE BOY"

This rhetoric of the Japanese as "immature" within the U.S. hegemony bears a striking similarity to the theorization of postwar Japanese mentality as "Little Boy" explicated by Murakami Takashi. Murakami is a contemporary male Japanese visual artist whose works are inspired by *otaku* (primarily young male geek) subculture/pop culture.[4] Both his artistic works and his theorization of postwar Japanese culture have been increasingly gaining international attention since the late 1990s. He defines Japanese art, mainly paintings and drawings, from the traditional to the contemporary as "Superflat," that is, something which neither has any depth/hidden truth beneath the two-dimensional surface nor makes clear distinctions between high and low art, both of which typify Western modern art ("A Theory of Super Flat Japanese Art" in *Superflat* 9–25).

Murakami also applies the concept to his analyses of postwar Japanese culture and society in *Little Boy*, a bilingual (Japanese with English translation) catalogue of an exhibit of the same title he organized in New York in 2005. First, he declares that "'Super flatness' is an original concept of the Japanese," although now they have been "completely Westernized"[5] ("A Theory of Super Flat Japanese Art" 5, also qtd. in "Superflat" 155–156).[6] He then extends his terms to include how Japanese culture was "super flattened" by the U.S. Occupation and the continuing American influence ("Earth" 101). In his idea, "monotony" in the name of social equality, or flatness in his term, was brought about by U.S. domination, and it affected the traditional Japanese aesthetic sense of flatness in a negative way ("Earth" 101; "Superflat" 152). In other words, the traditional aesthetic of two-dimensionality was transformed into a superflat, monotonous aesthetic as a result of the U.S. hegemony.

Murakami equates such monotony in postwar Japanese society with a system that does not mature the people: "Postwar Japan was given life and nurtured by America. We ... were taught to live without thought. Our society and hierarchies were dismantled. We were forced into a system that does not produce 'adults'" ("Tokyo Pop" in *Kôkoku Hihyô*, cited in "Superflat" 152). Thus, in "Superflat" Japan live the Japanese who have been "Little Boys" ever since an atomic bomb "Little Boy" ended the war.

Murakami's theory of "Superflat" is another example of "nationalism as aesthetics," which emanates from Japan from the 1990s onward. Its cooperation with the United States in the Gulf War and the Iraq War shook Japan's pacifist constitution, which was created under the surveillance of SCAP, and yet, contradictorily, has been in danger of violation by Japan's participation in U.S.–led international affairs. This irony forced the Japanese to reconfront the fact that Japan is still under U.S. hegemony. Murakami's nationalist sentiment is manifested in his lament for postwar Japanese who have become "Little Boys" without the "vigor" that imperialist Japan supposedly (in nostalgic memory) possessed ("Earth" 111).

Another equally important issue about Murakami's theory of "Superflat" is, as Marilyn Ivy points out, the absence of women, even though the catalogue *Little Boy* includes a few women artists (502). In his writings, he avoids using the term *shônen* (boy), and instead uses a gender-neutral term *kodomo* (child). However, with the English translation "Little Boy," his basic attitude of excluding women is clear. A further example is in his suggestion that contemporary Japan is marked by "a sense of impotence" ("Earth" 137). These examples imply that his concern is the feminized and childlike status imposed on Japanese men by the "adult male" of the United States.[7] From such a stance, it would not be difficult to imagine a resurgence of the desire to regulate women's bodies as self-sacrificing or self-effacing "good wives, wise mothers," which is another side of the desire to bring back masculinist Japan.

It is therefore interesting that KATHY performed in 2002 at GEISAI ("art festival"), organized and chaired by Murakami for the purpose of developing a unique form of Japanese art.[8] Through GEISAI, he attempts to challenge Western art with what he thinks of as unique Japanese art (*The GEISAI* 7), by which he means postwar Japanese art created through the appropriation of negative, mutated postwar Superflatness. He tries to turn the status of "Little Boy" in the Superflat space into the positive uniqueness of contemporary Japanese art ("Earth" 149; "Superflat" 161). At this event, the members of KATHY performed and sold copies of their first video *Mission/K*.[9] The performance of "Little Girls" came out of Murakami's masculinist and nationalist event as if to challenge such ideologies.

Reconsideration of Japanese Women's Bodies

WHO AND WHAT IS KATHY/KATHY?

The members of KATHY do not reveal their identities and never talk about their works in public. It is commonly assumed that it is a Japanese troupe[10] and that the members are female. Other basic information about them is available at their website: they claim that they are under surveillance by a powerful yet unseen entity called Kathy and that they have to fulfill missions constantly assigned to them by Kathy.[11] Also, other information can be found as "rumors" in several art magazines/journals. "Rumors" say that they are skilled dancers with a background in classical ballet.[12] Also, they are well known in the field of contemporary dance (Sakurai, "Skills" 204). Moreover, according to one rumor in an article in the culture magazine *Dazed and Confused Japan*, their boss Kathy is "a typical American" (Harada 25), although the article does not specify what it means by "typical."[13] From these, it is reasonable to conclude that KATHY's parodies of Western dance are their means to display their Westernized/Americanized Japanese bodies as well as to wittily denaturalize the "organic" beauty and grace of Western/American dance. Since what they do in their performance is the mission assigned to them by Kathy, one may say that their parodies are also ordered by Kathy and hence they have no agency. However, I wonder if a performative force with a generic Western name would really have those under its surveillance make fun of Western traditions. If this were the case, this performative force would strangely turn out to be a deconstructive force. I will come back to this point again at the end of this essay. Suffice it to say that the members are exploiting the very situation over which they are supposed to have no agency. As Carol Martin points out, "The performers [of KATHY] disbelieve in their own agency as they obey Kathy's commands and believe in their own agency as they create ways to subvert Kathy's commands" (53).

THE END OF THE U.S. OCCUPATION AND CONTINUING SPLIT OF JAPAN'S VOICE AND BODY

The central issue of KATHY's parody of *Singin' in the Rain* seems to be having Kathy or "a typical American" as their boss. The original film begins with the split of voice and body and ends with their unity. This appears to parallel the situation of immediate postwar Japan, that is, transformation from the defeated voiceless nation into a full-fledged nation independent of the U.S. occupation. Whether intentionally or not, the parallel between the film and their parody seems too clear for mere coincidence. The film depicts Hollywood in 1927 when the industry shifted from silent to sound cinema, which visualizes body with voice as the "totality" or as the "organic" (Doan 363–4). It also traces the process in which male characters split two female characters' voices and at the same time, literally appropriate their bodies, only to finally bring these disjointed elements together into one woman's body. Below is a summary of the film.

Don Lockwood (played by Gene Kelly) is a superstar in silent films, but the studio he works for decides to shift to sound cinema. This causes Don trouble, since blond bombshell Lina Lamont, who always plays the role of his lover in their films, has a shrill voice and an uncultured speech style, which do not match her beautiful appearance. His lifelong friend and colleague Cosmo Brown (Donald O'Connor) comes up with the idea of having Don's real life lover Kathy Selden (Debbie Reynolds), who has the same name as the performance troupe KATHY, dub Lina. With Kathy Selden's help, the film turns out to be a great success. Lina insists that her contract allows her to keep Kathy as her voice, without acknowledging this to the audience. But after the movie's premiere, when the stars come onstage in person and perform, Don and Cosmo pull open a curtain to reveal Kathy, who is standing behind it while dubbing Lina's voice (just as she does in the film). Hence, these men return Kathy's voice to her body. Thus, as Peter Wollen argues, "The underlying theme is that of nature as truth and unity, versus artifice as falsehood and separation" (55).

The year 1953, when *Singin' in the Rain* first came out in Japan, is also the year marking the beginning of a democratic, independent nation of Japan, at least formally. Japan was supposed to be able to regain its "organic" body after the U.S. occupation was over in 1952, but that really was not the case. Japan was dependent on the United States politically, militarily, and economically. For instance, the United States–Japan Security Treaty of 1951 granted the United States the right to maintain its military bases in places such as Yokohama and Okinawa. In 1960, the then Prime Minister Kishi Nobusuke tried to revise the 1951 version to make it more equal, but it was renewed with only partial modification, leaving the fundamental power relationship between Japan and the United States unchanged. As Yoshikuni Igarashi writes, the new version made Japan recognize again that "Japan gained concessions only through actively recognizing and internalizing U.S. strategic interests in East Asia" (134). Thus, Japan, although officially independent of the United States, had to internalize the U.S. policy in its newly reborn national body. Japan's voice and body were split.

Singin' in the Rain also has some aspects of the folk musical, which "projects the spectator into a mythicized version of the cultured past" (Rick Altman qtd. in Wollen 55), that is, Hollywood as "a site of Americana" (55). A traditional American value in the film is the "happy family," manifested as the couple of Don Lockwood and Kathy Selden (55). Although the occupation was over, the film might have functioned as a tool to teach the Japanese the value of the American "happy family" in contrast to Japan's pre-war and wartime imperialist "family." The American version of family is based on an idealized democratic, heterosexual, and romantic relationship, with the United

States/Don as husband and Japan/Kathy Selden as wife. Indeed, the Kathy Selden/Debbie Reynolds character is cute and depicted as young and sweet in contrast to Lina Lamont, who is depicted as adult, sexy, evil, and manipulating. This cute Kathy Selden/Debbie Reynolds character may have represented the U.S. ideal model of what Japan should be. As the film looks to the past for the mythicized American cultural essence, the performance troupe KATHY seems to resort to this classic film to trace postwar, mythicized Japanese women's bodies as a reaction to the installation of American values.

KATHY's choice of *Singin' in the Rain*, whether intentionally or not, evokes the fact that Japan continued to be dubbed by the United States even after the occupation; although the film ends with the unity of voice and body, Japan as a nation has not been able to achieve such unity. Indeed, "Good Morning," the musical number to which the members dance, precedes in the original film the moment when Cosmo comes up with the idea of dubbing; right after the number, he demonstrates the effect of dubbing to Don by having Kathy dub himself, singing "Good Morning."

FAILURES TO PERFORM AMERICAN

The members of KATHY perform Americanized Japanese women, wearing blond wigs and pastel-colored dresses and dancing like Broadway dancers, as if not only to ridicule the masculinist construction of Japanese women's bodies as national essence but also to display their bodies as the products of inevitable Americanization. As long as the resurgence of Japanese women's bodies as the national essence is the byproduct of the U.S. "reinstallation of the modern," performing American will just end up reinforcing or affirming U.S. hegemony in Japan. Although performing American may effectively belittle Japanese masculinists' critique of Americanized Japanese women, it still reinforces Japanese women's status as the national essence. In addition, although Japanese women acting like Americans may threaten Japanese masculinists, they would probably look like model Americanized Japanese to the eyes of Americans who aim at transforming Japan into its democratic, female "partner." Kathy Selden, with whom the members of KATHY seem to identify, is actually a good girl who helps an adult man (Don Lockwood) make a successful film by allowing him to split her voice and body. As if to reconsider their Americanized Japanese bodies, the members of KATHY, covering their faces with black tights, perform American while comically showing their failure to perfectly become American, and at the same time, they also make fun of classic American female stereotypes.

Choreographically, there is almost no similarity between the dance of Gene Kelly, Donald O'Connor, and Debbie Reynolds and that of the three members of KATHY, except a few steps from can-can and hula toward the end. Unlike the original version, KATHY's dance has some mime movements; for instance, in "Good Morning" they lower their bodies and writhe with their heads in their hands, then quickly shift to skipping with their arms swinging. They also mime a German drinking a glass of beer to "Guten Morgen!" In this sense, their dance shows more synchronization of lyrics and body movements than the original. However, the important point is that it is not the members who are singing. They use the audio recording of the song, and therefore, they are dubbed by American actors/characters. They cover their faces with black tights and hence have no mouth, making it explicit that they cannot speak for themselves.

The segment of KATHY's dance to "Good Morning" starts with a shot of forests, a grass field adjacent to the forests, and blue sky on a beautiful, bright sunny day. As a prelude to the number proceeds like the overture to a musical show, the camera moves around the forest and starts running fast on the grass, as if looking for someone. Almost at the end of the prelude, the camera stops, and we see the members of KATHY lying in a line on their backs in the field. A dark-colored image framing a screen, which looks like the frame of a fish-eye lens, appears for the first time in this shot and remains during the rest of the performance. It gives the viewers the impression that they are watching the members through Kathy's surveillance camera. At the same time, however, the camera lens sets up the stage for the members to expose the making of the dance or the constructed nature of performance. When Kathy Selden's line "Good mornin'" is heard, the member in the middle swiftly raises her upper body, with her right arm raised to her shoulder height, her elbow bent to make a right angle, and her palm facing forward. It is supposedly a gesture of greeting, but together with her movement like that of a clockwork doll or a robot, it also looks like an oath, pledging that she will dance an American dance to American music, a mission assigned by "a typical American," Kathy. The others on the sides also raise their upper bodies right after the one in the middle, and each of them does a similar but slightly different gesture. This seems to emphasize that they are slightly in a panic, since they have been discovered by Kathy while they are lazily lying down, resting on the ground. Kathy Selden's voice singing "Good mornin'" is like a wake-up call demanding that they perform Kathy/Americanization.

From the immediate refrain of the same melody starting with, again, "Good mornin'," the members start dancing in unison until the end of the lyrics. They put together movements from different Western/American dance traditions, such as ballet, Charleston, and Broadway-style dances. The result looks like a showcase of Western/American dances that these faceless women (with black-tights obscuring individual facial features) are bound to perform as a routine in Americanized postwar Japan.

Performativity is, according to Judith Butler, the authoritative power of compulsory citation and repetition of naturalized practices, which creates and binds subjects (226–227). Thus, Americanization is a performative, since only by accepting the U.S. occupation and constantly internalizing U.S.–defined modernity, could the newly born, democratic nation-state of Japan come into being. Ever since, Japan has been functioning as America's loyal "partner" in the global arena. Likewise, Japanese women's bodies (constructed as the national essence in reaction to such modernity) are also a performative; the category of "good wives, wise mothers" has been reified as the national essence and those who cannot conform to it have been socially stigmatized.

Simultaneously, this same sequence, as performed by KATHY, also deconstructs Western/American dance traditions. The members of KATHY take one movement from a certain tradition and perform it only for a short while, and then abandon it to move on to another movement from a different tradition. Moreover, within these traditions, the dancers are required to look like they are performing beautifully and naturally without any effort; in contrast, the members of KATHY do not try hard to look that way. Rather, they show how much effort it takes them to dance. For example, in a later sequence, they perform the can-can for a brief moment as the characters in the film do, but the way the members shake their heads suggests that they are gasping for breath (although we cannot see their mouths). Thus, while their dance looks like their obedience to Kathy as a performative force, it also manifests their subversive attitude. The space framed by the camera lens functions both as the space under surveillance and as the space where the way such surveillance operates is exposed.

Butler maintains that a performative is not always successful in its attempt to bind and produce subjects. This is so because gender and sexuality are not natural but constructed, and therefore not everyone can fit perfectly or cite and repeat the norms, even though they try (231). She sees the possibility of resistance to and subversion of the heteronormative, masculinist social structure in this failure to cite and repeat. As a strategy for such purposes, Butler examines the hyperbolic performance of queerness: "[t]he subject who is 'queered' into public discourse through homophobic interpellations of various kinds *takes up* or *cites* that very term as the discursive basis for an opposition" (emphasis in original 232). The members of KATHY employ the same strategy. They hyperbolically show their failure to dance American dance, thus exposing Americanization as a performative. Moreover, by hyperbolically performing classic American female stereotypes and comically messing up gender construction, they also reveal gender and Japan's feminized status in its relation to the United States as a performative.

After the lyrics are all sung, their movements in unison start to collapse. This makes a sharp contrast to the original dance in the film, which starts with each character dancing different movements and then shifts to all three dancing in unison after the lyrics end. When the American voice is gone, KATHY's parody of Western/American dance becomes more extreme and funnier. For instance, one of the members simply walks to the middle of the screen, as if she is bored and bothered, but suddenly, she acts like she notices that Kathy is watching her and she starts doing a turn *à la seconde*, a movement that is typically performed by a male ballet dancer. Thus, even though she looks like she is again interpellated by a call from a performative, she only partially fulfills it; she dances, but fails to perform the gender assigned to her. This is followed by other failures. For example, another dancer crosses in front her, trying to dance but merely staggering. She moves out of the screen but soon comes back with a third troupe member. Citing a classic ballet *pas de deux* in which a male dancer kneels and supports a female dancer in *arabesque penchée*, one of the members lowers her body and looks ready to catch the other's hands, but the former drops the latter. Here again, not only is one of the members playing the role of a male dancer, but also, reminiscent of childish play, they mess up the stereotypical gender construction in which a male dancer supports a female dancer.

Indeed, from the very beginning of their dance, the members of KATHY make fun of stereotypically American feminine dance movements and postures. After they answer Debbie Reynolds' "Good mornin'" call, they flap their skirts and move their shoulders up and down. In another moment, they raise their arms and slightly bend their upper bodies backward, which is a typical posture to show off glamorous female bodies. They also push their buttocks out to the camera lens and turn their faces to it like women in advertisements. Moreover, they mimic the typical Broadway musical spatial structure; three of them form a slope by adjusting their height with various postures. Their bodies create a sculpture, displaying depersonalized female bodies. Although all these movements and postures are supposed to be feminine, lovely, and beautiful in a traditional sense, the black tights covering the members' faces turn these stereotypes into something very ugly. In this way, they seem to be making fun of the U.S. "reinstallation of the modern" which defines Japan as its Americanized feminine partner.

Thus, while the members of KATHY embody the fact that they are bound to perform American in postwar Japan, they also expose the fact that Americanization as a performative is not always successful. They emphasize that they do not let Americanization abject their "bodies." In using this term,

I do not mean bodies charged with the "Japanese feminine essence," but rather a concept that I will expand on in a moment. If we follow Murakami's idea that Japan has been infantilized by the United States, KATHY's performance might appear at a first glance to be a declaration of their "unique" and "cool" childishness in contrast to the adult United States. However, I would argue instead that KATHY challenges such Japanese masculinists' nationalism as aesthetics.

KODOMO SHINTAI (CHILD BODY)

In a similar vein to Murakami, dance critic Sakurai Keisuke characterizes contemporary Japanese dancers' bodies as "*kodomo shintai* (child body)" ("Kodomo shintai" 33). In a very essentialist way, he contrasts Westerners' bodies with Japanese bodies, and claims that even in a daily movement such as walking, the difference between Westerners' movements and Japanese ones are obvious; while the Westerners cannot help moving smoothly, the Japanese move jerkily (33). Then he concludes that the former have more rigid control over their bodies, while the latter only have "loose" control over theirs (33). He expands and applies this idea to what he calls the "basic pattern" of Western and Japanese contemporary dance. According to him, orthodox Western contemporary dance is based both on "Western, built-up bodies nurtured by dance history" and on "a high level of skills which is made possible by the solid educational system" ("Skills" 205).[14] In contrast, Japanese contemporary dance has neither of them, but instead, it has Japanese dancers' "children's bodies" (205). Although he seems to be somewhat aware that bodies are not natural but constructed, his argument often slips into essentialist rhetoric.

Like Murakami, Sakurai suggests that this seemingly negative "nature" of Japanese dance could be a unique tool to counter Western, masculinist hegemony in contemporary dance ("Sloppiness" 181). The problem here is that his attempt to discover something uniquely Japanese to counter such hegemony is another example of nationalism as aesthetics. His theory supports the clear binary between Japan/child/female and the West/adult/male, and he celebrates "children's bodies" as the remnant of pure Japanese bodies remaining uninfluenced by the West. Uchino Tadashi speculates, "Sakurai tries to isolate Japan's contemporary dance culture and vocabulary within a global standard of dance and discourse. His goal is to protect Japan's dance culture from the continuing pressure coming from romantic ballet, modern dance, and diverse contemporary dance practices" (58).

Based on the framework of Japan/child versus West/United States/adult, Sakurai describes the members of KATHY as "good students" of Western dance, who, like Western postmodern dancers, make full use of their built-up bodies and techniques in order to perform "silly" ("Skills" 205).[15] Paradoxically, he defines "children's bodies" as lacking self-control, yet he includes in this category KATHY's bodies, which are trained in Western dance. Regarding KATHY's "childishness," he points out that the members often use the ballet technique *en pointe* (standing on tiptoe), which was originally invented to stay balanced, for the precisely opposite purpose of losing balance, thus emphasizing their childlike, Japanese bodies (206–7). Despite the essentialist aspects in his theory of "child body," Sakurai convincingly argues that the members of KATHY possess Westernized techniques yet deconstruct them. What he fails to consider, however, is that KATHY seems to challenge rather than to celebrate the supposed "uniqueness" of Japanese bodies.

KATHY AS *MODOKI*

As long as essential Japaneseness is constructed in the dichotomous framework of Japan and the West, taking childishness as a badge of honor does not fundamentally change Japan's relationship to the West/U.S. nor does it negate Japanese women's bodies constructed as byproducts of Western/American-defined modernity. In the frameworks of Murakami and Sakurai, Japan keeps defining itself through the lens of the West. For them, Japan is defined as a negative: it is not Western/American. In contrast, Iida's formulation of nationalism as aesthetics suggests that unique Japaneseness is imagined in the context of Japanese culture permeated by Western/U.S.–defined modernity. Thus, not being American does not automatically lead to being uniquely Japanese. Rather, it should lead to not being essentially Japanese. Therefore, I would argue that the members of KATHY perform their failure to dance American dance not to mark their unique Japanese bodies, but to deconstruct such uniqueness and eventually to overcome the binary of Westernization/Americanization and the construction of essential Japanese women's bodies. For this purpose, they are parodying the American musical.

KATHY's parody evokes Sakabe Megumi's theorization of the aesthetics of *modoki*, which parodies the god in various traditional Japanese performances. Referring to ethnographer and poet Orikuchi Shinobu's research, Sakabe defines *modoki* as a prototype of Japanese performance, offering a Japanese version of mimesis (87–90). What needs to be mentioned before my discussion of *modoki* is that, Sakabe, who specializes in Western philosophy, tends to Orientalize Japan, although he is aware that too much emphasis on Japanese uniqueness would lead to nationalism (Sakabe 15). I introduce his discussion of *modoki* as a useful tool to explain KATHY's performance, but I do not mean to emphasize that *modoki* is an essentially and uniquely Japanese aesthetic practice, since such an idea clearly goes against my argument that KATHY is trying to deconstruct "unique" Japanese women's bodies.

Modoki's performance is generated by the dynamics of two opposite ends. It makes fun of and parodies the performance of those who play the roles of gods and/or spirits in sacred rituals, but at the same time, it conveys the meaning of their performance to the audience. A good example of *modoki* is found in the role called *Sanbasô* in the traditional celebratory performance *Okina*.[16] While the actor playing the role of the god wears a white mask and performs in a serious and sacred manner, the actor playing the role of *Sanbasô* wears a black mask, and makes fun of, contradicts, and parodies the god. However, at the same time, *Sanbasô* interprets the god's esoteric performance and conveys its meaning in a plain form to the audience. In short, *Sanbasô* as the *modoki* criticizes the god, but at the same time, he is the god's loyal interpreter, and through such performance, the *modoki* dynamically and constantly transforms himself from a human being into something like the god and vice versa (Sakabe 89–102). Thus, the *modoki* rejects fixity, transgressing the boundary between the god and human being. However, the *modoki* does not attempt to be the god or even to transcend the god. Sakabe emphasizes this by alluding to Bakhtin's theory of the carnivalesque; after the performance is over, the *modoki* faces the fact that it is not the god after all (106). What the *modoki* does is to draw power from his mimesis of the god. This power lets the *modoki* demystify the idealized image of the god and present an alternative to the static, single meaning/truth that his counterpart the god embodies. Through its body, the *modoki* visualizes what is not in the single truth, by contradicting and parodying the god.

The *modoki*'s function of presenting an alternative through mimesis of the god is similar to Brecht's theory of "not ... but," which demands that the actors imply to the audience that what they are not doing on stage is an alternative to what they are doing on stage. Thus, "not ... but" prevents the audience from the total identification with what they are seeing on stage as the single Truth. Elin Diamond combines Brechtian gestus with feminism and calls it "'gestic' feminist criticism" (44). It disrupts what is constructed as organic femininity and brings about the historicization of women's experiences, which are not recorded in masculinist history. Gestic feminist criticism makes visible both the idealized/naturalized image of women and what does not get naturalized (Diamond 45–54).

Following Diamond who applies feminism to Brechtian gestus, it is possible for us to apply feminist perspectives to Sakabe's discussion of *modoki*. In parodying Americans, the members of KATHY are performing *modoki* to present an alternative both to Americanized Japanese bodies and to idealized or naturalized Japanese women's bodies, which are byproducts of Americanization. As *modoki*, the members draw power from Americans by performing them, and hence threaten Japanese masculinists, who feel castrated by the United States and also who have an idealized image of essential Japanese women. By such performances, the members bring the idealized image of Japanese women down to earth. With their background of classical ballet, they can interpret Western/American dance. Moreover, by showing their bodies performing Americans under the surveillance of Kathy, they convey to the viewers what it means to be Americanized, or more specifically, how much their bodies are bound by "the reinstallation of the modern" by the United States as a performative. Yet, at the same time, they make fun of and parody American dance or the idealized image of America and American female stereotypes. Thus, this *modoki* serves both to critique such a binding force and to present an alternative to Americanized Japanese bodies without presenting them as "essentially" Japanese women's bodies. As *modoki*, the members parody and contradict the masculinist and essentialist dichotomous thinking of Japan/female versus the West/the United States/male. Moreover, as *modoki*, they reject fixity, as embodied by the fact that they do not have unified bodies, which would mark their single identities. They wear blond wigs and Western-style party dresses, but the black tights on their faces and the white tights on their arms and legs turn them into unknown creatures.

Women Dubbing Women

To further speculate how KATHY disrupts the unified, organic bodies of Japanese women, I will now look at Kathy Selden's role and the complicated process of dubbing employed in *Singin' in the Rain*. The group name KATHY, intentionally or not, encourages viewers to identify the troupe with her. As mentioned above, Kathy Selden is a good girl, who sacrifices her prior ideas for her lover Don Lockwood. When they first meet, she tells him that she does not respect silent film actors, since they neither talk nor act but "just make a lot of dumb shows" as opposed to respectful stage actors "speaking ... glorious words." She even tells him that he is just a "shadow on film" without "flesh and blood." Thus, she despises the body/voice split. However, after they are involved in a romantic relationship, she decides to lend her voice to his film project. This pattern is similar to the relationship between Japan and the United States. As a good Americanized girl, Japan lets the powerful adult male (the United States) split her voice and body.

In *Singin' in the Rain*, Kathy's voice is returned to her body by these men in the end, but we do not know what happens to her afterwards. We are simply given a shot at the end of the film in which Don and Kathy hug and kiss each other in front of the billboard of their film also titled *Singin' in the Rain*.

featuring them as stars. *Singin' in the Rain* is usually seen as Kelly's film, rather than Kelly and Debbie Reynolds', due to the control he possessed over the production as a co-director and co-choreographer, as well as his starring role.[17] In addition, as Stephen Prock argues, reflexivity between characters and actors in the film further blurs diegetic and extradiegetic realities (312). For example, Gene Kelly and his character Don Lockwood share an almost identical process to stardom and, as movie stars, they discover Kathy Selden and Debbie Reynolds. Moreover, Wollen points out Kelly's obsession to establish the priority of the male dancer, with his masculine, athletic body, which in turn diminishes the presence of women's bodies and forces them to be something like shadows of male bodies (57).

With these facts in mind, it seems reasonable to assume that Don Lockwood and Kathy Selden's *Singin' in the Rain* would probably be like "Kelly's" *Singin' in the Rain.* Kathy Selden and Debbie Reynolds are both subordinate to Lockwood/Kelly, even after their voices and bodies are unified. Furthermore, even Kathy Selden/Reynolds is replaced by another female dancer/actress Cyd Charisse in "The Broadway Ballet," a long dance piece in *The Dancing Cavalier.* Charisse never speaks or sings in the scene. Only her dancing body is needed. As Steven Cohan observes, "The female figure is ... punished (Lina) and redeemed (Kathy) in the narrative and then, in the ballet, silenced completely in order to be eroticized as pure spectacle (Charisse)" (63). Female bodies are being united and split, exploitable at men's own sweet will. Female voice is either ugly (Lina), dubbed (Kathy), or completely silenced (Charisse). Female bodies, in contrast, are always on display — either as sexy-bodied Lina/Charisse, or as cute-bodied Kathy.

At first glance, it may seem that the performance group KATHY's possible identification with Kathy Selden is visualizing this obedient body of a woman. But the black tights which mask the members' faces add a comical yet uncanny tone to such identification. A look at the background of making *Singin' in the Rain* may explain such uncanniness. In the film, Kathy Selden dubs Lina Lamont, but in reality, Debbie Reynolds is also dubbed. Wollen writes that her singing voice is dubbed by Jean Hagen, who plays the role of Lina (56), and Cohan writes that when Kathy dubs Lina's singing and speaking, Reynolds' singing voice is dubbed by Betty Noyes and her speaking voice is dubbed by Hagen (59). Thus, it is not clear which part of Reynolds' voice is dubbed by whom, but at least, Jean Hagen is involved in this complex process of dubbing. This fact first tells us that, although the film is over with the happy unity of Kathy Selden's voice and body, such unity is never attained extradiegetically. This eternal split resonates with KATHY's mouthless/voiceless bodily performance. According to Cohan, it was the male director's(s') decision to employ such dubbing in the film. Cohan refers to

Hugh Fordin's assertion that co-director Stanley Donen mentioned that Reynolds was dubbed, since her regional accent was considered unsuitable for Lina's supposedly sophisticated speech in *The Dancing Cavalier* (59). I would argue that the members of KATHY, by hyperbolically performing this male-created split, employ it as a means to counter the unified, essentialized image of Japanese women's bodies.

Returning now to KATHY's performance, we see that after a series of failures, the members resume dancing in unison to "Good Morning." Here, we see that they are enjoying the "mouthless" state. In the sequence of their dance in unison is inserted a scene in which three of them approach the camera lens and pretend to kiss it in an overly flattering manner. This is as if showing hyperbolically and comically that they are obedient, gendered female, Japanese subjects produced by "typical" American Kathy. At the same time, it suggests the irony that even if it wants to, Japan cannot kiss the United States, since Japan was not given a mouth by the U.S. reinstallation of the modern. Similarly, although they pretend to enjoy Western tea (elegant tea cups are associated with femininity in Western culture) balancing gracefully on tree branches, they have no mouths and therefore cannot drink anything. During this tea party, another member is doing barrel leaps (a technique both used in ballet and Broadway-style dance) behind them, and the camera shifts its focus from the two on the tree branches to the dancing one. The members emphasize the fact that they have no mouths and hence no voice and yet their bodies (represented by one dancing member in this scene) are dancing Western/American dance. Furthermore, while evoking the postwar situation of the Japanese, they seem to be enjoying and celebrating this split (or even cyborgian) state. It is as if they are demonstrating that, although the split of voice and body has been imposed on the Japanese, they can take advantage of such a split in order to disrupt the belief in Japanese femininity as an organic whole, which is the other side of modernization. In this sense, another *modoki* is working here.

One more *modoki* may be working if we consider that, in a sense, Jean Hagen speaks for herself, in a very oblique way, through Kathy Selden/Debbie Reynolds' body. Considering that Lina tries to speak for herself in the premier but nobody wants to listen to her and yet her "fake" voice in *The Dancing Cavalier* attracts the audience, it may even look like a complicity between Kathy/Reynolds and Lina/Hagen to have a woman's muffled voice heard. I am aware that I am conflating the two different levels: what the characters are doing in the film and what the actors are doing outside of the film. Also, I am aware that this complicated process of dubbing was not the choice of these actresses but that of male director(s). However, if we just focus on this phenomenon that a body of a seemingly obedient girl functions as a medium for a "bad" woman who tries to have her suppressed voice heard, it seems reasonable to consider that Kathy Selden/Debbie Reynolds is a *modoki*, performing a good obedient girl and yet has a "bad" woman's voice heard through her body. The members of KATHY without mouths/voice resemble Kathy Selden/Debbie Reynolds whose body has other women's voices.

In their parodies of "Good Morning," the disrupted bodies of the members of KATHY offer a space where the present and the past meet. They bring immediate postwar Japanese history into the present and visualize the continuation of U.S. hegemony. Their bodies historicize Japanese women's bodies and become a site where the women could possibly share their experiences, deconstruct their bodies as Japan's national essence, and transform them into something unstable or unknown. In her discussion of gestic feminist criticism, Elin Diamond summarizes three temporalities within a single stage figure in Brechtian theater, that is, the historical subject or historicity of a character, the character, and the actor. When watching such a figure, the audience's gaze is constantly split into three, and in the process, they, as historians, also reject fixity/truth and attempt to capture meaning, based on historical and dialectic comparisons (50–51). In regard to the bodies of such actors and audience, Diamond writes: "If feminist theory sees the body as culturally mapped and gendered, Brechtian historicization insists that this body is not a fixed essence but a site of struggle and change" (52). Likewise, the bodies of the members of KATHY open up a space for struggle and change, having the audience historicize Japanese women's bodies constructed as natural.

Moreover, this space transgresses national boundaries, as embodied by the members' strategic identification with the American woman Kathy Selden. I do not mean that they are identifying themselves with Kathy Selden in the realist way. Rather, by covering their faces with black tights and making fun of American female stereotypes, they are identifying themselves with Kathy Selden as a *modoki*. Thus, KATHY's "identification" with an American woman is not charged with the power relationship between the occupier and the occupied. Such transnational "identification" may result from KATHY's desire to get out of the fixated status of Japanese women narrowly defined as the national essence, and instead to form a space where women can share their experiences, not bound by national boundaries and the power relationships which accompany them.

Conclusion: Toward the Playground of Little Girls

After the scene of tea, the members of KATHY go back to their dance in unison to "Good Morning." Citing Western/American dance traditions, their movements become more extravagant and spectacular toward the end.

However, the members do not literally replicate them, since, unlike these traditions, their movements do not build up organically. They still consist of bits and pieces from different traditions.

Citing a typical movement in musical films, at the end of the song, they move out of a camera lens. Traditionally, this means that the dancers are proudly moving forward to the future, and this is exactly what KATHY repeats. However, in their case, it has an ironic twist; the future to which the members are moving forward is outside of Kathy's surveillance camera. It is as if they are saying to this unsubstantial entity, "We just follow the American dance tradition, and then, we end up moving out of your surveillance camera. Sorry, but it's not our fault."

Thus, the unsubstantial entity Kathy is invented by the members as a parody of an unknown power operating in global capitalism, in which the United States still holds the hegemonic position. Henri Lefebvre calls the modern space produced by capitalism "abstract space," in which not only social labor but also "state (political) power" is abstracted (49–51). In global capitalism, which blurs national boundaries, the location of power becomes more and more abstracted. Yet, we are bound to live in such an abstract space, constantly interpellated by unseen, unlocatable power. This is the very situation that the members of KATHY strategically exploit. Although they actually design their own performances, they blame this unknown power for their deconstructive performance and thus abstract their responsibility in a parodic way. As Carol Martin speculates, "KATHY's performances are designed to confuse the spectator's notions of cause and effect, of action and responsibility" (53). This way, the members avoid directly confronting the performative force and yet they contradict it. KATHY is a *modoki* of Kathy.

By citing the very tradition of American musicals, they leave the space created by the tension between U.S.–defined modernity and Japanese masculinist reactionary ideology. In the space they newly enter, the members might ponder what it means to be Japanese women. Or rather, they might speculate on what it means to define national identity. In this space, the unknown bodies of these Little Girls would constantly transform into something else and never get fixed. In such a space, Little Girls play around, with abundant possibilities of what and who to become.

NOTES

1. The video is available at some art shops such as NADiff.
2. See her article "Lingering Heat and Local Global J Stuff."
3. *Shingeki* is Western-style theater, but literally means new theater, as opposed to *kabuki* and other Japanese traditional theaters as old. It was established in the early twentieth century under the influence of Western realism theater.

4. He mainly produces paintings and installation art works, and his well-known pieces include, for instance, a gigantic female figure, which looks like an eroticized anime character. For more of his works, see the collection of his art works *DOB in the Strange Forest*, and *Little Boy*, a catalogue of an exhibit he organized in New York in 2005, for example.

5. When I quote from *Superflat* and *Little Boy*, I refer to the English translations. However, the translations do not always convey what Murakami writes in Japanese. The original English translation that I quote here is as follows: "Super flatness is an original concept of the Japanese, who have been completely Westernized." It might be confusing, since it sounds like Superflatness was originally invented by the Westernized Japanese. However, what Murakami means in his writing in Japanese is that Superflat is an essentially Japanese concept, which has been passed from generations to generations, even before the Japanese experienced Western influence.

6. I use two of his articles compiled in *Little Boy*. Henceforth, when I refer to "Earth in My Window," I note "Earth" in a parenthesis, and when I refer to "Superflat Trilogy: Greetings, You are Alive," I note "Superflat." It is different from his book titled *Superflat*.

7. The total absence of women in his essays, whether intentionally or not, does stand out, particularly when they are juxtaposed with one of the other essays in the catalogue, the one about contemporary artists, many of whom are women, written by a female art critic Matsui Midori. In this essay titled "Beyond the Pleasure Room to a Chaotic Street: Transformations of Cute Subculture in the Art of the Japanese Nineties," she traces the genealogy of Japanese contemporary art in the 1990s, and one of her main points is that women, simply regarded as consumers before, started to be involved more in the production of art, and this contributed to the shift in the meaning of innocence (which is a typical image attached to girls) from a "narcissistic mask to the agency of spontaneous creation" (225).

I need to note here that although Murakami does not mention "Little Girls" in his theory, as Matsui notes in this essay, he actually organized a group exhibit of four woman artists in 1999 in Tokyo. The title was *Tokyo Girls Bravo*, named after the work of Okazaki Kyôko, a representative woman comic writer who was active from the mid–1980s to the mid–1990s. Matsui argues that Murakami sees a possibility in these girls to develop future aesthetics of Japan by appropriating the "unnatural" state of postwar Japan (229–230). However, I would argue that it is indeed odd that he never mentions women in his theory if he really finds such a possibility in girls. Later in 2002, Murakami edited the collections of works of ten Tokyo girl artists at the turn of the century (such as drawings, paintings, photographs, and stuffed animals). In this bilingual book (Japanese and its English translation) also titled *Tokyo Girls Bravo*, he has one page of brief introduction, in which he applauds the girls' creative power, but at the same time, he manifests his masculinist desire toward these girls as follows: "The 'Tokyo' of the 21st Century (sic) has finally passed through its maturity, and is only now getting good and decaying. Like horse meat is best a little past its time, 'Tokyo' and its residents are just now getting tasty. / This is the 'Tokyo' where these girls live: overripe, but still with a smell of bright red blood, sweet and wholesome, coming from somewhere" (5). Aside from his argument that Tokyo is now finally mature, which seems to be contradictory to his theorization of postwar Japan as Little Boy, in the remark above, he seems to show his desire to consume these girls.

8. It also aims at nurturing new talents for such art, and providing an educational space for aspiring artists who want to learn how to market their works. Beginning in

2002, GEISAI is held twice every year. KATHY participated in GEISAI-2 in 2002, GEISAI-3 and 4 in 2003. For more detailed information for the event, see the bilingual (Japanese and English) book *The GEISAI*, compiling the works of artists who received awards in the events (and the predecessor Geijutsu Dôjô) from 2001 to 2004. See also its official website: http://www2.geisai.net/. The website is also bilingual (Japanese and English).

9. In their booth, they created a room with a TV screen showing *Mission/K*. In their performance in the room, they did not dance, but they simply stood, lay down, or sat on the floor ("'GEISAI-2' Ôza Kunrin!!; gyakushû no hasha tachi GEISAI-3 e no yabô ôi ni kataru!? ['GEISAI-2' Champions Rule!!: Champions of a Counterattack Discuss Their Ambitions for GEISAI-3!?] 156).

10. For instance, it is introduced as one of the most interesting Japanese performing art groups in a journal *Eureka* (July 2005 issue).

11. The URL of KATHY's website is http://www.zzkathyzz.com/.

12. This rumor is found in articles such as Sakurai Keisuke's "'Kodomo no kuni no dansu' dayori: Gijutsu no 'zenyô ni tsuite [Letter of 'Dance in the Children's World': On 'Making Good Use' of Skills"] in the journal *Butai geijutsu* [Performing Arts] 5 and Uchino Tadashi's introduction of the group in the literary magazine *Eureka*.

13. However, as far as I know, this is the only "rumor" about Kathy being an American. Dance critic Kimura Satoru mentions that the members of KATHY look French: see, for example, "Imadoki no 'odoriko' no yûmorasu de setsunai shukumei" ["Humorous Yet Painful Destiny of 'Showgirls' of Today"] in the journal *BT* (November 2003, 180).

14. Sakurai writes in Japanese. All the quotations from his writings are my translation.

15. As examples of Western dancers who attempt to deconstruct modern dance, Sakurai lists William Forsythe and Jan Fabre ("Kodomo shintai" 206).

16. The status of *Okina* is complicated, since, given as a special status in *noh* repertoire, "it is *noh*, yet it is not *noh*." As mentioned, *Okina* has a celebratory dance/song, and is usually performed in a special occasion such as New Year or the opening of a new theater (Sakabe 91).

17. See his book *Singin' in the Rain*.

9

Motherland and Mothers-in-Law: African-American Wives in African Plays

Kevin J. Wetmore, Jr.

"How much does the American Negro know?"
Ato in *The Dilemma of a Ghost*
Ama Ata Aidoo

"Why should I know anything about Africa?"
Mama in *A Raisin in the Sun*
Lorraine Hansberry

Lorraine Hansberry's *A Raisin in the Sun* was one of the first contemporary American plays to engage the larger relationship between the people of Africa and the African diaspora. The play, especially when compared to African drama of the same period, demonstrates the similarity in the movements in Africa and the United States — independence and civil rights being the major themes in the respective dramas. Hansberry's play, especially though the character of Joseph Asegai, also clearly demonstrates an emerging interest in the African diaspora — Africa in African America and African Americans in Africa — that would see echoes in African dramas in which African Americans (and in particular the trope of the African-American wife) began to appear as characters.

A Raisin in the Sun demonstrates the transition from the pre-war awareness of Africa by African Americans as posited by Mama, who sees the Africans as primitive heathens, much as the white media depicts them, and the understanding of Africa by the post-war generation, as embodied in Beneatha.

Beneatha complains, "All anyone seems to know about when it comes to Africa is Tarzan" (Hansberry 57). Beneatha's concerns are not simply misrepresentation, though. Tied in with her own family's struggle against segregation and racism, Beneatha identifies with the African struggle for independence. While Mama gives money at church to save Africans from heathenism, Beneatha fears "they need more salvation from the British and French" (57).

Beneatha finds a foil as much as an ally in Joseph Asagai, a Nigerian at Beneatha's college. Beneatha takes her connection to Africa very seriously. Asagai gently mocks her for it, imitating her for approaching him in order to find her own identity. He further teases her as being different from other African Americans as "assimilationism is so popular in your country," but she will not acquiesce to it (63). Asagai, however, is not merely a pure symbol of a pure Africa. Hansberry gives us a more complex character who is a bit of a Lothario with a reputation for having many girlfriends. He undergoes a change during the play, however, moving from a gift-giving, playful campus Casanova to a man who asks Beneatha to marry him and be a doctor in Africa. He makes it clear that although their struggles are similar on the surface, and perhaps even related, Nigeria's problems are very different than African America's, and the grass may be greener for each. We might also note that Beneatha's feminism is in counterpoint to her Africanism, a point that will be echoed in Rotimi's play. At the end of the play, Asagai asks Beneatha to "come home with me ... to Africa" (136). These two ideas have been linked in the play: Nigeria and home. The play ends with her announcing to the family that she has been asked, but it is unclear whether or not she will go. In one sense, African-American theatre since *Raisin* has been exploring the relationship between the Motherland and her American children.

The sixties, however, saw several African plays that one might see as sequels from the other side of this relationship, plays in which African-American women return to Africa with their African husbands. These plays offer a very different conceptualization of the relationship between African America and Africa than Hansberry's. In this essay I shall focus on two plays in particular: Nigerian Ola Rotimi's *Our Husband Has Gone Mad Again* and Ghanaian Ama Ata Aidoo's *The Dilemma of a Ghost*, with a few additional comments on J.C. deGraft's *Through a Film Darkly*, all of which feature African men with American (or in de Graft's case, European) wives.

Interestingly, I know of only one play from this period in which an African woman dates an American man (whose ethnicity is never made clear, he is simply called Alvin and is identified as a "Yankee"), and that is the sketch "Childe International" from Wole Soyinka's 1964 revue *Before the Blackout*. Titi, the daughter of "Politician," is a modern young woman, much to her father's chagrin, and she is dating "a Yank ... his father is a big official at the embassy," whom she has invited to dinner without asking her father's permission (Soyinka 59). Alvin shows up early, refers to her father as "Pops" and "your old man" and asks him if he's really a "Big Shot" (61). The politician drives the insulting and insufferable young American from his house, telling him to tell his father "to give [him] some home training," so he knows how to behave properly toward traditional Africans (61). Although Soyinka's satirical target is clearly both sides of the home-grown generation gap, the sole American on stage for less than fifteen seconds still gets side-swiped hard as a target, too. Boorish and believing it charming, disrespectful and believing it friendly, rude, crude, and completely devoid of self-awareness or an understanding of others, Soyinka's American is an object of scorn.

Ola Rotimi's play is a comedy in which an army major, running for his nation's highest office, has married Liza, an American woman, without telling her that he already has two wives. While the play is a satire on African (in general) and Nigerian (specifically) politics and ideologies, Liza is portrayed as a catalyst and a model for African women who inspires her fellow wives to enter politics. Ama Ata Aidoo's play explores the attitude of the African women toward their American daughter-in-law and her attitude towards them, and how the two societies misunderstand one another. Whereas Eulalie Rush Yawson has idealized Africa, believing when she goes to Ghana with her Ghanaian husband she will "belong somewhere again," after growing up in the racist United States. Her husband's family rejects her as the descendant of slaves who does not know how to interact within the African family unit.

In both plays, African-American women are constructed as Other within Africa. Each play uses the figure of African-American woman within the African family to explore both the relationship between Africa and the United States in general and African America specifically. Whereas many plays in the United States at this time (such as those by Baraka, Hansberry, and Walker, to name but a few) focus on the direct relationship between African America and Africa, the African plays from the same period focus on the differences between the two groups, and constructs a more complex relationship within pan–Africanism. One in which African America remains related, but distinctly foreign.

One of three Nigerians awarded scholarships to study theatre abroad, Rotimi was in the United States from 1959 to 1966 (Dunton 11; Coker 54). He earned a BFA from Boston University in 1963, followed by an MFA in playwriting from Yale in 1966, supported by a Rockefeller Fellowship (Coker 54). His thesis play, *Our Husband Has Gone Mad Again* was written in October and November of 1965, with considerable rewriting during rehearsals in New Haven and again after the play's first Nigerian performance (Dunton 148). At Yale the play was directed by Jack Landau and won the Student Play of the Year Award for 1966 (Coker 54). Upon his return to Nigeria, Rotimi presented the play in September 1966 at the University of Ife.

Although incredibly popular in Nigeria, and very much reflective of a Nigerian idiom, the play was conceived, written and produced originally at Yale in Connecticut. At the time, the American theatrical world (and especially the African-American theatrical world) was profoundly shaped by Hansberry. Rotimi found himself in issues very similar to those of the fictional Asegai. Rotimi was very involved in African politics in Boston and New Haven, but not in African-American politics or causes.[1] *Our Husband* is a play about African politics, albeit one written in America, with a literal African-American character (Liza was born in Kenya, met Lejoka-Brown in Congo but has lived much of her life in the United States, which has shaped her world view). Rotimi himself admitted that his play had roots in his own domestic situation in New Haven in 1965, as he had recently married Hazel Mae Gaudreau, a (white) French Canadian student at Yale:

> Perhaps some of the problems inherent in a cross-cultural marriage might have impinged on my subconscious sufficiently enough to find expression in aspects of this play.... But what is true is that the basic inspiration for *Our Husband* derived from a "Dear Abby" letter column in a local Boston newspaper where a lovelorn woman was seeking advice on how to curb the amorous excesses of her lover.... When I started writing *Our Husband Has Gone Mad Again* the ultimate goal was to laugh at ... er ... political charlatans, of whom there are many in Africa.[2]

While "Dear Abby" may have been the initial impetus to write a play about African politics, I posit that Rotimi's play, written in New Haven in 1965, emerged in a theatrical milieu profoundly shaped by Hansberry's play, and that Rotimi's play maintains important similarities and differences from its predecessor, not least of which is its focus on satire over drama. Both plays feature the intermixing of the domestic with the social, and the exploration of the relationship between people in the Motherland and in the Diaspora. Both plays feature a man who has a desire to rise in the world, but who is disempowered by the women in his own house, Major Lejoka-Brown in *Our Husband* is flummoxed by his three wives, whereas Walter finds himself emasculated in his own house also by three women: his mother, his sister and his wife. The key difference is that Rotimi's play is set in a place where people of color are empowered and run the government, whereas Hansberry's play is set in a place where people of color are disenfranchised, specifically by an institutionally racist nation, government, and neighborhood. Thus, their overall political and social concerns are different.

Rotimi's play begins with the arrival of Major Lejoka-Brown's wife Liza from America. Like Beneatha, Liza's background is medicine. Beneatha

planned to become a doctor, Liza is one. The major planned on entering politics, which would enable him to "chop a big slice of the National cake"
(Rotimi 4). This stated motive is the concern that Beneatha expresses — that
once imperialism ends, the corruption is so set in the culture that the exploita-
tion continues, this time by people of color. It is this figure that Rotimi seeks
to mock. And unfortunately for the Major, his African-American wife does
not know he already has two wives who will be her "sisters in marriage." The
first is his brother's wife, whom his father married to him in absentia after
his brother's death. The second he recently married because "she is the daughter of the President of the Nigerian Union of Market Women," and her by
his side would help him win the upcoming election (10). Lejoka-Brown has
been keeping the women separate in order to use all three to win the election, planning to get rid of the other two and settle down with Liza after he
wins.

Liza, however, arrives early, goes to her husband's home and finds the
other wives. She is nonplused that her husband is already married. They are
nonplused that she mistakes them for domestic servants. Initially there is no
kinship between the women. Sikira (wife number 2) calls Liza "the black-
white woman who spent her whole life roaming the streets of America" (15).
Liza is therefore also part of a trope in African drama of the African-American wife who is out of place in Africa. While such relationships might be a
metaphor for the relationship between Africans and African Americans, as
embodied by a romantic relationships (primarily between African men and
African-American women), they also might be seen to be indicative of a reality on the ground of postcolonial Africa — as African men traveled abroad for
education, they came home with foreign wives.

One of the first plays to deal with this issue was Ama Ata Aidoo's *The
Dilemma of a Ghost* (Ghana, March 1964) in which Ato Yawson marries Eulalie
Rush while a student in the United States, and his American bride comes to
Africa to find conflict with her in-laws because she neither understands Africa
nor her place in it. Eulalie refers to her husband affectionately as "Native
Boy." In the playful argument that opens the play, Ato tells her she speaks
"like an American" and she takes issue that she is no different than African
women (Aidoo 9). He asks if she "must drag in the differences between your
people and mine" every time they argue (9). She announces that she has found
a place where she belongs. Unlike racist America, she believes as a woman of
color she will be accepted unquestioningly in Africa. This is not to be so. Esi
Kom, Ato's mother, and the other women in his family do not accept his new
wife.

When Ato announces his marriage to his family, they assume he has married a white woman, and bemoan the fact. He replies, "But who says I have

married a white woman? Is everyone in America white? In that country there are white men and black men.... I say my wife is as black as we all are" (17). While this news comes as a relief, it is followed by the revelation that as an African American, Eulalie's ancestors were slaves. The family panics and weeps: "My grand-child has gone and brought home the offspring of slaves [*Women's faces indicate horror.*] A slave, I say" (19).

Eulalie is also challenged by the new environment. She is frightened by funeral drumming in the neighborhood, admitting that she knew there would be drums in Africa but thought "they would sound like jazz" (25). Esi Kom brings the young couple a sack full of snails to roast and eat, which Eulalie promptly throws away. Esi accuses her son of falling victim to American ways: "And what, my son? Do you not know how to eat them now? What kind of man are you growing into? Are your wife's taboos yours? Rather your taboos should be hers.... These days, the rains are scarce and so are snails. But the one or two I get for you, you throw away" (33). After a year of marriage with no children, his entire family gathers to ask for the gods' blessing and to perform rituals designed to increase fertility. Ato kicks them out, too ashamed to explain that he has agreed to not have children until Eulalie wants them. She rails against his family: "Have they any appreciation for anything but their own prehistoric existence? More savage than dinosaurs. With their snails and their potions!" (47). She asks him why she must always do what his family wants. She asks why he "can't ... preach to your people to try and have just a little understanding for the things they don't know anything about yet?" and when he asks what "the American negro" knows, she tells him never to compare African Americans with "these stupid narrow-minded savages" (48). After which, he slaps her and leaves the house.

Esi confronts Ato and learns the truth. She forgives Eulalie (who is not present) her affronts: "No stranger ever breaks the law.... My son. You have not dealt with us well. And you have not dealt with your wife well in this" (51–2). As often in African drama and African culture, the answer is proverbial:

> Before the stranger should dip his finger
> Into the thick palm nut soup,
> It is a townsman
> Must have told him to [52].

In other words, the stranger only knows how to behave properly when told how to do so by someone from within the culture. Until properly instructed in how to behave, the stranger will remain ignorant (and potentially offensive). Ato failed to properly teach his African-American wife how to behave and how to be a part of her African family. The fault of her misbehavior lies with her husband's failure.

It is not the blame in which we are interested, however, so much as the construction of the African American, who in this case feels linked to Africa by virtue of her historic ethnicity but knows little to nothing about African culture, nor displays any interest in learning. She is disrespectful, rude, and selfish. When offered a delicacy such as snails, she throws them away. She claims the privilege of African descent, but knows nothing of African culture, language, rituals, family rules and obligations, or beliefs. When the family's concern for her seeming inability to bear children (they do not know she is using contraceptives and Ato will not tell them) she casts aspersions on their intelligence and their ability to comprehend and sympathize with others. Her attitude is pejorative at best and racist at worst. She is a petulant child who thinks she understands everything when in fact she knows nothing.

In the three plays noted thus far, the American characters are disconnected from Africa, un–self-aware, and capable of great rudeness and discourtesy. While Liza is presented in a much more positive light than Eulalie or Alvin, she is still Other, and ultimately interferes in African politics. Another play that engages the same themes, except the wife is English instead of American, is J.C. de Graft's *Through a Film Darkly*, in which Fenyinka has married Janet Wilson after studying in England. The two of them live in Ghana. Unlike Eulalie, who assumes she understands Africa because she is of African descent, Janet knows her own limitations, and seeks to understand her husband's culture better from within. She wants to meet Ghanaians, speak the languages, learn to make Ghanaian dishes like palm soup. Fenyinka's friend John is hostile to Janet and in fact, "can't stand" whites in general (de Graft 34). As their friend Addo explains, "I know some people who didn't have it easy in Europe — and America" (35). While Janet's willingness to engage Ghanaian culture stands in counterpoint to Eulalie's insistence on her own cultural superiority, both women are distrusted in part because they are westerners, and Europeans and Americans cannot be trusted too much by Africans.

John reveals that his hatred springs from his own negative experiences in England. He fell in love with a white woman named Molly, who "was the only girl who would talk to me without making me feel like a stranger," but who was actually merely using John for her own anthropology research (53). "It takes courage and faith in himself for an African to keep his humanity outside of Africa ... particularly among white people," notes John (57); which is also a key message of Edgar White's *Lament for Rastafari*, another play that explores relationships within the African diaspora and constructs the United States as a place unfriendly to foreigners.

In considering these plays in total, we might note a few key aspects in how they construct America and Americans. One might first note that Americans, even African Americans, know little to nothing about Africa. They do no know how to interact respectfully and they have no sense of propriety. Second, America is seen as a place of education and marriages, where young African men go to get degrees and wives. Third, Africans in America must be careful, as Americans are judgmental, prejudicial, and even racist, especially toward Africans, and even African Americans are capable of looking down on Africans. Through the metaphor of marriage, these playwrights have looked at the relationship between Africa and America and found it to be a complex and challenging one indeed, and one in which America does not understand, appreciate or value its spouse as much as it should.

NOTES

1. Martin Banham, email to author, 10 March 2004.
2. Ola Rotimi, interviewed by Dapo Adelugba (19 November 1975, unpublished, n.p.).

10

Marking the Nation from the Outside: Vietnamese Americans as Abject in the Vietnamese Play *Dạ Cổ Hoài Lang*

Khai Thu Nguyen

In *Dạ Cổ Hoài Lang*, one of the most popular and long playing spoken dramas in Ho Chi Minh City since official declarations of market reform in 1986, a Vietnamese American girl, known as The Girl, asks the question "What is homeland?" to an audience in the city's 5B Small Stage Theatre. To the Vietnamese audience, The Girl can represent the sexual promiscuity, excess, materialism, loss of tradition, and hyper-rationality in American culture that leads to her complete disconnection to Vietnamese identity. Yet her question marks at once the existence of a Vietnamese identity to be lost, and a dispersal of such coherence in a nation shifting from war-time nationalism to post-war market reform and global integration.

Since the end of the Vietnam/American War and the entry of North Vietnamese Communist troops into Saigon in 1975, the coherence of national boundaries has been persistently tested with the mass exodus of Vietnamese refugees leaving through official immigration programs or "throwing themselves into death" in the open seas (Takaki 30). Within the country itself, collectivization of the South led to the dispersal of people from their homes into New Economic Zones, and an underground existence for those who snuck back into the cities. Those who left Vietnam became displaced citizens of the world who struggled for acceptance into host countries, often facing rejection and the return home. Ambivalently accepted as immigrants, members of diasporic communities such as Vietnamese Americans participated in America's refugee dispersion policy that scattered Vietnamese immigrants throughout American cities to limit their influence (Hien 66–67). Since 1975, the Vietnamese Communist Party (VCP) has faced the challenges of constructing national identity and coherence in the context of mass exodus and internal displacement.

The United States has played an important role in the State's construction of national identity in both the period of the Vietnam/American War and postwar market reform. The defeat of Americans, a powerful modern military force, reinforced the Vietnamese Communist Party's role as the vanguard in Vietnam's liberation from forces of colonialism and neocolonialism, and affirmed the effectiveness of the Party's construction of the nation's modern identity. After the end of the Vietnam/American war, state power would be critically challenged by failures of collectivization in the South, the emergence of factions that took advantage of the State's Southern failures, economic devastation resulting partially from the international embargo led by the United States, and increasing dependence on foreign aid from the Soviet Union. In response to these crises, the Sixth Party Congress declared a national policy of *đổi mới* (renovation) in 1986 that instituted market reforms, decentralization, de-collectivization, and a policy of global integration inviting international tourism and foreign investment. Vietnam's renewal of relations with the United States, secured through formal normalization and the end of the economic embargo in 1994, visibly marked the country's performance of a new global and integrative identity.

Vietnamese theater has begun to reflect its changing relationship to America. Unlike propaganda plays of the Vietnam/American War era that portray the American as a stereotypical enemy that is arrogant, uncompassionate, and materialistic, plays such as *Dạ Cổ Hoài Lang* ambivalently stage healing between Americans and Vietnamese through the transition figure of the Vietnamese American. The focus on the Vietnamese American experience by author Thanh Hoàng, who confesses he has never been to the United States but has heard many stories about the experience from narratives of Vietnamese Americans, forms a part of the Vietnamese imaginary of America that serves to consolidate Vietnamese identity. Through its portrayal of the assimilated and the unassimilated Vietnamese American, the play stages the Vietnamese American as an abject figure that affirms the existence of a coherent Vietnamese nation through his loss and longing for a geographic and cultural unity that he knows in his memory. At the same time, the play dramatizes the Vietnamese American as simultaneously a privileged spectator that has license to speak for and legitimate the authenticity and value of the Vietnamese nation. While the play seeks to define a coherent and distinct Vietnamese identity through the Vietnamese American, audiences' identification with the play relies on their very consciousness of transnational ties and regional diversity that resist a homogenous view of the nation. Portraying the Vietnamese American as simultaneously an abject and elevated figure to paint the nation as both culturally and geographically distinct, and globally integrative, *Dạ Cổ Hoài Lang* marks the anxieties of a nation that struggles to define its geographic and cultural boundaries in its transition from wartime nationalism to post-war globalization.

Vietnamese Americans as Abject

According to Julia Kristeva, abjection is a process where the subject comes to being through the repetitive delineation of borders around the self, and the "jettison[ing]" (Kristeva, *Powers of Horror* 2) of that which is deemed horrific and sickening. The abject is not an object but "simply a frontier" (9), simultaneously a constituent element and radical other that defines and continually challenges the boundaries of the subject. To Kristeva, one of the best examples of the abject is in the body: "As in true theatre ... refuse and corpses *show me* what I permanently thrust aside in order to live.... My body extricates itself, as being alive, from that border.... If dung signifies the other side of the border, the place where I am not and which permits me to be, the corpse, the most sickening of wastes, is a border that has encroached upon everything" (3). Extending the process of abjection to analysis of subject formation in social contexts, Judith Butler defines "the abject" as something that "designates here precisely those 'unlivable' zones of social life which are nevertheless densely populated by those who do not enjoy the status of the subject, but whose living under the sign of the 'unlivable' is required to circumscribe the domain of the subject" (3). As Karen Shimakawa has pointed out, Kristeva suggests the psychic process of abjection as integral to the way that we can conceive and experience nation and nationalism on a social level (4).[1] Shimakawa argues that Asian-American performance demonstrates and resists the process of abjection of Asian Americans in the formation of American nationhood (4). Scholars such as Shimakawa have also used the apparatus of abjection as a way of "linking the psychic, symbolic, legal, and aesthetic dimensions of national identity as they are performed (theatrically and otherwise)" (4).

Following scholars who use the apparatus of abjection to connect the social, aesthetic, and affective dimensions of national identity, I argue that the play *Dạ Cổ Hoài Lang* demonstrates the process of abjection in the formation of national identity in post-war Vietnam, in which the Vietnamese American plays an abject that is both jettisoned and constitutive of Vietnamese identity (and therefore becomes an easy subject of identification). As abjection involves an anxious repetitive process where the abject is perpetually rejected but never quite separated from the subject, the Vietnamese American is repeatedly jettisoned and re-incorporated, radically excluded and elevated, in the building of the nation. At the same time, if abjection allows the consolidation of Vietnamese identity through negation, Vietnamese audience members' identification with the play depends on their very awareness of the heterogeneous identity of the nation and its transnational ties.

Dạ Cổ Hoài Lang is known as one of the most popular and long-playing spoken dramas in the South since the 1990s, and one of the most well known Southern plays to achieve national recognition. Author Thanh Hoàng[2] wrote the play in 1994 at a creative camp sponsored by the Association of Vietnamese Artists, receiving lukewarm feedback. The play, however, went on to win the Gold Medal at the government-sponsored National Professional Theater Festival in 1995 with performances by Thành Lộc, Việt Anh, Hồng Vân, and Quốc Thảo.[3] From 1995 through 2007, the play performed over 500 times at the 200-seat 5B Small Stage Theatre, changing casts three times to feature Lê Vũ Cầu, Thanh Hoàng, Hồng Vân, Phương Linh, Ngọc Trinh, Quốc Thảo, Cao Minh Đạt, and Việt Anh. The play was instrumental to the careers of several Southern actors. The role of Ông Tư, for example, was one of the defining roles in the career of the famous actor Thành Lộc. The actor, who would later become the star and artistic director of the popular IDECAF theater, drew a large audience for the play with his popularity as a comedic actor.

According to the playwright Nguyễn Thị Minh Ngọc, the play was one of few to pass political and emotional requirements to gain both the approval of the State and an enthusiastic audience, satisfying the three mandates of "aesthetic quality," "profitability," and "conforming to official policy" that she argues as virtually impossible to achieve in theater after market reform ("Đi Tìm Người Yêu").[4] After showing seventy times at the 5B Small Stage Theatre under the direction of Công Ninh, it was promoted by the Performing Arts Department of the Ministry of Culture and Information to perform for the "50th Anniversary of National Independence" in Hanoi in 1995, becoming one of the only Southern plays to tour and gain general acclaim in Hanoi.[5] In August of 2007 at the fiftieth anniversary of Vietnamese theater under the Vietnamese Communist Party, it was one of two plays representing spoken drama in the South. The play marked the birth and growth of the privatization of theater in the South after *đổi mới*, helping the 5B Small Stage Theatre lead a new private-government partnership model, in the wake of market reforms and reductions of government funding in the arts.

Reflecting what the author Thanh Hoàng calls the orientation to "reconcile" and integrate globally ("*Dạ Cổ Hoài Lang:* Cổ Mà Không Cổ"), the play expresses a transnational identification with diasporic Vietnamese,[6] and the "deep sadness and suffering of those Vietnamese afar" ("Thanh Hoàng: 'Tôi là người sống hướng nội'"). Set in an unspecified but snowy city in the United States, the play dramatizes the experience of Ông Tư, a Vietnamese American immigrant of 65 to 70 years of age who cannot adjust to the life he regularly describes as "cold" in the United States. Alienated from his Americanized teenage granddaughter who misinterprets his closeness to her as sexual abuse, he spends his days in an insane asylum where he is forced to stay because his "Vietnamese" behavior of ancestral worship and remembrance of the past are interpreted as insanity. The play begins as Ông Tư sneaks out of the asylum to commemorate his wife's death anniversary at home and struggles with his granddaughter, who is not concerned with the death anniversary, but rather her boyfriend's birthday. He shares his memories of his homeland with his friend Ông Nam, talks to his granddaughter's boyfriend (Young Man) about his observations of Vietnam after the Young Man's visit, and dies on the rooftop of his house while looking down on a forest with the shape of an "S," resembling Vietnam. Before his death, however, his granddaughter is finally able to understand him better by reading her father's diary retelling the story of his traumatic journey from Vietnam by boat. Concluding that her "grandfather is [her] homeland," she vows to journey back to Vietnam with him. Though he dies before she can, the play suggests a transnational Vietnamese identity born out of shared trauma and suffering.

Concerned with real life problems experienced by Vietnamese immigrants in America, the play performs a global Vietnamese identity and a collective unity between Vietnamese and Vietnamese Americans through shared loss and displacement. The first wave of Vietnamese immigrants left Vietnam in 1975, consisting mainly of educated American and South Vietnamese military officers and their families. They were followed by refugees on boats, at least ten percent of which died on the journey. This second wave of refugees included ethnic Chinese, Christians and Buddhists escaping religious persecution, and civilians fleeing the State's "nation building" policies that included the re-education of former South Vietnam affiliates and "counterrevolutionary elements" (Thomas 47) in camps, the drafting of citizens to New Economic Zones to adapt to primitive and undeveloped land, and the implementation of the "hộ khẩu" family registration system that discriminated against persons with "bad family background."[7] By 1987, more than half a million refugees were granted refuge in the United States, building large communities in Los Angeles, Orange County, and Santa Clara County. Vietnamese American refugees faced problems that included downward occupational mobility, difficult assimilation especially in the older generation, and conflicts between generations (Freeman 13; Smith and Tarallo 82–83). As refugees who are forced to flee, they often experienced a "double crisis" of adjustment and loss in their separations from their homes and families and struggles to assimilate (Freeman 11). These displacements of identity often produce "severe psychological distress" as well as a strong longing to return to their countries of origin (Freeman 11–12).

Playwright Nguyễn Thị Minh Ngọc argues that *Dạ Cổ Hoài Lang* stands out as a play that addresses the "sensitive topic" about the relationship between Vietnamese and Vietnamese Americans.[8] The relationship between the two groups is historically one of ambivalence, involving both strain and identification. As refugees who were affiliated with the South Vietnamese regime or fled Vietnam because of the policies of the State, many Vietnamese Americans, especially in the older generation, shared an "anti–Communist" sentiment and hostility to the Vietnamese regime. These communities organized early support of the embargo against Vietnam and resisted diplomatic normalization between the two nations. The Vietnamese regime, too, was fearful and anxious about Vietnamese diasporic anti–Communist organizations, often warning about the dangers of *việt kiều*[9] terrorism in its media and cultural portrayals of diasporic Vietnamese. Reforms during *đổi mới* and normalization of Vietnamese-American relations has led to growth of remittances from Vietnamese Americans to Vietnamese family members, and increasing numbers of diasporic returns to Vietnam. Yet meetings between *việt kiều* and Vietnamese are sweet reunions and also stark reminders of the wide differences in financial power, mobility, and cultural perceptions. Since *đổi mới*, Vietnam has continued to court returning diasporic Vietnamese by easing immigration regulations and adopting rules streamlining investment and the buying of property for overseas Vietnamese, opening the way for successful *việt kiều* entrepreneurship (Symons). More frequent interfaces between Vietnamese and Vietnamese Americans reveal the duality in the process of abjection involving both identification with, and radical exclusion of, Vietnamese Americans in the construction of Vietnamese identity.

Dạ Cổ Hoài Lang demonstrates the ability of Vietnamese audiences to identify with the struggles of Vietnamese American communities and recognize Vietnamese American stories of displacement as their own:

> In the 80s and 90s, the circumstances of Ho Chi Minh residents truly resembled the situation in the play, many families had to leave the country and separate, so the story on the stage reached deeply into the hearts of the spectators. It is also the story of the loss of culture, the sadness and struggle of the Vietnamese in a foreign land, which shook the spirit of the audience [Hoàng].

While identification closes the gap between Vietnamese and Vietnamese Americans, the experience of loss also becomes displaced onto Vietnamese

American identity. Author Thanh Hoàng expresses the dual motive of the play to articulate Vietnam's openness to global integration while building Vietnamese nationalism: "When our country opened its door, I saw that people were so oriented towards the outside, so I decided to write a play to remind people about the banyan tree and the ferry dock" (Cát Vũ). The only actor to play Ông Nam in the history of the play's production, Nguyễn Việt Anh articulates how abjection involves an ambivalence between identification with, and "jettison[ing]" of, Vietnamese American identity in the formation of Vietnamese identity: the play has "helped us better understand the situation of the Vietnamese abroad, and also to encourage our youths to love their country" (Cát Vũ).

The play relies on binaries between America and Vietnam to emphasize fundamental difference and consolidate Vietnamese identity as sentimental, empathetic, and connected to heritage. As the author describes, the play occurs "in a place where life is most modern — America," where the mixing of Vietnamese and American culture leads to the juxtaposition of "a birthday celebration with a death anniversary," of "prayer, and love making" (*Dạ Cổ Hoài Lang: Cổ Mà Không Cổ*"). Vietnamese Americans play tragic figures that affirm the existence of an authentic Vietnamese identity through its loss. Ông Tư's experience in America is filled with a longing for the past and for Vietnam. For Ông Tư, a kite represents the continuity between generations and a harmony with nature in Vietnamese culture that he can no longer experience in America. He reminisces about how much his son had loved flying kites, things that "you can let fly to the depths of the sky." "With just one thin string ... it stays connected to the person that has raised it (laughter)" (Thanh 3). He laments, "The old live through memories. I don't have anything else to think about but the memories of home" (4). For him and his old friend Ông Nam, "home sickness" is an experience causing disorientation and a "profound state" of "muddle headedness" (*quẩn trí*) (11). The loss of home results in mental and physical sickness that Ông Tư and his friends experience collectively. According to Ông Nam, the "old geezers" who come to America "miss home so much they become a little mad" (11).

The men's homesickness is synonymous with madness when they seek to retrieve their homelands in symbolic ways. Ông Tư transforms his son's living room and the stage into his homeland with drawings on sheets of "rooftops made of leaves," and "bamboo bushes" representing idyllic landscapes of the Vietnamese countryside (Thanh 12). When he lets Ông Nam see the paintings that he has created on old bed sheets hung throughout the stage, the audience too enjoys a pastoral image of the traditional Vietnamese countryside with a small road, a river, and a banana leaf house, through which to re-imagine the nation. In another scene, with Ông Tư, Ông Nam climbs to the rooftop of his house, a place where "I can see my country" (12) by looking down at the forest in the shape of an "S." A memory of a coherent Vietnam in the shape of an "S" is projected onto a diasporic subject who, having left a colonized, divided, or war-torn Vietnam, may have never known such unity. Dying on the rooftop while looking longingly at the image of his homeland, the Vietnamese American is constructed as a stranded and immobile character, not a figure empowered to cross national boundaries.

The play stabilizes the homeland through the image of an unchanging and geographically situated female lover. Ông Tư and Ông Nam share love for a woman in their past that they remember for the rest of their lives. Along the bank of the river that Ông Tư draws on the old bed sheets, he wins over the woman they both love with the song *Dạ Cổ Hoài Lang* ("She yearns for her husband upon hearing the sound of the midnight drum"). The lover, who becomes Ông Tư's wife, situates the nation by acting as the source of longing for both men, while never severing her ties from its geographic space. Ông Nam recalls, "She got to die in the soil of the country. But you [Ông Tư] and I die over here, who knows how it will be?" (Thanh 15).

The song that he uses to woo his wife, *Dạ Cổ Hoài Lang*, also the title of the play, is the original song that gave birth to the *vọng cổ* main melody of the traditional "renovated opera" form *cải lương*, a widely popular melodramatic form in the South. The play cites the historical circumstances in which Cao Văn Lầu wrote the song, when he was forced by his parents to part with his wife because she could not bear him a child. Expressing his loss of home through a central Southern melody, the play uses a regional performance form to represent the loss of the nation as the loss of the woman. The stories of deep longing of unassimilated Vietnamese Americans mark the imaginary of a geographically grounded nation in their memories, a nation that gains coherence and authenticity from a projected distant memory of it as a place of tradition, sentimentality, and continuity.

On the other hand, the assimilated Vietnamese American, The Girl, represents the radical difference between American and Vietnamese culture. The critic Nguyễn Thị Minh Thái argues that the play is about "a granddaughter who is born and raised in the land of foreigners, who becomes 'Americanized' and does not know what *homeland* is, lives the conventional American pragmatic lifestyle, paying no attention to love or honor, only caring about herself and her wealth" ("*Dạ Cổ Hoài Lang*: Vở Diễn Xuất Sắc Của Sân Khấu Nhỏ TP Hồ Chí Minh"). The assimilated Vietnamese American fully embodies "America," and its excess, sexual promiscuity, materialism, disconnection from tradition, and hyper-rationality. The Girl represents the complete perversion of traditional Vietnamese feminine identity in her adoption of sexual freedom. Making kites out of pictures of sexy photographs that disgust her grandfather, she responds to her boyfriend's suggestion "Shall we make love?" with "OK!" turning off the lights in the living room and on the audience and filling the dark stage with "noises that denote love-making" (9). She provokes grandfather's indignation as he articulates his view of Americans: "So much freedom it's total chaos! If they want to have sex, they have sex...!" (Thanh 10). Disconnected from the older generation (represented by the lack of respect she has towards kites), The Girl is concerned with only celebrating her boyfriend's birthday, and throws the incense commemorating her grandmother's death to the ground. Such a picture of sexual promiscuity and lack of respect for tradition has once caused an audience member to stand up and slap Phương Linh, the actor playing The Girl, retells author Thanh Hoàng ("*Dạ Cổ Hoài Lang: Cổ Mà Không Cổ*").

If the kite expresses a natural continuity and sympathy between man and nature, and father and daughter, in America the relationship between Ông Tư and his granddaughter is mediated by the artificial and impersonal language of American liberalism and the law. Refusing to let him use her birthday cake and candles for the death ceremony, she warns him that "he infringes upon the personal freedom of others" (Thanh 7). The Girl had in fact taken her father to court after he had spanked and left bruises on her, and warns her grandfather that she can call the police to take him back to the asylum if he touches her: "The law protects us" (7). While the play dramatizes *tình cảm* (sentiment) as a source of collectivity and community in Vietnamese society, The Girl lacks compassion and reads her grandfather's paternal affection as sexual perversion and abuse. As the ideal Vietnamese woman in the old men's memory embodies an authentic and geographically situated nation, The Girl stands for the complete aberration of the norm, displaying a mechanical logic of American capitalism that results in loss of human compassion and national origin, manifest in her question "what is homeland?"[10]

A Vietnamese theater instructor's comments about the meaning of the play reveals how empathy for Vietnamese Americans consolidates a sense of Vietnamese identity that is distinct and incompatible from American identity:

> I feel very touched when watching this play. I feel a great love for the elderly abroad. Even though their material needs are more than sufficient, even plentiful, they are still very lonely. We can generally speak of the difference between American and Vietnamese culture.... Briefly we can say that the Vietnamese are oriented towards sentiment, feeling. Relating to family, different generations live together in one home, taking care of each other through every meal ... grandfather kissing grand-daughter, grandmother kissing granddaughter, is a matter of course ... people are close to nature, living with the river, the water, the stream.... And these very normal things seep deep into us, taking root deep inside each of us, turning into our very blood and skin — something called *homeland*.... That is why the two

old men were "shocked" when they had to live in such a new atmosphere. Why they had to die![11]

Indeed the consolidation of Vietnamese society around "sentiment, feeling" occurs through the abjection of Vietnamese American figures that represent American identity and the melancholic loss of and longing for an existent Vietnamese authenticity. As the playwright Thanh Hoàng explains, it is precisely "the stories of the elderly who are lonely in foreign lands, searching for images of their homeland by hanging up onions, garlic, and peppers in their houses" that make him poignantly aware that "homeland was something that can't be replaced ... [that] surpasses rich or poor, space and time" ("Thanh Hoàng: 'Tôi là người sống hướng nội'"). As the first actor to play Ông Tư, artist Thành Lộc identifies with the Vietnamese Americans' loss of homeland precisely through his own nostalgia for a lost past and lost forms of tradition he connects to his father, the People's Artist Thành Tôn, performer of the traditional opera form *hát bội*:

> In the last days of his life, he was still so passionate about *hát bội* that he forgot his own sickness. In the small room, when the students would come to ask about characters in the operas, he would immediately jump out of his chair and perform the movements in the small four by two meter room. Once his dance was finished, he gasped for his breath but his face showed profound happiness. Even when he was in the Nguyen Trai hospital, when the artist Kim Thanh came to ask about the character Châu Xương, he immediately jumped off the bed and performed a scene. A week later he died [Hoàng].

Comparing the play characters' imaginary of nation and homeland to his own memory of coherent past in the image of his father and *hát bội*, Thành Lộc articulates a longing for a past he sees as quickly dissipating in Vietnam.

Local and Transnational Ties

Indeed while *Dạ Cổ Hoài Lang* affirms the coherence of Vietnamese national identity through abjection, audiences' ability to empathize with the story depends on their own recognition of the heterogeneity of the nation, and their own awareness of the nation's transnational ties. In the narrative entitled "Where is homeland?" for example, author Thu Nguyệt mentions the power of the play *Dạ Cổ Hoài Lang* to stir the hearts of audiences, using the play to talk about nationalist sentiment. Yet her ability to identify with the loss of the characters' homeland is built upon her own longing for local origin and her own awareness of the heterogeneity of local identity forming distinct visions of nation. Thu Nguyệt compares her homesickness in her travel from her hometown Đồng Tháp to the city of Ho Chi Minh to the old men's transnational displacement: "You don't need to go all the way to a foreign country like the two old men in the play to miss home, miss the country, miss the nation. Only traveling 150 miles from Đồng Tháp to Sai Gon, only going to the Miền Tây train station, do I already miss home!" (Thu Nguyệt). She describes her own inability to identify with the folks from the city despite having lived in the city for years; she still chooses friends from the countryside and struggles to understand her "close friend" from the city who knows every nook and corner of Sai Gon, dances on the stage during karaoke without a care, and pragmatically lectures her against giving money to pan-handlers using a logic that merges "the good and the bad like blades of grass growing side by side." To Thu Nguyệt, the "cold" city is a place of transnational flux where one "passes through" but never "lives." At the same time, however, her nieces and nephews long for the city whenever they are far away: "Wherever I go, when I return to the city I feel an inner burning; seeing the lights of the city I feel a strange happiness!" Her narrative emphasizes the heterogeneity of the nation, particularly in the title "What is homeland?" that suggests that home acquires an unstable definition that changes from different points of view. Indeed while *Dạ Cổ Hoài Lang* is a play that builds a distinct national identity through the abjection of Vietnamese Americans, writers such as Thu Nguyệt identify with the play precisely through their own struggle to pin down their "homeland."

Furthermore, while the play uses the Vietnamese American to mark the existence (and loss) of an authentic Vietnamese identity, it at the same time offers reconciliation precisely through the shared experience of displacement. The play attributes The Girl's hyper-assimilation and loss of identity to the experience of trauma in migration linking Vietnamese and Vietnamese diasporic identity. She is "Americanized" ("*Dạ Cổ Hoài Lang*: Vở Diễn Xuất Sắc Của Sân Khấu Nhỏ TP Hồ Chí Minh") from being raised by a father who denies his Vietnamese identity after his journey from Vietnam on a boat he describes as a "coffin for a hundred people awaiting death from hunger and thirst" (Thanh 24). The experience of guilt from turning his back on his people, epitomized by his silence as he watches his people board a ship he knows will be immediately raided by pirates, leads him fully to reject Vietnamese identity, while also melancholically longing for his past. The play acknowledges the experience of trauma leading to the Vietnamese American ambivalence towards Vietnam, while offering the possibility of reconciliation through recognition of shared suffering. It is by finally reading her father's diary describing his experience of migration that The Girl connects with her grandfather's displacement and crosses the wooden plank separating them in the final scene before the grandfather dies.

Vietnamese Americans as the Modern (Masculinized) Subject

The Vietnamese American affirms the existence of a stable Vietnamese identity through his loss and longing for a culturally and geographically situated homeland, but the ability of the Vietnamese to identify with the play's narrative depends on their transnational tie with diasporic Vietnamese, and an awareness of the heterogeneity of local and national identity. While the play uses Vietnamese Americans to create a fixed national identity, it shows as well the very transformation of the concept of national identity from a fixed, coherent and geographically placed idea to one that accounts for heterogeneity and transnational linkages. The orientation towards building of both a culturally distinct and a globally integrative national identity in the postwar leads to the dual function of the Vietnamese American in the Vietnamese imaginary as both a jettisoned and elevated figure that is given authority to critique and affirm Vietnamese society from without.

If *The Girl* represents the perversion of Vietnamese culture by embodying American excess, sexual promiscuity, and heartless pragmatism, her boyfriend, the Vietnamese American Young Man, is a masculine embodiment of a new nation with international links. He demonstrates a respect for traditional Vietnamese culture, and the new identity of the nation as modern and transnational. The Vietnamese American Young Man appreciates and desires to understand his cultural background, journeying back to Vietnam and returning to America to retell of his experience. Like an ideal Vietnamese American, he desires to give back to his country by returning after he has finished his education (Thanh 20). Moreover, he acquires his modern and masculine identity through his enforcement of proper behavior in his interactions with The Girl. When The Girl chastises her grandfather for hanging up the sheets of pictures of the Vietnamese countryside, her boyfriend holds her back; and when she insults her homeland by comparing it to the "crazy and muddled brained" old men, he enforces respect of Vietnam by slapping her. His opposition to The Girl creates a positive masculine international identity in contrast to a feminine embodiment of cultural contamination and submission.

If the old men Ông Tư and Ông Nam can only dream of a Vietnam in their memories, The Young Man's international travel allows him to gain the perspective to affirm the growth and renovation of the nation, acknowledging that it is "still very poor ... but these times are a lot better than the past ... people are beginning to be more comfortable." He describes a progressive and international Vietnam that strives for education, economic development, and the acquisition of foreign languages, since "without studying languages, it would be impossible to talk to foreigners" (Thanh 19–20). The Vietnamese American becomes the new transnational citizen empowered to speak for and legitimate the value of a global Vietnam. He acts as an ideal *việt kiều* who is not pompous or distancing like those that "newspapers in America have written about," but "appears just like common folk" (*giả dạng thường dân*) (19), merging easily into common society to see "real" Vietnamese life. The Young Man declares Vietnamese identity as performable and capable of re-incorporating diasporic Vietnamese, in a new performance of openness and global integration. The play invokes the idealized woman that situates a geographically and culturally distinct nation, to replace her with a new, masculine figure of transnational exchange and mobility.

In *Dạ Cổ Hoài Lang*, Vietnam is both a country with a distinct identity incompatible with foreign cultures such as America, and a transnational site connecting different experiences of suffering and displacement, offering new possibilities of Vietnamese masculinity. As a play that attempts to build a fixed and distinct Vietnamese identity while at the same time provoking identification through transnational empathy, it reveals the dual process of abjection that creates opposing imaginaries of the Vietnamese American. The play negotiates the state's dual needs in the post-war to build national identity and integrate in global capitalism. In the globalized order, the "other" is no longer a distinct American, French, or Chinese "other" of the past, but a diasporic subject that forms the boundaries of the nation at the same time as his body, location, and hybrid identity mark the dispersal of identity and nationhood. *Dạ Cổ Hoài Lang* stages the Vietnamese American, but it is less about a Vietnamese American that one can recognize, and more about Vietnam's own story of itself— its anxieties and questions about national delineation and the role of tradition in a society undergoing rapid transition in globalization — creating visions of spectators, looking back at itself.

NOTES

1. See Julia Kristeva, *Nations without Nationalism*, trans. Leon S. Roudiez (New York: Columbia University Press, 1993).

2. Thanh Hoàng graduated from the College of Theater and Film in Ho Chi Minh City in 1984 and wrote his first spoken drama called *The Dream of the Prisoner* in 1989. He is working on a sequel to *Dạ Cổ Hoài Lang* that stages the main character (Ông Năm) bringing the body of a friend (Ông Tư) back to the "homeland." Ông Tư's son Nguyễn emerges as a character that forgets past conflicts, returns to Vietnam, and arranges a marriage between his daughter and a Vietnamese "born in America but who loves his homeland with all his heart." The author is from Bạc Liệu, where the songwriter Hà Văn Cầu wrote the base song for the "renovated opera" *cải lương* of the same title, *Dạ Cổ Hoài Lang*. See "Thanh Hoàng Viết Kịch Bản *Dạ Cổ Hoài Lang* Tập 2 Thanh Hoàng Writes the Sequel to *Dạ Cổ Hoài Lang*]," *Việt Báo*, February 26, 2007,

http://vietbao.vn/Van-hoa/Thanh-Hoang-viet-kich-ban-Da-co-hoai-lang-tap-2/40188 657/181/ (accessed November 15, 2008). Originally published in *Người Lao Động Newspaper*.

3. Along with the playwright, these actors also received individual gold medals for their performance.

4. Thanh Hoàng reiterates this point when he mentions that the play succeeds by balancing "education," "entertainment," and "aesthetic quality." See "Thanh Hoàng: 'Tôi là người sống hướng nội' [Thanh Hoàng: 'I Am an Introspective Person']," *Vietnam Express*, July 21, 2003. http://www.vnexpress.net/GL/Van-hoa/San-khau-Dienanh/2003/07/3B9C9DB3/ (accessed November 20, 2008). Originally published in *Thanh Niên* newspaper.

5. Members boasted having the attendance of high-level officials of the Party, including Prime Minister Võ Văn Kiệt, at their performance at the Ho Chi Minh Mausoleum in Ha Noi.

6. The performance of reconciliation between Vietnam and America is staged through the Vietnamese American. In an earlier version of the play, Thanh Hoàng stages a reconciliation between the Vietnamese and American when Ông Tư is dying and an American doctor pretends to be his son to say the final goodbye. However, rather than choosing to stage such a symbolic reconciliation, the actor Thành Lộc orchestrates a revision in which Ông Tư dies on top of the rooftop, looking down on the site of the "S" shaped forest in memory of Vietnam, while his granddaughter traverses the symbolic plank separating the cultures to come towards him. Thành Lộc explains, "I don't like foreigners infringing into the spirit of Vietnamese people. This tragedy was created by the Vietnamese and no one has the right to intrude." See Hoàng Kim, "Thành Lộc và *Dạ Cổ Hoài Lang* [Thành Lộc and *Dạ Cổ Hoài Lang*]," *Thanh Niên*, July 26, 2006, http://www.thanhnien.com.vn/2006/Pages/200630/156878.aspx (accessed November 15, 2008).

7. See Joe Thomas, *Ethnocide: A Cultural Narrative of Refugee Detention in Hong Kong* (Aldershot: Ashgate, 2000), 43–51.

8. Nguyễn Thị Minh Ngọc, phone Interview with the author, January 15, 2009.

9. This term literally translates to "Vietnamese sojourner" and refers to Vietnamese people living outside of Vietnam. It used predominantly by the Vietnamese to refer to overseas Vietnamese.

10. This line was stated in a performance attended by the author in June 2007 at the 5B Small Stage Theater, but is not in the manuscript. In the manuscript, she insults her homeland when talking to her boyfriend: "You love your homeland. But look at these two old men. That's the picture of your homeland. Crazy and muddle brained like that." Thanh, 23.

11. E-mail message to author, December 14, 2008.

PART III. AMERICA THROUGH MUSICALS ON THE WORLD STAGE

11

Hair in Sarajevo: Doing Theatre Under Siege

Nenad "Neno" Pervan

Throughout the world, 1992 was the year of positive changes. The United States just elected Bill Clinton, a reform-oriented president. Eastern European countries, including Russia, were plunging into democracy after decades of oppression under Soviet rule. Just three years after the tragedy and massive crime at the Tiananmen Square, China was slowly beginning to change its ways, and open its doors to the rest of the world. After decades of dictatorial regimes, all over Latin America new and democratically elected governments were coming to power. The world, as we knew it for many years, divided and ruled by the principles of the Cold War, was re-inventing itself in front of our eyes.

At the same time, for the peoples of former Yugoslavia, especially those who lived in then federal unit of Bosnia and Herzegovina, the four years of nightmare was just beginning. That nightmare, known as the Bosnian war of the nineties, brought the greatest destruction in human lives and property in Europe since World War II. Hundreds of thousands of civilians were killed, thousands of women raped, and concentration camps smaller in size but similar to those from the Nazi era, were operating again. The capital of Bosnia and Herzegovina, Sarajevo, was in the midst of all of that horror. The city of roughly half a million residents, squeezed between hills and mountains, provided a perfect opportunity for the Serbian aggressor to conduct one of the worst and harshest sieges since the three and a half year long German siege of Leningrad, Russia during the second world war. Without water, power, food or heat at the subfreezing temperatures, Sarajevo's residents suffered immensely under the Serbian mortars, grenades, rockets and sniper fire. In almost four years of the siege, 12,000 Sarajevans died, more than 60,000 were wounded or crippled, and about 120,000 pre-war residents left the city. In the midst of that madness, one of the things that helped people survive and preserve sanity was art.

Even during this violent siege, Sarajevo's actors, directors, filmmakers, musicians, painters, designers, sculptors, dancers, poets and writers were as active and productive as any other artists in the world. Even more so, their need to create and explain to themselves and the rest of the world about what was going on and why propelled them to challenge their motives and inspiration as far and as deep as the human imagination can reach. There were numerous examples of unusual, creative, extremely important works of art. A poetry book by Zlatan Fazlić-Fazla was written and then published on a lowest quality toilet paper, because that was the only kind of paper available. After witnessing a Serbian mortar kill and wound dozens of citizens waiting patiently in line for bread, a cellist from Sarajevo returned to the place of the massacre day after day to perform for an hour and keep alive the memories of the innocent people killed. He was always there at noon, dressed in his concert tuxedo, ready to perform for 22 days, one day for each individual who died. Mortars or snipers almost killed him on many occasions, but he carried on. There was also a series of caged birds made of wire and put in cages by a Sarajevan sculptor, Fikret Libovac. He kept making them throughout the siege with their heads sadly pointing towards the floor, and with their bodies tired and unwilling to fly. Finally, at the very end of the war, the last one lifted her head towards the sun, getting ready to fly away into the freedom. There are hundreds of examples similar to these.

Theater was one of the main forms of this artistic resistance to the hatred, fear and humiliation created by the war. New plays were written and performed under the unthinkable conditions. One of the most remarkable theatrical undertakings came during the first year of the war, when a large group of actors, directors, dancers, designers, and musicians came together to produce a wartime Sarajevo version of the famous Broadway musical *Hair*. The group gathered to rehearse for six months under heavy, non-stop shelling and everyday sniper fire without food, water, or power. They risked their lives for the simple act of showing up for rehearsal. What was their motivation? How did they decide to risk their lives and produce the show? Anybody who has ever decided to create a theatre show, knows that one of the most important factors that has to be taken into account is an answer to a simple question: *Why?* Why are we doing this? The question has to be asked, and final production must be an answer to that question. That makes work on a production purposeful.

It is important to closely examine the circumstances of the production of *Hair*, the way it was cast, conceptualized, rehearsed and performed. Those people's answer to their *Why* was so clear and powerful, that even though it was often a life risking effort to simply come to the theater during the three year long run, nobody ever missed a performance.

Geo-Political Background

To fully understand the severity of the war and the gravity and horrendousness of the situation which Sarajevo was in between 1992 and 1996, one has to understand the set of circumstances that led to the Bosnian war. At the moment of its demise in 1991, Yugoslavia was a country that consisted of six federal units (de-facto states with the right to self-determination), namely; Bosnia and Herzegovina, Croatia, Macedonia, Montenegro, Serbia, Slovenia, and two autonomous provinces within Serbia — Kosovo and Vojvodina. The country was populated by six equal nations and numerous minorities. Yugoslavia came out of World War II as a winning nation. Its leader, Marxist Josip Broz commonly known as Tito, managed not to fall under the Soviet rule, and sustained the country's socialist order without antagonizing the West. For more than forty years, Yugoslavia, one of the founders of the Non-Alignment movement, was a bridge between two antagonized blocks and it became a peaceful place in the middle of the divided Europe. Following Tito's death in 1980, freedom of expression improved rapidly, and as a result artistic expression blossomed in every possible way. This peaked during the fourteenth Winter Olympic Games, held in Sarajevo in 1984. At the same time, however, old nationalistic tendencies, held suppressed under Tito, had been re-ignited. Led by its nationalistic leader Slobodan Milošević, Serbia, the largest nation in the Union, tried to homogenize its power over the other nations. That instantly provoked reaction from the others, especially from Serbs' traditional rivals, Croatians. Slovenia, Croatia, Bosnia and Herzegovina (in the given order) all claimed independence from Yugoslavia in 1991. Backed up by the powerful Yugoslav Army, Serbs opened several fronts. After six months, bloody conflict in Croatia claimed tens of thousands of lives and resulted in Croatia (as well as Slovenia) being recognized as independent countries. The Serbian offensive then moved to Bosnia and Herzegovina. Being a mix of three people, Serbs, Croats, and Bosnian Muslims (Bosnians), Bosnia and Herzegovina was particularly vulnerable to the nationalistic hysteria. Superior in arm power and heavily backed by the Milošević's government in Serbia, Bosnian Serbs put almost two thirds of the country under their control, and completely surrounded the capital, Sarajevo. The siege will last for almost four years, including some of the harshest winters ever recorded in this area, with temperatures dropping to 8 degrees Fahrenheit. People were dying from sniper bullets, shrapnel wounds, mortars, diseases, even common cold. The citizens of Sarajevo dropped their body weight on an average of between 25 and 30 pounds. However, the city stayed resilient, and its mixed national and religious structure survived throughout the war.

Because the siege was so cruel and severe, many urban Serbs chose to stay and defend the city, despite the fact that their fellows Serbs were fighting on the other side. Sarajevo is located between the mountains, with basically only two main roads to enter and exit the city. That gave the Serbian side the opportunity to besiege it based on the medieval tactics combined with modern weaponry. Serbs brought a massive amount of heavy artillery pieces and tanks and dug them all around the city. More than two million artillery projectiles were shot at the city throughout the course of the siege. Their tactics were to starve, kill, freeze and wound the population until the point of unconditional surrender. To avoid that, Sarajevans of all nationalities organized themselves in an attempt to keep life flowing. Production of the American musical *Hair* was one of the direct results of those efforts.

The Choosing and Adjustment of the Script and Casting Process

When the war broke out in April of 1992, Sarajevo quickly found itself completely surrounded and under the enemy's fire. Most of the people picked up a little weaponry that was available in the city, and went to the front lines to defend their homes and families. Besides the enemy outside of the city, there were a lot of criminals, thugs and war profit-makers within Sarajevo, which made the situation even harder. Under these grave circumstances and after the first shock of being hit by the war was absorbed, people started to look for the ways to keep their life as normal as possible. Theatre workers started to look for the scripts, musicals, plays, and anything that would allow them to artistically respond to the events around them. The need to produce something was urgent and imminent. There was very little, if any, food and water and these artists instinctively turned to their other sources of energy by turning to their talent and creativity. The main theatre building in Sarajevo, Narodno pozoriste (National Theatre), was completely shut down. National Theatre is located at the riverbank in the very center of the city and it was completely unprotected from the Serbian fire from the hills, making it to risky to even enter the building. However, there were two other, smaller theatres located very close to the National Theatre that were much safer and made production possible. Within the first couple of months of the war, little by little, most of the functioning technical devices such as costumes, useful set pieces, small props, make-up, even power generators, were transferred to Pozoriste mladih (The Youth Theatre), and Kamerni teatar '55 (The Chamber Theatre '55). In the long run, this move was crucial for the survival of theatre in the city throughout the entire war. The costume shops in both small theatres were operational, and artists began to gather and organize themselves in an attempt to revive theatre production under the wartime circumstances. This organizing came not just as a result of the instinctive need to create, but also from the need to resist the enemy, and fight humiliation that was generated by the life under the siege.

The first step in the process was choosing the script. After meeting in The Chamber Theatre in early May of 1992 and discussing several plays, scenarios, and librettos, a small group of theatre workers chooses to produce Sarajevo wartime version of *Hair*. This famous American musical, written by James Rado and Gerome Ragni, with music by Galt MacDermot, opened off–Broadway in October of 1967 in Joseph Papp's Public Theatre in New York City. After an immediate success, production moved on Broadway in April of 1968 and ran consecutively for 1,750 performances. *Hair* dealt with numerous controversial issues considered taboo at the time. Some of the themes that the musical was dealing with included sexuality (full nudity was introduced on the stage), the use of illegal drugs, as well as the issues of race and religion. However, one of the main themes that provoked Sarajevo's artists to choose *Hair* was the dominant anti-war sentiment developed in the original version as a response to the United States involvement in the war in Vietnam.

The creative team, including a director/choreographer, set and costume designers, two rock musicians, and a co-director,[1] approached the original version with passion. The 1979 film version of *Hair*, directed by famous Czech director Milos Forman, was extremely popular all over former Yugoslavia and every member of the creative team was familiar with it. *Hair* was often performed on stages in Yugoslavia, and one of the previous productions was made in Sarajevo. After searching through the available theatre archives in the city that were not yet damaged or destroyed, they were lucky to find a translated version of the Broadway original, as well as the music sheets with the lyrics in English. Due to the popularity of the movie version, the songs were well known among the city's population. Therefore, the call was made that the spoken dialogue was to be delivered in translation, but the songs should remain in English. The feeling was that translating the lyrics from English into the local language would probably end up being extremely awkward. In the spoken part of the musical, the emphasis was put on the parts that were dealing with issues of war and peace, draft, abuse of the political power, and the people's power to say no to the tyranny, war, suffering and occupation. Other themes within the musical were touched on as well; however large parts of the script were cut. Furthermore, a well-known and widely popular local poet[2] wrote several additions to the lines that were directly addressing local situation and issues. This added component allowed the performers, especially actors, to personally connect with the story, and brought the emotional aspect of the show to a whole new level. After making these decisions and additions, the next step was to cast the show.

Since the movement through the city was extremely limited and dangerous, a curfew from 9 P.M. to 6 A.M. for civilians was enforced throughout the entire four years of the war, and most of the telephone lines were non-operational, the only way to reach potential cast members was through word of mouth. In the city of the size of Sarajevo, the artistic community was very tightly knit. Everybody who was a part of that community pretty much knew everybody else. The word quickly spread throughout the community and very soon members of the team were actually forced to turn some people down due to the numerous limitations of the production. The main difference between this process and the standard casting process, which usually becomes a competitive and often humiliating and nerve-breaking event, was that neither fame, nor money, nor the "being the best in the pack" mind-frame, were motivational forces behind the decision to join this production. Everybody wanted to do it because it was a question of survival; not just a simple survival, but survival with dignity. The final result was the casting of four actors, seven dancers, four singers and four rock-musicians.[3] Together with the creative and organizational[4] teams, they were to develop and deliver their version of the famous musical, for an occasion re-named *Hair, Sarajevo, A.D. 1992.*

Directorial Concept

From the very beginning of the rehearsal process in June of 1992, production was faced with many difficult problems. They were able to secure the performance space in The Chamber Theatre, but rehearsal space was not always available and due to the wartime circumstances in the city, walking around and trying to find one was not an option. Every available square foot of the Chamber Theatre was used for rehearsals. There was no power, and gasoline powered generators were used only for the performances and extreme emergencies. The members of the band could not use their electrical equipment, and all the way to the final dress rehearsal they practiced and rehearsed on acoustic instruments. Very often, the only source of power was simply a used car battery that would be sufficient to provide obscure sources of light for a very limited time periods. Singers sang without the help of microphones and amplifiers.

While rehearsing during daytime, some of the performers were spending their nights as soldiers on the front line fighting the aggressor. They were tired and sometimes completely exhausted. Others suffered from tremendous weight loss. For these, and several other technical and organizational reasons caused by the siege, it was clear from the beginning that performing all the songs and putting together the entire two and a half hours long production would not be possible. The length of the play was reduced to one hour and the burden of the performance was equally divided between actors, dancers and musicians. The band was permanently on the stage, and occasionally some of the singers were given small acting and dancing assignments. Only two male and two female actors performed various characters, while dancers would become those same characters during the musical numbers. That meant that each scene was broken into speaking and musical segment, but instead of actors acting, dancing and singing there would be two or three versions of each character. For example, the well known military draft scene between the characters of Claude and members of the Army's medical commission, would start with Claude's character being portrayed by an actor, which would shift into another performer singing Claude, as well as a dancing version of the same character. One character would equally be shared by two or three performers. This approach allowed director/choreographer[5] to build his vision of the musical around the Tribe. This concept is introduced in the original version where character of Berger and his group are introduced as the Tribe, and everybody else within the musical is a part of the establishment. In the Sarajevo version, everybody on the stage was a member of the Tribe that seeks "peace, flowers, freedom and happiness." Those ideals were taken directly from the original musical and the hippy movement. On the other hand, those outside the stage, theatre and the city, those who are holding positions on the hills and continuously shelling Sarajevo, belong to a different Tribe. This Tribe of highlanders who are keeping the city under siege were perceived as nothing but savages who hated Sarajevo and its cultural and urban values. While creating and developing this concept for the production, authors[6] constantly kept answering their artistic "*Why?*"

This clash-of-the-Tribes approach allowed the authors to explore the actual reasons for nationalistic hatred that had torn Bosnia and Herzegovina and Sarajevo apart. At the opening of the show, in added lines written by local poet,[7] an actor[8] said:

> I can no longer live in this city made to prison.
> Nor in this country made to hell.
> Nor in this world made to brothel.

> I hate this fucking world in which children
> Must lay down on the ground in horror
> When flock of pigeons flies over their heads
> Thinking it was a machinegun fire.
> I hate darkness of basements
> In which our children grow like mushrooms.
> I hate highlanders who fire mortars
> At children who pick cherries.

This poem shifted into "Aquarius," the opening song of the musical which sends the message of piece, love, harmony and understanding. The show continued with this struggle between the message of peace, love and happiness proclaimed by the original *Hair*, and the one of frustration, death and distraction that started in Sarajevo in 1992. At the end of the show, after the cosmopolitan, inter-cultural and very optimistic version of "Let the Sun Shine In," the Band continued to play the "Hare Krishna" song, and actors invited the members of the audience on the stage to join in a collective dance and song of love. The Tribe of good eventually wins the struggle. That was the message that *Hair, Sarajevo, A.D. 1992* desperately needed to send to the rest of the world.

The Band and the Musical Arrangements

Starting in the early sixties, Sarajevo began to develop a very strong and authentic rock scene. Some of the greatest rock bands of the former Yugoslavia, which had a very vibrant, highly profitable and widely popular rock and pop scene, originated in Sarajevo. In the early nineties, right before the war begun, most of those bands were touring Yugoslavia and selling their records in hundreds of thousands of copies. Members of those bands that stayed in Sarajevo after the beginning of the war wanted to get involved in the cultural activities. Working on *Hair* was very attractive to many of these artists due to the nature of the musical and its strong rooting in the hippy movement and rock sound.

The creative team chose two male and two female superior rock vocalists[9] to share the burden of 11 songs that made the cut out of 29 from the original Broadway version. It was a prevailing opinion within the artistic team that the original music arrangements of songs lacked the strength and musical power which was needed to address this almost diabolical situation that was developing in and around Sarajevo. They felt that both music and the lyrics were excellent, but that the music part was a bit too soft for the circumstances. After assembling the band with a standard rock formation with lead guitar, drums, bass guitar and two keyboard and synthesizer players,[10] they began to re-arrange[11] the songs. The final result was much firmer, often hard rock sound, filled with strong and clean guitar solos and powerful riffs, supported by an unstoppable rhythm section and emotionally complimented by the couple of keyboards.

The authors of the project knew that the majority of the audience would be young. That was one of the reasons that the strong hip-hop influences may be heard in some of the arrangements. All these musicians were between twenty-five and thirty-five years old, they all knew each other very well, and they all performed together sometime in the past. The concept of the Tribe fitted perfectly into their rock mentality, and the band and the musical segment of the show became the dominant force within the production. Four singers[12] were the most prominent feature of the show. Their forceful vocal and emotional energy mixed perfectly with the severity of the situation and poetic and idealistic message of *Hair*. They carried the rest of the cast through the show. Their voices and energy behind them provided the last necessary push for everybody else to endure the harsh conditions, bombs and bullets, hunger and thirst, and to deliver not overly complicated, but definitely demanding assignments within the show.

Design, Actors and Dancers

At the time when the work on the production have started, it was almost impossible to produce materials, or find the qualified people who would be able to transform those materials into costumes and set design. The entire work on the project was done on the voluntary bases. The situation in the city was deteriorating on a daily bases, and to avoid a trap of spending to much time in search for fabrics and materials, costume designer[13] made a choice to talk with performers, and find the solution in their own, private closets. Everybody started digging through their (or in some cases their parents) old stuff, revisiting sixties and seventies. Everything they found was combined with the costumes that were available in the Chamber and Youth Theatre costume shops. The final result was a surprisingly personal collection of costumes that never obstructed the happenings on the stage. Sixties and nineties met in the best possible way.

The set designer[14] worked in a more symbolical manner. With a help of an experienced, skilled carpenter,[15] she was able to build series of abstract elements that covered back wall of the theatre. Each piece was hand-painted by the designer. When finished, these geometrically and size-wise different objects, were unmistakably reminding the audience of being surrounded by the cruel, merciless force. Large, human size dolls were built and mixed up with the performers all over the stage. These faceless, scary objects reflected the severity of the siege and cruelty of the aggressor. Throughout the show they were moved around and used as set pieces and props at the same time. The stage stretched deep into the audience. This allowed performers to connect with the viewers on a very personal level. Audience members would sing, and in some cases even stand up and dance, together with the members of the ensemble. Due to this personal kind of set up, the acting style was more intimate, and often directed towards the audience. The goal was more to share the message of the show with the audience, then to create the clean characters as they were originally written. In many occasions, actors spoke directly to the people, and this created a very deep and personal bonding between the two.

Because of the shortage of electricity, most of the generated power was used for the musicians. That resulted with show being lit with as few light sources as possible. This approach resulted in a very simple, sometimes even obscure lighting design that perfectly reflected the state in which the citizens of Sarajevo were struggling at the time.

Choreography and dance mixed several styles and influences. The most powerful moments were coming through numerous duets based mostly in a classical ballet. The often hard and loud sound of rock music was in a sharp contrast with a soft and even romantic movement of classically trained dancers. This contrast underlined the importance of love and beauty serving as the survival tools amidst the desperate life under the siege. However, to stress the importance of the resistance many dance numbers were choreographed in a much more contemporary style. This constant switch between classical and contemporary was another way to bridge the gap between the Broadway and Sarajevo productions. Through these dances, the hippy rebellion of the sixties was transformed into the pain, suffering and resilience of Sarajevans.

The Show

At noon, on November 14, 1992, *Hair, Sarajevo, A.D. 1992,* opened in The Chamber Theatre '55. This small theatre could not seat more than two hundred people and on that day every single seat was occupied. Despite heavy shelling and very cold weather, Sarajevans chose to come. They sat in between the rows, stood on their feet, and even had other audience members sitting in their laps. Still, a large number of people could not make it to the theatre. As soon as the performance was over, artists took a short fifteen minute break, the stage was quickly re-set and the show was performed again in front of another full house. The reception was fantastic. The energy flow between the performers and the audience was unique. People joined in singing and dancing. There were tears, there was pride, and there was hope that the horrendous situation can not continue forever. The message of love from the original Broadway version was finding the place in the hearts of those who watched. However, the new message of resilience and resistance was also developing under the pressure of the siege.

Another very important aspect of the show was its national structure. Bosnians, Croats, Serbs, Jews were all members of the creative team, cast and crew. Everything that was happening in Bosnia and Herzegovina at the time clearly suggested that living together and in peace with other nations is not possible, and that the country has to be partitioned through war and horrible methods like ethnic cleansing. *Hair, Sarajevo, A.D. 1992*, using the American musical's message of brotherhood, tolerance, and anti-war, undeniably proved that the peoples of Bosnia and Herzegovina can and should live and work together, as they did throughout the centuries. It showed Croatian and Bosnian leaders not to expect the Sarajevans to turn against their Serbian neighbors who decided to stay in the city. In essence, show was able to stay true to the spirit of Sarajevo that kept the city together for centuries, without being afraid to clearly point out who was the real aggressor and how to defeat him. American hippies became the model for Sarajevan unity.

Between the opening day and April of 1993, the show was performed fifty-three times in front of the full houses. The show generated great interest outside Sarajevo and Bosnia and Herzegovina. Every international journalist accredited in the city during the war reported about it. The United States and several European countries have shown interest to see the show. After long negotiations, the warring factions agreed to allow the production to fly out of the city on a world-wide tour that was supposed to end in the United States.

On April 13, 1993, the cast and crew were waiting in downtown Sarajevo to be picked up by a bus that was supposed to take them to the airport while short truce was enforced. The bus never came. Somebody high in the political hierarchy has changed his mind and *Hair, Sarajevo, A.D. 1992*, was not allowed to leave Sarajevo. Despite their disappointment, the artists continued to perform their show. There were twenty-one more performances until the war finally ended in December of 1995.

Conclusion

Following the end of a four year war, as people were trying to cope with the harsh aftermath of the siege, the artists who produced and performed the show went on with their own lives and careers. Like many Sarajevans, many of them left the city and tried their luck all over the world. Some of them stayed in the city. Throughout the years, I had a chance to talk with several of them. Their opinions about the war and the siege, about the different aspects of the show and what it achieved, vary. However, they all agreed about one point; starting a theatre project without clearly answering the question *Why*, makes the effort pointless.

In an everyday world, we can not produce and participate in every theatre project like our lives depend on it. However, we should keep in our minds that undermining the power and importance of our own art by choosing our projects without really knowing what will be their cultural, artistic and social relevance makes our work unimportant and ordinary. Those who created and performed *Hair, Sarajevo, A.D. 1992*, proved that any work of art should always aim to be important and extraordinary.[16]

NOTES

1. Director/choreographer: Slavko Pervan
   Co-director: Kaca Doric
   Costume Designer: Amela Vilic
   Set Designer: Lada Pervan
   Lead Guitar: Amir Beso-Lazy
   Lead Singer: Srdjan Jevdjevic
2. Added Poetry: Marko Vesovic
3. Singers: Srdjan Jevdjevic, Amila Glamocak, Dragana Ilic, Igor Zerajic
   The band: *Guitar and Vocals*—Amir Beso-Lazy, *Keyboards*—Boris Bacvic and Dusan Vranic, *Bas*—Samir Ceremida, *Drums*—Izudin Kolecic
   Actors: Admir Glamocak, Gordana Boban, Suada Topolovic, Zeljko Stjepanovic
   Dancers: Jelena Solaric, Emira Sahinpasic, Lejla Nezirovic, Irma Ugrincic, Mirce Hurdubae, Mesud Vatic, Adnan Dzindo
4. Organizers: Lila Simic, Franjo Ripis
5. Director/Choreographer: Slavko Pervan
6. Script Adaptation: Slavko Pervan, Kaca Doric, Marko Vesovic
7. Poetry: Marko Vesovic (Translation in English: Nenad Pervan)
8. Actor: Admir Glamocak
9. Singers: Srdjan Jevdjevic, Amila Glamocak, Dragana Ilic, Igor Zerajic
10. The band: *Guitar and Vocals*—Amir Beso-Lazy, *Keyboards*—Boris Bacvic and Dusan Vranic, *Bas*—Samir Ceremida, *Drums*—Izudin Kolecic
11. Musical Arrangements: Amir Beso-Lazy, Srdjan Jevdjevic
12. Singers: Srdjan Jevdjevic, Amila Glamocak, Dragana Ilic, Igor Zerajic
13. Costume Designer: Amela Vilic
14. Set Designer: Lada Pervan
15. Master Carpenter: Esad Landzo
16. This article was written through personal interviews with many of the original participants. Special thanks to Slavko Pervan and Lada Pervan for their insights and stories.

12

Japanese Women/American Men: National Identities and the Takarazuka Revue

Jessica Hester

Attack and destroy the germs
The germs in our heart-minds
Get rid of them now
Quick, quick expel them
Attack and destroy the germs
The Anglo-American[isms] in our heart-minds[.][1]
— *The Battle Is Also Here*, 1943

The 1860 Japanese mission to America, which included three diplomats from the Tokugawa Shogunate and an entourage of seventy-four people, provides some of the first records of Japanese perceptions of Americans and American culture. The Tokugawa era was notoriously closed to foreign, particularly Western, influence, one of its mottos being "Revere the Emperor, Expel the Barbarians" (Henshall 67), and this mission towards the end of that era indicates an increased perception that Japan needed to look more closely at its interactions with the world outside of Asia. The documents of the mission reveal numerous differences in American and Japanese attitudes, some of which cast an interesting light on the travelers' experiences and expectations of theatre and women.

The delegation, visiting San Francisco first, provided their first experience with theatre in America, and the unusual sight of women performing female roles struck them as strange. They later attended a Chinese theatre performance, appreciating that event significantly more, as it "'was like a Japanese play.'"[2] The performance tradition in Japan saw men playing all characters, both male and female — a convention that, in the public theatre, grew out of a desire to control the offstage sexual negotiations that were common in the early years of kabuki theatre. On the east coast, theatre managers issued invitations to the Japanese delegates, hoping that their exotic presence would attract audiences, ostensibly coming to see the Japanese as opposed to seeing the plays being presented (Beasley 62–63). The Japanese, on the other hand, found many American trends both alien and disturbing. Throughout the trip, they were perplexed by what they observed as the deferential treatment of women, and particularly the presence of women at official functions (61, 65, 70).

For hundreds of years women did not perform professionally in Japan, but in the early twentieth century a new genre developed — the all-female musical revue. In as much as kabuki emerged in the 1600s as popular culture entertainment to please the middle class, the most successful of these revue companies, the Takarazuka Revue, is engineered for mass appeal, and both it and kabuki present idealized manifestations of gender. Kabuki's *onnagata* performers, men specializing in female roles, have fascinated Western scholars for years. Takarazuka, on the other hand, gives audiences female performers, *otokoyaku*, specializing in male character roles. Just as the *onnagata* reveal to audiences archetypes of sixteenth century femininity, the *otokoyaku* perform a similar function regarding twentieth century masculinity. It is through these performances that *otokoyaku* enact the status that eludes Japanese women offstage, often through the representation of Americans and American culture.

Neither stage performances nor the histories of them can be separated from their cultural and political contexts. The theatrical stage provides a space in which national issues are played out, either providing a forum for alternate views of these issues, or reinforcing the status quo. Theatre can be seen as a process that "stages the private and public anxieties of a people who are what they are because of history" (Wilmeth and Bigsby xvi). The staging techniques used by Takarazuka have been shaped by both Japanese and Western theatrical conventions, but the performances have been influenced just as much by political tensions between Japan and America, particularly in the decades immediately following the occupation.[3] Women performing male characters on the Takarazuka stage have revealed "private and public anxieties," in many ways about gender, but have also been used to assert Japanese nationalism, frequently in relation to American identities. Gender, sex, and national identity are terms that have an eternal presence in scholarship about Japanese theatre, but typically that scholarship analyzes the performance of male actors, with a particular fascination with the kabuki *onnagata*. The

Takarazuka Revue falls both within and outside of traditional Japanese performance conventions. Borrowing stylistically from kabuki, Stanislavski, Broadway, Las Vegas, and European cabaret performances, Takarazuka simultaneously represents everything and nothing at all.

The Takarazuka shows are performed in two parts: story and flash. The first half is (typically) a love story with dialogue and singing interspersed. After intermission, the company performs a flamboyant musical revue, which often has no connection to the first half of the performance. Many of their shows have been productions of American musicals and, although they did not perform any American shows while I visited Japan in July and August of 2007, I was excited to see at least how the company presented the masculinities that appeared on their publicity posters, which, curiously, present *otokoyaku* who look neither completely male nor female, Japanese nor Western. I convinced two friends to join me, with the promise that the show would be transformative, and sat between them to gauge their reactions. Understandably, they were uncertain, particularly after watching a four-and-a-half hour Kabuki version of *Twelfth Night*, during which I palpitated on the edge of my seat and they, well, did not palpitate.

Then it began, *Valencian Passion*, set in Spain following the end of the Napoleonic Wars. I thought I was watching an Elvis movie —*Jailhouse Rock*, perhaps. The star *otokoyaku*, Yuga Yamato, plays Fernando, a rebellious young man hungry to restore Spanish rule to his country. Yamato, in profile on a high platform, is silhouetted against an orange background that bleeds into a deep crimson hue at floor level. Her contralto voice is mesmerizing, as is her presence. The woman to my right is converted, immediately moving forward on her seat, whispering to me, "I love it." The man to my left is entranced, but not transformed; he knows that this performance is not directed at the straight male audience member. As one of only five men in the theatre, it is clear that one of the key elements of the Takarazuka Revue is that of only women performing, primarily, for other women. Although the Revue was marketed as a family entertainment in the mid-twentieth century, it is now recognized as having an almost completely female fan base.[4]

The plot of *Valencian Passion* is not complex — primarily revolving around young Spaniards resisting French rule, all the while negotiating love with beautiful and virtuous young women. The wooing onstage is supposed to be an idealized performance of romantic pursuit — complete and controlled tension between gentle caresses and powerful embraces, passion and distance, respect and lust. Yamato is charismatic, wooing two women at once — the first is the virtuous woman to whom Fernando is betrothed, the other is a singer, Isabela. Fernando and Isabela have several smoldering scenes in which they cling to one another while singing passionate duets, and by intermission it seems that the majority of the audience is ready to follow Yamato backstage.

The second half of the show is like a high-octane Las Vegas musical revue: *Cosmic Festival: Space Fantasista!*, about the birth of the cosmos. Yamato is again the star of the show, playing Fantasista. The actual connection to the cosmos is vague, but the episodes are fascinating. At one point Yamato's female love interest begins a scene as virtue in bondage, dressed in a white Grecian-style peplos, and ends the scene in black leather with thigh-high boots, transformed into a dominatrix. The finale centers on the light-up staircase that takes up the entire back of the stage, and, during the curtain call, each actor descends the stairs in increasingly elaborate concoctions of feathers — the plumage increases as the minor actors are dwarfed by supporting actors, and everyone on stage looks tiny when Yamato makes her final entrance. Yamato seems diminutive herself for the first time, overwhelmed by the feather cape that seems to extend three feet on either side of her body.[5]

Conflict on the Takarazuka stage, in the guise of war, sword duels, or the cosmos in bondage, is aesthetically satisfying. The tension may be emotionally charged, but in the performance I saw, it was also pretty. Keeping unpleasantness at bay is part of the Takarazuka Revue management's business strategy. While the strategy makes for an easily controlled publicity network, research on the company and its history is not welcome. As anthropologist Jennifer Robertson and others have made clear, detailed research on the Takarazuka Revue is difficult, as the archives are closely guarded and performers can typically only be interviewed with a chaperone present. Robertson, whose research focus was sexual politics, was blocked from seeing the files that would most pertain to her work, and received a phone call warning her that, if she were Japanese, she would not be allowed into the archives at all. Robertson's caller said of the Takarazuka administrators, "They're mean. They have their ways. They could twist your arm the way developers do when they want to force people to sell their land." (54). Robertson was allowed to continue, but was closely monitored and only able to see materials considered "safe" for the company's public image. So it is not surprising that the sources of information regarding the Takarazuka Revue come from the company's public relations staff, performance reviews, articles that analyze the company from a distance, and Robertson's articles and book.

The Takarazuka Revue was founded in 1913 by railroad executive Kobayashi Ichizo as a tourist draw to Takarazuka City. Kobayashi based his idea for an all-female revue on the success of a Western-style boy's soprano group that entertained customers in the Mitsukoshi Dry Goods Store in Osaka (Robertson 4). He particularly wanted to provide audiences with wholesome entertainment, a counterpoint to what he considered the disreputable kabuki troupes that were popular at the time (Singer 162). He recruited female performers and had them trained in the style of the musical revues popular in Western Europe at the time. The company performs their own versions of Japanese and European plays and novels, in addition to American musicals, dance revues, adaptations of novels, and original texts based on both Japanese and Western content. A 1990s Takarazuka Revue brochure advertises the performances as "an instant history ... [and] a playback of how the Japanese see and interpret the West" (Sischy 88). Or at least the parts of the West that translate well into catchy musical numbers, elaborate costumes, and flashy spectacle.

The performers are divided into two categories: *Musumeyaku*, female character roles, and *otokoyaku*, male character roles. Both the *musumeyaku* and *otokoyaku* play to the extremes of gender stereotype, and are, as Robertson puts it, "products of a dominant social ideology that privileges masculinity in men" (12). Part of the *otokoyaku* training includes studying male sex symbols to learn their movements, gestures, and behavior, so they are better equipped to portray ideal men in their performances. Of the common celebrities emulated, several are American, notably Clark Gable, James Dean, Elvis Presley, Marlon Brando, and Jack Nicholson (12–13).

The development of the Takarazuka Revue is linked to Western performance at almost every step. In acknowledgement of the French revue's influence, performers are referred to as "Takarasiennes," after "Parisiennes," a subtle but important element of their connection to non–Asian theatre. The 1920s and 1930s became critical years for Takarazuka, both in terms of popularity and style. The Takarazuka Grand Theatre, which seats 3000, was built in 1924, followed in 1934 by a similar theatre constructed for the revue in Tokyo. During this period of growth, the influence of Western theatre increased: Beginning in the 1920s, Takarazuka directors were sent to the United States to study theatrical styles and staging techniques; in 1930, performers ceased wearing the traditional whiteface makeup, which is still used in kabuki, replacing it with greasepaint and other Western-style stage makeup techniques; in the 1930s, Constantin Stanislavski's psychological realism acting methods were introduced to the revue (Robertson 5, 124, 12, 60).

By the time World War II began, Western, and specifically American, performance culture was an intrinsic element of the Takarazuka Revue. At the same time, Japanese nationalism became a dominant theme of wartime theatre. This uniquely positioned Takarasiennes, who, already performing dual genders, now used Western acting techniques to inhabit those genders while conveying anti–American rhetoric. The *otokoyaku's* performances took on new meaning as "some forms of previously assimilated difference and otherness were newly coded as pathogenic in the rhetorical climate of war" Robertson 132–134). These "pathogens" appeared as distinctly Western, as the lines from the 1943 revue *The Battle Is Also Here* make clear: "Attack and destroy the germs / The Anglo-American[isms] in our heart-minds[...]" (qtd. in Robertson 133).

Songs like this made the Takarazuka Revue an important part of Japan's wartime nationalist language, particularly given its status as theatre for mass culture, and attending the performances became a patriotic act. In this way the Takarazuka Revue functioned similarly to theatrical genres in the West during politically charged times, at which point, "...theatrical nationhood in the era of mass politics foregrounds the representation of national citizenship as national spectatorship" (Kruger 186). Takarazuka was able to meet this need largely because of its pop culture appeal. Going to see the Revue was a lighthearted family activity; the political message may have been embedded, but the surface was all fun. Osaka housewife and long-time Takarazuka fan, Kitamura Kazuko, began attending performances in the fourth grade, during World War II, when the troupe temporarily replaced the deprivation of life during wartime with a glittering fantasy world. As Kitamura said, "It was like a fantastic dream to me" (qtd. in Singer 178).

The popularity of Takarazuka is indicated by the Tokyo Takarazuka Theatre's inclusion in the 1944 "Regulations for the Control of Theatrical Production," which, among other things, sought to reduce the frequency of large gatherings of people in case of air raids by closing nine major theatres in the Tokyo entertainment district (Okamoto 24–25). Despite the success of the revue and its wartime rhetoric, however, the *otokoyaku* complicated representations of national identity. In 1941, Takarazuka Revue stars were forbidden from dressing as males, suggesting that "playing" at masculinity might have been perceived as dangerous (135). Clearly, the issue was not simply performing an opposite gender, as male actors specializing in kabuki *onnagata* were not affected. Instead, the presence of women creating tantalizing images of men onstage had to be restrained.

After World War II and the American occupation of Japan, the use of gender in Takarazuka to comment on national identity shifted, particularly in relation to the production of American musicals. *Otokoyaku* are able to perform multiple identifications, in many ways because they are ideal masculinities inhabiting female bodies. It is in this liminal space, marked as pop culture, that the company's female performers effortlessly delineate the national identity markers of "Japanese" and "American." Played against the *musumeyaku* ideal femininities inhabiting female bodies, "generic American gender markers are constructed and performed in opposition to dominant assumption about Japanese gender ideals" (Robertson 77). *Musumeyaku* portray characters that reinforce feminine ideals, while *otokoyaku* might play an ideal Japanese masculinity or its opposition.

The Takarazuka production of *West Side Story* (1968) offers a sense of how gender and national identity uniquely operate in this sphere. Some members of the Takarazuka management wanted to block the production because the crudeness of rough New York City street gangs conflicted with the status of the Takarazuka stage as a place of "beauty and elegance." They also complained that "Japanese women should not portray coarse American characters," as their finer attributes would be scarred by the experience. The production, nevertheless, went forward, but the essential conflicts the musical seeks to trouble disappeared. The ethnicities in *West Side Story*, however problematic, were conflated into a general "American" character, and the politics surrounding Tony and Maria's relationship, Italian American and Puerto Rican, evaporated, replaced by an emphasis on the "'purity' of their impossible love" (Robertson 77). This theme is consistent with many of the Takarazuka productions, like *Valencian Passion*, with the primary love interests entirely devoted to one another, but their union opposed by more powerful forces.

The 1977 premier of the Takarazuka Revue's musical version of *Gone with the Wind* reveals another perception of Americans. Instead of casting a leading *musumeyaku* as Scarlett O'Hara, the character was played by a top *otokoyaku*. The director explains:

> The *otokoyaku* have an erotic appeal that is missing in *musumeyaku*. The rationale for having an *otokoyaku* play Scarlett O'Hara is to revive her original femininity while at the same time retaining the sensuality of her "male" gender, thereby doubling her charm [qtd. in Robertson 82–3].

When *otokoyaku* are called upon to play strong female characters, they are typically Euro American. Takarazuka managers and directors feel that the *musumeyaku* must have a certain degree of virtue and innocence, which would be jeopardized if asked to portray female characters with unabashed sexuality (Robertson 83). The leading *otokoyaku* enjoyed another rare experience with *Gone with the Wind*—facial hair. For the first time, leading *otokoyaku* wore false beards and mustaches to help convey the specifically American masculinities called for by the production. Haruna Yuri, the first Takarasienne to play Rhett Butler, wore her mustache offstage to "feel more 'natural' and convincing" as the American icon (13). The story of *Gone with the Wind* was considered quintessentially American, but, as such, it could not be performed in characteristic Takarazuka style. Just as the street gangs represented a dangerous foreign presence in *West Side Story*, Scarlett O'Hara's bold sexuality was interpreted as a hazard that is specifically American.[6]

James Michener's novel *Sayonara* (1953) offers an American view of Americans in Japan, specifically through the lens of the dually restrictive American military and Takarazuka Revue administration. Set during the

Korean War, *Sayonara* chronicles the shift in Major Lloyd "Ace" Gruver's perception of the Japanese after he falls in love with Takarazuka Revue's *otokoyaku* star Hana-ogi. At the beginning of the novel, Gruver is disgusted by the number of American servicemen dating and marrying Japanese women, who he sees as unattractive: "They're all so dumpy and round-faced. How can our men — good average guys — how can they marry these yellow girls?" (Michener 7). His attitude toward the beauty of Japanese women changes after seeing Hana-ogi's performance in the Takarazuka Revue's *Swing Butterfly*.

    Swing Butterfly is a retelling of Giacomo Puccini's *Madam Butterfly*, a burlesque of the opera that gave power to the Japanese geishas and made American military men look like buffoons. When Gruver first sees the show he is disgusted, particularly with Hana-ogi's performance as Lieutenant Pinkerton. Aside from Pinkerton appearing as "arrogant, ignorant, and ill-mannered," Gruver is amazed that the actress playing the character simultaneously exudes both masculinity and femininity, saying, "It was this that made her version of Pinkerton so devastating. She was all Japanese women making fun of all American men" (94). Despite his frustration with the show, Gruver becomes obsessed with Hana-ogi, and they fall in love, although neither one can speak the other's language. When he sees the performance again after falling in love with Hana-ogi, his view is decidedly different. He sees the humor in her parody of Americans, becoming aware that she had been studying his own mannerisms, and reproduced them with a comic edge. Gruver's understanding was directly connected with the personal nature of the satire — he was able to laugh at himself, and, at the same time, see the connection to American military personnel in general.

    Part of the power of Takarazuka performances, as suggested by Gruver's perception of Hana-ogi's dual presence on stage, is the parallel image of both male and female in the *otokoyaku*'s appearance. The tension brought out by this performance of gender makes political satire and commentary particularly effective; in its absence, the Takarazuka Revue takes on a different kind of presence. The 1957 film version of *Sayonara*, starring Marlon Brando, includes no reference to *Swing Butterfly*. Instead, Hana-ogi is shown in a series of ten-second clips performing characters from various shows, most of whom were female. The name Takarazuka Revue is not mentioned, and instead Hana-ogi is the star of the fictitious Matsubayashi Girls Revue. The stage shows were performed, not by Takarazuka singers and dancers, but by members of the Shochiku Kagekidan Girls Revue.[7] The Shochiku Revue, founded in 1928, became the main rival for Takarazuka, and was known as dramatically more erotic. The *otokoyaku* performers with Shochiku were also known as more masculine than the Takarazuka performers, both on and offstage (Robertson 6, 148). The use of the Shochiku Revue, particularly given the innocent nature of the clips shown in *Sayonara* and the absence of *otokoyaku* performers, says more about Hollywood aesthetics than the novel's agenda. Perhaps filmmakers felt that a female love interest that specialized in performing male characters would be unacceptable for Western audiences.

The film provides no direct reference to Hana-ogi, or any performer, specializing in portraying characters of the opposite gender. Michener's novel makes a brief reference to kabuki *onnogata*, but the film creates an entire sub-plot around kabuki star Nakamura, played by Ricardo Montalban. The character first appears getting ready backstage, with only his genitals covered. Layers of costumes then conceal Montalban's muscular body, and he enters the stage as a woman. Although introduced as an *onnogata*, subsequent scenes show Nakamura playing male heroes on the kabuki stage, which would never occur in a professional kabuki company. Like the character of Hana-ogi, Nakamura is not presented as an actor who specializes in gender manipulation. Instead, they are both simply actors, who *might* occasionally portray the opposite sex. The cultural complexities of men and women on the Japanese stage are nonexistent in the film.

In contemporary Tokyo, fortunately, the intricate performances of gender are not hidden. A show at the bar *Kingyo* (Goldfish), known for the skills of its dancers, many of whom are transsexual, an additional perspective on Americans in Japan is presented. *Kingyo* had been recommended because, as it was phrased to me, one of their regular dances addresses American politics in Japan during World War II. The show began with a lip-synched pop song and glow-in-the-dark costumes, followed by several perky (and really fun) dance numbers, each one accompanied by quick changes and moveable set pieces. The floor at *Kingyo* illuminates like a disco floor, rises and falls, and, like the Takarazuka Revue, has a light-up staircase. The show was fabulous.

Midway through the ninety-minute set, dancers slowly walk onstage wearing kimonos, while a gentle melody is played on a samisen. The song is a serene version of the pop hit "Hana" by Okinawan Shokichi Kina,[8] and the mood immediately changed from modern pop to traditional elegance. Two characters run on, dancing and playing together: a boy and a girl, who, based on their all-white costumes, look to be from the 1940s. The other dancers sit on the edge of the stage observing the young couple as they flirt with one another. Two American marines, wearing World War II uniforms, enter. They chase the boy away and enact a stylized rape of the girl, leaving her in a heap on the floor. As the dancers in kimonos care for the girl, three columns light up above the stage, each with a Japanese kamikaze pilot saluting to the sky. The dancers perform a sequence of entrances and interactions — the boy, kimonos, kamikaze pilots, girl — ending with the girl and boy reunited, the Japanese soldiers standing onstage saluting, and a World War II Japanese warplane moving above the stage.[9] The simplicity of that final moment was overwhelming, and, as the audience applauded and shouted, I thought of how revealing it is to see history and national identity from another set of eyes.

NOTES

1. Quoted in Robertson 133.
2. W. G. Aston, trans., *Nihongi: Chronicles of Japan from the Earliest Times to AD 697* (reprint, 2 vols in 1, London, 1956) II, 195. Quoted in W. G. Beasley, *Japan Encounters the Barbarian: Japanese Travellers in America and Europe* (New Haven: Yale University Press, 1995) 63.
3. The American occupation of Japan was from 1945 to 1952.
4. The Takarazuka fans can be obsessively devoted to their favorite stars, the top stars always being *otokoyaku*. Analysis by almost every Westerner who has researched Takarazuka has theorized the homoerotic nature of the Revue's fan culture. The 1994 documentary *Dream Girls*, by Kim Longinotto and Jano Williams, attempts to draw out the assumed lesbian undertones of Takarazuka, but, as they had extremely limited access to the Revue, the film's argument comes across as a simplistic read on an otherwise complex subject.
5. Yuga Yamato, perf. *Valencian Passion*, by Yukihiro Shibata, dir. Yukihiro Shibata and Satoru Nakamura, Takarazuka Grand Theatre, Takarazuka City, Japan, 25 July 2007.
6. For more on *Gone with the Wind* in Japan, see Kevin J. Wetmore, Jr., "From *Scaretto* to *Kaze to tomo ni sarinu*: Musical Adaptations of *Gone with the Wind* in Japan" in *Modern Japanese Theatre and Performance*, edited by David Jortner, Keiko McDonald, and Kevin J. Wetmore, Jr. (Lanham, MD: Lexington, 2006).
7. *Sayonara*, dir. Joshua Logan, perf. Marlon Brando, Red Buttons, Miiko Taka, Ricardo Montalban, Miyoshi Umeki, and James Garner, Warner Bros., 1957.
8. Otake Tomoko, "Go! Go! Kingyo!" *Japan Times* 13 February 2005.
9. *Roppongi Kingyo*, dir. Shozo Tanimoto, Tokyo, Japan, 2 August 2007.

13

Taiwan Style *I Love You, You're Perfect, Now Change* by Lancreators

Llyn Scott

The closing of Off-Broadway's second longest running musical, *I Love You, You're Perfect, Now Change* (LPC) written by playwright/lyricist Joe DiPietro and composer Jimmy Roberts, on July 27, 2008, was preceded by the launch of two different Chinese international premiers in Shanghai and Taipei. From May 9 to June 3, 2007, Shanghai Dramatic Arts Centre (SDAC), in cooperation with Broadway Asia Entertainment, transferred their 2006/2007 LPC production in Mandarin to the Westside Theatre for a limited run of twenty-three rotating performances with the resident American company. During the same period, Lancreators, a Taiwan-based musical theater company founded in 2005 by Chia-yi Lin, was in rehearsal for an English language production of LPC to open at the Crown Theatre in Taipei. The Crown Theatre performances by Lancreators from November 3 to November 30, 2007, marked the first long-run of a single show in Taiwan, four days longer than the SDAC visiting production in New York; however, immediately after their success, Lancreators mysteriously disbanded. The SDAC production returned to Beijing to begin a multi-city tour throughout China. Circumstances involving the state of musical theater in Taiwan, financial pressures, subversive directorial approaches to LPC's American style humor, and other conflicts contributed to the brief fame of Lancreators.

Lancreators reacted to the news about the American and SDAC Off-Broadway repertory productions, both directed by Joel Bishoff, LPC's original director, with competitive instincts. The young company ambitiously set

201

out to create a different and innovative premier production in Taiwan. Taking his cue from the word "change" in the musical's title, the director of Lancreators set out to re-interpret LPC as much as possible in accordance with The Rodgers & Hammerstein Theatricals license. For example, he invited Brook Hall, a Broadway-trained choreographer residing in Taipei, to enhance selected songs with dance movements and choreography. Furthermore, Lin departed from the original Broadway production cast of two couples or just four actors by adding one additional couple for the "blue" cast (six actors) and two extra couples for the "green" cast (eight actors) and assigning them to perform on alternate nights. Based on my observations made during nineteen hours of rehearsals and one performance, five interviews with company members, and follow-up research, I will attempt to trace how the localized and personalized interpretation of LPC produced by Lin successfully achieved a Taiwan style. Inadvertently, the conflicted ambitions of Lin to imitate the American Broadway musical style and yet produce a distinctive Taiwan version of LPC contributed to the final break-up of Lancreators.

Lancreators and Broadway

Chia-yi Jackie Lin, founding director of Lancreators, developed a passion for Broadway musicals long before he entered the theater department of Taipei National University of the Arts in 2000. The only son of a wealthy construction company owner, Lin describes himself as a spoiled child. On one of his frequent trips to New York City, he purportedly bought tickets to attend thirty Broadway and Off-Broadway shows in twenty days. Less interested in graduating than in directing a "graduation" play, Lin, in partnership with his sister as producer, directed his first musical, Stephen Sondheim's *Into the Woods*, in March 2005, for the campus theater under the auspices of TNUA. Although the production failed to earn him a diploma and temporarily disrupted the supply of family money, it sparked the hopes of many young adults in Taiwan seeking opportunities to train and perform in musical theater. On his own, Lin held auditions, secured two company managers, and started hiring local dance teachers to train his newly acquired talent in jazz and tap dancing and singing. According to an interview in the *Taiwan Review*, Lin stated that Broadway is not "just the name of a place or a genre," it is a "standard" ("East of Broadway"). Broadway musicals served as models with which he trained company members to become "versatile performers" who can sing, dance, and act ("East of Broadway").

This was the case twenty years ago when Taiwan's first professional theater group, the Godot Theatre Company, began performing. In an interview to commemorate their tenth anniversary, founding artist director Chi-ming Liang confided in an interview for *Taiwan Review* that after viewing over one hundred American dance musicals in one year, "he realized the untapped potential of combining western and eastern theater, music, dance, and graphic arts in highly effective ways in Taiwan" ("Celebrating"). In contrast to Liang's forecast of a flourishing musical theater environment, however, journalist Ying-ying Shih, who also performed in LPC, reports that today "Taiwanese musical productions ... are struggling to make ends meet" ("East"). She goes on to suggest that Taiwan corporations readily fund foreign musical tours, but turn down proposals from local artists. In a news release for his Taipei production of *Smokey Joe's Café*, by Jerry Leiber and Mike Stoller, choreographer/director Hall described Taiwan's "tradition of adopting foreign performing traditions and combining them with local skills and theory" ("Interview"). Is the problem a lack of Broadway versatile talent as Lin implies? "One Million Stars," a popular weekly television talent show sensation in Taiwan since it first aired on CTV in January 2007, auditions hundreds of contestants from around the island hoping to win one million Taiwan Dollars (about $30,000 US) in prize money and sign a professional recording contract. While Hall confirms, "[t]here are some incredibly talented people here," but he adds that local artists have almost no experience in authentic Broadway style dance and voice ("Interview"). Conversely, modern dance in Taiwan led by the prestigious Cloud Gate Dance Company under the direction of founder and head choreographer Hwai-min Lin established an international reputation over twenty years ago. Besides, hip hop in Asia began in Taiwan where today nine out of ten boys hanging out in the popular Shihmingding area do hip hop ("I Hip Hop").

Training in Broadway dance style was a priority for Lancreators from the beginning. Operating out of a basement studio in a suburb of Taipei City, company manager Mu-hao Clinton Lin, was assigned the challenging job of scheduling weekly dance and other stage training classes for company recruits who all held down various kinds of jobs around the city. For nearly a year after *Into the Woods*, Lin, a philosophy department major, worked as a volunteer in charge of the company training program. One of the youngest company actresses, Pin-ling Chen, said the three performance classes or about twenty to thirty hours of training per week were essential for her to learn to imitate the Broadway style ("Troupe"). Actress/singer Ying-ying Shih agreed that the dance training in tap and jazz arranged by Lancreators was useful, although not all of the dance coaches were effective teachers. In an interview after LPC closed, choreographer Hall explained that the Broadway style is not only about dance, but also intense moments. A veteran of Broadway musicals, Hall elaborated his point by adding, "In a musical, the characters need to express themselves so deeply, they have to sing about it.[1] Hall observed that such overt communication is a culturally and psychologically foreign concept in Taiwan society, and the reason musicals are so appealing. Speaking as a former theater major from St. Edwards University in Austin, Texas, Hall reflected that acting and musicals both require commitment, i.e., performers must believe what they are doing onstage. During the LPC rehearsal period, Hall mentioned that he was extensively involved in coaching actors and singers to perform with stage presence that conveys confidence and ownership.

On the other hand, actress Shih complained about the lack of adequate speech and voice training for company members who had not studied or lived abroad.[2] Whereas Shih earned a master degree in art education from Harvard University and Shi-en Lesley Hu, one of the experienced actress/singers in the company, graduated from Taipei American School, went abroad to study, and received her Bachelor of Arts degree from Syracuse University. Nevertheless, in very few instances, deficiencies in American English speech patterns or pronunciation detracted from the performances overall. Even though Lin had to direct from Mandarin translations for all the musicals Lancreators produced, he rejected suggestions either to perform a musical in Mandarin or to act in Mandarin and sing in English relying on the bi-lingual fluency of lead company members to coach other cast members instead. Lancreators most seasoned performer, Yi-ray Chiang, is an outstanding example of Taiwan talent who performs equally well in English, Mandarin, and even Hoklo and Hakka, two Chinese dialects spoken by over seventy percent of the population in Taiwan.

By June 2007, a new producer Wu-ming Jerry Chen, production manager for Semiscon, took over company management and Lancreators was onstage again with *Let's Broadway*, a musical revue of twenty-one songs and dances from Broadway shows including "Heart and Music" from *A New Brain*, "Cell Block Tango" from *Chicago*, "The Full Monty" from *Let It Go*, and "You Can't Stop the Beat" from *Hairspray*. Convinced that he had learned the secret of Broadway musical success, Lin produced a more lavish and costly production than *Into the Woods* at the Metropolitan Theater in Taipei. Technical director Jin-yuan Eugene Yang suspended a spectacular marquee with one thousand light bulbs above the setting for "The Full Monty" musical number to recreate the ambiance of 42nd Street. Besides the scenery, other features of the production such as the three-foot long glossy poster and ninety-two page all-color programs fulfilled Lin's expectations to "wow" the audience ("East of Broadway").

The Taipei audience failed to meet box office expectations and a three day run left the company exhausted and unpaid. In a tearful curtain speech director Lin alluded to the bond that existed between himself and the company, "I know everyone onstage." At this, according to Mu-hao Clinton Lin, the onstage cast broke down and cried in a teary aftermath of emotional release in front of the audience. Mu-hao intimated during a follow-up interview that young artists and performers dreaming of professional careers in Taiwan are more interested in a chance to perform than in payment. After LPC closed, company member Chien-heng Brendon Chen, owner/designer of Brendon Jewelry, admitted that he remained with Lancreators on the understanding that his original jewelry designs would be showcased as accessories with LPC costumes. As we will see later, lack of professional management undermined the high ideals of Lancreators. In retrospect, the stage machinery for which Lin paid $3,000 U.S. to create a "crack" onstage for *Let's Broadway* was one of the causes for the eventual collapse of Lancreators ("East of Broadway"). Setting and costuming were not the only areas affected by drastic cost-cutting measures for LPC.

Production debts and pressure from unpaid artistic team members, forced Lancreators to produce another Broadway musical as quickly as possible in anticipation of generating enough revenue to pay-off the accumulated debts of both productions. The success of *I Love You, You're Perfect, Now Change* on Off-Broadway and frequent comparisons between the musical and two widely popular American sitcoms, "Friends" and "Sex and the City," convinced Lancreators LPC was the right choice. SDAC producers reached the same conclusion in Beijing where LPC was billed as a "celebration of the modern-day suburban mating game...." ("I Love You"). American journalists announced with satisfaction that Chinese and Americans were playing the same game ("How Do You Say"). Once into rehearsals, though, Lancreators was confronted not only by the scope of LPC, literally from dating to dying in song, dialogue, and dance in twenty-one scenes, but also by issues related to selling a foreign show to the local Taiwan audience. Contradictory comments about the Mandarin LPC productions held first at the 2007 Beijing Theatre Festival and then the Westside Theatre in May-June 2008, foreshadowed the difficulties ahead for Lancreators.

I Love You, You're Perfect, Now Change Is Changed

The controversy concerned the issue of localization, i.e., to what degree the original libretto was changed to suit a Chinese audience. In an article for *Playbill*, Kenneth Jones credits Nick Rongjun Yu with adapting the translation of LPC to Chinese taste ("Chinese Staging"). In response to the New York tour publicity boasting the director had reworked the show for a Chinese audience, a reviewer for the *New York Times* wrote, "[f]or Mr. Bishoff did such a thorough job that the Chinese version is just like the English version" ("Wacky"). On the other hand, Michael Sag, senior manager of Broadway Asia Entertainment, co-producer of the New York tour, stated that the musical was "tailor-made" for Shanghai and Beijing audiences ("I Love You"). More comments by violinist Jie Niu in the same China Radio International (CRI) English review allude to the power of LPC to make the audience "laugh and cry at the same time," and to recall the "bitterness of failing to find their true love" ("I Love You"). Describing its twelve-year run at the Westside Theatre, American reviewers of LPC mentioned the show was the most "marriage proposal friendly" musical on Broadway, but few if any observed that the audience wept during a performance ("Theatre Review"). Star cast member Qing-li Ma asserted that relationships in China and America are the same since Chinese young adults are familiar with "Sex and the City." According to Ma, LPC audiences in both countries are similar except that the audiences at the Westside Theatre laughed in all the right places ("How Do You Say"). If audiences were crying in Beijing and laughing in New York, but the musical content, according to translator Yu, was altered in only minor instances, a question arises about exactly what were those changes.

When Lancreators cast members watched video clips from the Mandarin production, their first reaction was disbelief. Manager Mu-Hao Clinton Lin described the tone of the Mandarin translation as too formal and literal. Lin cites Yu's translation of the closing lines of "Marriage Tango" as an example. Tyler and Zachary, the two sons who are supposedly in bed asleep, call from offstage, "Mom! Dad! The lizard's eating the guppies!" To which the passionately preoccupied parents retort, "Let 'em!" in the English version, or in other words, "Who cares!" In contrast, the Mandarin version of their answer conveys a sense that "if the lizard wants to eat the guppies, that's alright. Let him go ahead and eat them."[3] Another case in which a literal interpretation subverted the hint of sexual tension of a word occurred in the song "Lasagna Incident." Sag admits that in the translation process "[w]e changed small bits and pieces" ("I Love You"). In the English version, Diane invites Chuck over to her place for lasagna on their first date. The Mandarin translation substituted *daoxiaomien*, sliced rice noodles stir-fried with vegetables, meat, egg, tomatoes, green onion, and soy sauce. Although it may appear to have some similar types of ingredients, pasta and meat for instance, substituting *daoxiaomien* for lasagna missed the romantic/exotic flavor of foreign or ethnic food on a first date. Lasagna has become a popular culture marker and appears in several episodes of "Friends," the comic strip "Garfield," and in the movie *Clerks II* (2006).[4]

Making the musical's references familiar to the Chinese audience is a priority warns Sag. "If one brings material into China from overseas, he must change it, making it accessible to the local audience" ("I Love You"). Other changes pointed out by Sag occurred in the translation of the line by Man #1 in the Epilogue of LPC prescribing how the book of man and woman ought to be written:

> MAN #1:— endlessly crashing into each other, like two vengeful bumper cars, Romeo Romeo wherefore art thou Romeo, you played it for her you can play it for me, my man done did me wrong, chicks and ducks and geese better scurry, I got it bad and that ain't good, you make me feel like a natural woman, she was just seventeen you know what I mean, love to love you baby [LPC].

Sag mistakenly identified the lines as quotations from American movies; whereas, except for the second one, "you played it for her, you can play it for me," a line from Clint Eastwood's first film, *Play Misty for Me*, and of course the quote from Shakespeare, the others are lyrics from "Frankie and Johnnie," "Surrey with the Fringe on Top" in *Oklahoma*, Duke Ellington's jazz piece, Aretha Franklin's famous song, "I Saw Her Standing There" by the Beatles, and a song by Donna Summers. Nevertheless, the Chinese movie titles used in the Mandarin translation effectively produced the desired laughter to the satisfaction of the artistic team, reported Sag. Obviously, the missing element is the comical virtuosity of the performer who impersonates each of the eight quotations by imitating the original spoken or sung sources in rapid order. Lancreators attempted to avoid this type of trade-off when they decided to produce an all–English language version.

Ever since *Let's Broadway*, Lancreators has used the slogan "Broad *a New* Way" and for Chia-yi Jackie Lin, *change* was operative word in LPC's title, confided Mu-hao Clinton Lin in a pre-show interview. In Clinton's words, the director interpreted "now change" to mean "I'm different." The director persuaded the cast to discover new ways to make LPC characterizations and scenes different from other versions they had seen on Broadway and in London. For instance, by dividing the company into two teams and expanding the number of actors, the director aimed to capitalize on the company's variety of stage personalities to enhance the individuality of characterizations and scenes. During the rehearsal process from August to November, the cast accommodated the director's vision by trying different interpretations and often were coerced into accepting directorial instructions that eventually disrupted the tone of the musical and marred the acting. Furthermore, as a way of creating differences, the director and cast drew from personalized references to local society; therefore the original character relationships lost some of their American logic as an atmosphere of sentimentality subverted the American style of sarcastic humor in LPC.[5]

DiPietro and Roberts have crafted a fast-paced variety of episodes built into the libretto of LPC where each scene is a different parody on the various experiences associated with singlehood and marriage. In general, the episodes express symptoms of social anxiety disorder, gender stereotyping, and caricatures of age and stage. In scene one "Cantata for a First Date," scene two "A Stud and a Babe," scene six "The Lasagna Incident," and scene eight "Satisfaction Guaranteed," American obsessions are parodied such as desires for perfection in personal appearance, sexual attractiveness, and sexual performance exaggerated by advertising and consumerism trends. In scene two "I'm Busy, Busy, Busy," the parody turns to self-enhancement publications which analyze and even fictionalize every step and misstep in singlehood relationships. Young adults in America who play the dating game are such adept players in the dating game, they can narrate a vicarious date. In scene three "Single Man Drought," and "Why? 'Cause I'm a Guy," scene five "Tear Jerk," scene nine "I'll Call You Soon," scene ten "Scared Straight," scenes eleven and twelve "Wedding Vows," scene fifteen "Sex and the Married Couple," scene sixteen "The Family That Drives Together," and scene seventeen "Waiting Trio," DiPietro and Roberts extract sarcastic humor from a variety of predicaments between contrasting gender stereotypes that end with perfect solutions. In "Tear Jerk" for example, James discovers that Jane loves men who cry at movies; and James deconstructs the negative bias against male crying by seducing his date with tears. Internet matchmaking business is the object of parody in "Scared Straight" where two incompatible singles are terrorized into tying the knot by an unhappily single, convicted murderer. In "The Family that Drives Together," a bossy wife and mousey husband go for a drive that ends with a sarcastic twist. Instead of the expected scene implied by the song title, the family who "drives together, stays together," this trip ends with the husband singing "love ya, babe," to his perfect companion, the car. The treatment of exhausted married life in scene fifteen is cleverly visualized by an exhibition of stereotypical flashy feminine and macho masculine outfits worn over the couple's drab domestic-wear, satirizing the American obsession with glamorous sex.

The emotional situations in the following group of scenes resonated with Lancreators; therefore the directing approach to these scenes reveals insights into the ways by which foreign works are localized and personalized. In scene seven "And Now the Parents," scene thirteen "Always a Bridesmaid," scene fourteen "Whatever Happened to Baby's Parents?," scene eighteen "Shouldn't I Be Less in Love with You?," scene nineteen "Rose Ritz Dating Video," and scene twenty "Funerals Are for Dating" American stereotypes of age and stage of life are satirized. The director and cast felt the characterizations in these six scenes were familiar because, in their words, the scenes reflected the "every day life" that young people in Taiwan esteem. The highest praise from stu dents for films, plays, or even the content of a class lecture is that "it is just like our daily life."[6] The fact that these scenes revolve around family relationships signifies that in this company of under-thirty young adults, there was a strong identification with young children, older adults, and single women rather than the category of dating singles. In scene fourteen, a single acquaintance visits his friends who are now married and have a baby. This was a cast favorite in which the actor who played the new father squatted down in typical Taiwan body language to sing "The Baby Song" in completely Taiwanized image of the American father. Tearful interpretations dominated the tone of "Shouldn't I Be Less in Love with You" and "Funerals Are for Dating" as well. Manager Mu-hao Clinton Lin explained that from backstage the cast watched older members of the audience during these two scenes to see if the older patrons cried, and were gratified. In his words, "It's not only a show, we are putting real life onstage."[7] Since these directorial choices originated in a mutually shared sentimentality, then the portrayal of the late middle-aged wife in "Shouldn't I Be Less in Love with You?" who wore glasses on the tip of her nose and bent over while she sewed a coat for her husband illustrates a local negative age bias as well as blurred mother/wife roles. Several of the company actresses eagerly wanted to play the role of the wife because they were personally touched by the scene. No one seemed aware that the business of tailoring a coat would be logical for a mother, not a soul mate as represented in LPC. The effect of the common emotional ground, however, among the cast in the above six scenes intensified the sentimentality of Lancreators' version of LPC, and also restored some of their solidarity resulting from financial worries and frustrations communicating with the director.

The directorial choices applied to "Rose Ritz Dating Video" and "Always a Bridesmaid" drew attention to the perceptions of single women in Taiwan society. The Bridesmaid's lyrics and country and western music are perfectly suited to the scene. Lin substituted sentimentality for the sarcastic lyrics, "All those husbands are gone, but those dresses live on" and "I've lived life alone, but the terms are my own...." (LPC). The inherent textual irony of indestructible dresses, short-lived marriages, and survivor bridesmaid was circumvented leaving the talented comedian in the role of the Bridesmaid at a loss for the right emotion. The first hint that certain emotional contexts were problematic to interpret locally was apparent earlier in the director's interpretation of "Tear Jerk." At first, Yi-ray Chiang in the role of James reacted to the line of his movie date, "I just love men who aren't afraid to cry at the movies," with a double-take and knowing look before they both break down in a river of tears according to the stage directions (LPC). Although Chiang was following the logical motivation of the character, Lin adamantly rejected Chiang's acting choices and insisted that the audience ought to laugh at a male crying, not the feigned tears of a "jerk." The director flattened the intended sarcasm in this scene by imposing a literal reference to a local taboo. The director's tendency to localize and literalize LPC's innate American sarcasm was most apparent in "Rose Ritz," the scene that exceeded any other for its tearful sentimentality. The fact that the SDAC production omitted this particular scene suggests the sarcastic humor eluded the translator, or the scene with a divorcé advertising for dates was unacceptable to a Chinese audience, or the role seemed un-actable to a Chinese actress. In an interview after the show closed, actress Ying-ying Shih in the blue cast described the frustration she felt trying to satisfy the conflicting directions given by Lin. After weeks of wrestling with the role, she began to interpret the monologue in a way to evoke sympathy from the audience, and the "tears just came," she said. The director and other cast members encouraged her sentimental characterization of Rose and, according to Ying-ying, "I was proud of myself that for all fifteen performances, I cried in that scene every time."[8]

The same actress and the director were involved in a postmodern interpretation of "The Lasagna Incident." The tendency to deconstruct LPC's American humor with local sentiment suggests the motives for these changes are linked to a sense of identity in Taiwan. When Chuck walks away after making a date with Diane, the director inserted a parallel scene in place of the actor's exit. Chuck and another woman greet each other affectionately upstage. Diane sings "I Will Be Loved Tonight" while Chuck and the other woman go off together leaving the audience with the impression Chuck is not the shy young man he professed to be earlier in the scene. Mu-hao Clinton Lin explained that the director invented this upstage encounter because infidelity or cheating between men and women often happens in Taiwan society.[9] The director felt Diane was too naïve; therefore she deserved to be jilted. Further incidents revealing the director's cynical attitude toward relationships would occur as the show approached the opening date. The character of Diane was unaware of the irony created by the parallel scenes and the actress was directed to interpret the lyrics with tears of gratitude.

The three songs with the most tears, "Baby's Song," "Lasagna Incident," and "Rose Ritz," have an emotional quality in common which may be connected with changing social consciousness and national identity formation in Taiwan. Recent studies on crying are attempting to find a correlation between social contexts and emotions resulting in adult crying.

> Grief, sadness, joy, anger, frustration, self-pity, helplessness, and powerlessness are the most frequently reported emotions associated with crying [Vingerhoets and Cornelius 86].

Self-pity and helplessness may be two emotions the director and actors felt were justified in the above mentioned songs. How these relate to life experiences in Taiwan requires a thorough investigation into the relationship between types of humor and perceptions of national identity such as the one conducted by a research team at La Trobe University. The project gathers data from Australian comic media including films and television sit-coms to conduct a study on "how comic form and characters continue to influence ideas about our national character" (National Identity).

In the process of appropriating and localizing LPC, Lancreators gradually changed the American style of sarcastic humor into a combination of sentimentality and cynicism that reflected the perceptions and sensibilities of the director and cast. An uneven tone eventually eroded the Broadway style Chia-yi Jackie Lin had professed to admire earlier. Commercializing tactics toward the end of the run may have been prompted by dissatisfaction with the ambiguous, unmotivated shifts in mood and tone that affected the continuity of LPC's satire on the dating game, or the return of financial pressures, or some other still unknown reason. Lancreators persuaded the blue and green teams to allow professional models from a local agency to replace the regular casts in certain scenes for one performance. The producers did not expect them to perform well, but were banking on the well-known name of the agency and the novelty of models singing and dancing to increase ticket sales. The models surprised everyone with reputable performances, but not without extensive adaptation or transposition of the music to fit their vocal ranges. Other tactics had less positive effects. Cost-cutting measures marred the final production values. The director handed over the costuming to an inexperienced costume assistant who in turn sourced the costumes without a clear understanding of the characters or scenes. The costumes were delivered on the opening day, too late to make necessary adjustments. Other production work fell increasingly behind schedule; consequently, the scene designer was asked to enlarge a photograph of a street scene for the backdrop at the last minute. The scene was selected from the Internet and pictured a crowded, drab alley in a run-down section of Taipei, with no logical connection with LPC's slogan, "Love Is Coming," on one side and a 7-Eleven sign on the other. The company grew more disappointed as they realized the setting, lighting, and costumes failed to represent the mise en scène, not to mention suit the citified sophistication of LPC or the amount of time and talent invested by the actors. A year later, the cast is still waiting to be paid; the director fled the country; Ying-ying Shih will pursue her dream to perform in Broadway musicals, "'cause I keep coming back, to this lovesick mess..." (LPC). "Foreign aid" arrived to rescue the abandoned Lancreators' cast in the person of American choreographer and director Brook Hall, who with French producer,

Cédric Alviani, General Director of Infine Art & Culture Exchange, produced *Smokey Joe's Café* at the National Taiwan Arts Education Center on January 16–18, 2009, for standing room only (SRO) audiences.[10]

Conclusion

An American Broadway style, especially if it is interpreted as "broad a new way," remains foreign to local directors and producers. Lancreators succeeded in attracting an elite company of talented performers many of whom are continuing their stage careers under the direction of Brook Hall who became the first foreigner to direct a professional production of a Broadway musical in Taiwan. Does Lancreators' legacy represent a Taiwan style? Further case studies of local musical productions are necessary to determine which factors in the Lancreators' production derived from the director's individualistic personality and which signified local sensibilities. The creation of a new Taiwan style of musical was the goal of Lancreators, but the emphasis on being different at any cost contradicted and subverted the qualities that are intrinsic to the American style of *I Love You, You're Perfect, Now Change*. Striking a balancing between local sentiments and foreign humor, especially sarcasm, eluded the production of LPC by Lancreators. Lancreators director Lin inadvertently described his own company when he stated in the *Taiwan Review*, "Taiwanese musicals haven't fully matured yet" ("East of Broadway").

NOTES

1. Brook Hall spoke candidly about his relationship to Lancreators in an interview on 21 October 2007, at Checkers on the second floor of the Caesar Park Hotel.

2. Non-English majors in Taiwan typically do not read or speak in English. For English language plays on the university level, about thirty percent of rehearsals are devoted to coaching language skills such as pronunciation and inflection. Additionally, voice and diction training are necessary.

3. Quotations from *I Love You, You're Perfect, Now Change*, book and lyrics by Joe DiPietro and music by Jimmy Roberts, are taken from the rehearsal copy of the libretto published by the Rodgers and Hammerstein Theatricals Company.

4. Lasagna, as it is pronounced by Americans, has entered popular culture and frequently accompanies a romantic evening for two, somewhat like an order of take-out Chinese food.

5. While Lancreators chose not to localize proper names such as the name of the prison in "Scared Straight," Mu-hao Clinton explained in an interview on February 12 2008, that because Lancreators is a young company, they would have to try hard to be different. He said that at every rehearsal the actors were expected to bring many choices of approaches to their scenes and Chia-yi Jackie Lin would choose the best one. He wanted LPC to have many different aspects from scenes that would make the audience think deeply about life to a fashion show with designer clothes and jewelry.

6. Traditionally, education in Taiwan has been based on textbook and lecture learning styles. In recent years, the Ministry of Education in Taiwan is fostering more diverse teaching methods by requiring teachers in higher education to evaluate their teaching methods on the basis of core behavior skills and types of learning environments such as performance and adventure projects. The pressure on parents and students to compete for the best schools based on test results has forced students to spend most of their lives up to entrance into college in classrooms preparing for the next qualifying test.

7. In an interesting revelation about the negative age bias regarding over people over sixty in Taiwan, Mu-hao Clinton Lin said in the February interview that couples at that stage are tired. They spend their time working on unfinished jobs, and they don't have a bright new day feeling.

8. In an interview with Ying-ying Shih on February 22, 2008, Ying-ying described her frustration with the director who never fully explained how he wanted her to interpret different roles. She said that the interpretation of the characters had a lot to do with the personality of the director who set the tone for the production. According to Ying-ying, the interpretations of some roles such as those in "A Stud and a Babe" were influenced by Japanese culture.

9. Both Mu-Hao Clinton Lin and Ying-Ying Shih agreed that the other woman upstage in "Lasagna Incident" was Chia-yi Jackie Lin's idea. When he was asked about is reasons for adding the scene, he told them that he had a dark view of life and relationships; and he wanted the scene to have more depth.

10. *Smokey Joe's Café* is the longest running musical revue in Broadway history. The premier in Taipei is the culmination of a year-long dream of director Brook Hall. Counting on his own savings, the fantastic stage talent in Taipei, and an experienced coordinator, Brook made an all-or-nothing push to show Taipei audiences what Broadway musicals are all about and created a real Broadway phenomenon. <http://www.infine-art.com/smokeyjoes/englishindex.html>

14

The Great White Way Revived in Seoul: Korean Productions of *The Producers* (2006) and *Assassins* (2005)

Ji Hyon (Kayla) Yuh

Musical theatre, as a genre which developed during the twentieth century, tends to possess certain American-ness. While this has much to do with the settings and the contents of individual works, it also stems from the fact that musical theatre was developed in the United States. During the first half of the 1900s, when European countries still held onto the practice of classical forms of plays, Americans shaped and honed their new entertainment form and established musical theatre as a legitimate theatre genre. Especially for the musicals created in the U.S. by Americans, their American-ness is inherent in their themes and contents, as Raymond Knapp observes in his book *The American Musical and the Formation of National Identity*; "the American musical" made crucial contributions in "defin[ing] how America s[aw] itself" (228). Even with the rise of European musicals since the 1980s, the United States remained as the motherland of the musical theatre; Broadway is still the most valued venue for musical theatre, and the annual Tony Awards are the most prestigious and awaited awards in the world of musical theatre.

Different musicals engage different tools in displaying American qualities; sometimes they are explicitly stated through a character within the story, and other times they are more dependent on the general setting or subject matter of the musical. Also, depending on the political and social situations and preconceptions that people have of the United States, some messages will be embraced, while others will not. In other words, a certain representation of the United States to Americans living in the United States will be received differently by a group of people with other cultural backgrounds. Furthermore, how the audience responds to a certain image of the United States presented to them can reveal the already established notion of the United States among the audience. In this essay, I intend to look at particular examples within the Korean theatre community, in which musical theatre has grown so rapidly over the last decade. I will focus on the production histories and reviews of two very different American musicals presented in Korea: *The Producers* (2006) and *Assassins* (2005). I chose these two musicals because they seem to possess more apparent American-ness than many other musicals that opened in Korea in recent years. However, the images of the United States that these musicals presented were quite different from one another, perhaps even in opposition to one another. While *The Producers* revealed the United States as the idealized country where dreams could come true as long as you pursue them, *Assassins* depicted the United States as a society with inevitable limitations, a place where there were individuals who were marginalized and did not have their share of "American dream."

These different depictions of the United States, among other elements, were significant in determining the shows' success in Korea, because these shows either appealed to preconceived notions of the United States or rejected them. In other words, the audience members had a specific image of the United States that they expected from the musical, and naturally, they enjoyed and responded better to a show that matched the preconceptions of the United States that they had. By looking at the production histories of both musicals within the United States and abroad, and examining the process of cultural transfer from the United States to Korea, I explore how the United States is represented through musicals, and how Koreans responded to the specific images given to them in *The Producers* and *Assassins*. Chronologically, *Assassins* was produced before *The Producers* in Korea, but I will start the discussion with *The Producers*, which was better received by the audience than *Assassins*.

Adapted from the original movie of the same title, *The Producers* is the story of Max Bialystock and Leopold Bloom, two not-so-talented producer-wannabes who produce a musical to make a fortune by producing a sure-flop on Broadway. Their plan goes awry because the musical turns out to be a great hit, and they end up in prison for the fraudulent accounting records they kept for the musical. However, they never let go of their initial dreams of becoming producers, and they eventually make it to Broadway. The musical opened on Broadway in 2001, as a star vehicle production, having Nathan Lane and Matthew Broderick as the leading actors. The show was a hit right off the bat; despite the fact that the story was far from being politically correct, the audience was absolutely exhilarated every night, and the critics saw in the show the legacy of the masterpieces of American musical comedy during the 1930s. Accordingly, *The Producers* set a record by being awarded 12 Tony Awards in 2001, showing how well it was received in the United States.

Following in the footsteps of musical comedies during the 1920s and the 1930s, the show was full of offensive and sexist jokes that used to be very common until the late 1980s. For one, Max Bialystock, the mastermind of the big scam, made money by providing sexual pleasures to the Jewish old ladies who could not find other sources to satisfy themselves; and to top it all, Hitler was portrayed as a gay man, and he won the war in Max and Leo's musical-within-the-musical *Springtime for Hitler*. The level of comedy and satire was also heightened because Max Bialystock and Leopold Bloom, the producers of the flop, are Jewish. When creating the show, Mel Brooks, who created the musical as well as the original movie in 1968, certainly did not intend to ask for any political agenda or controversy other than creating a musical that was highly entertaining.[1] *The Producers* might have been unconventional in the sense that Max and Leo put up a show about the life of Adolf Hitler, but other than that, it employed conventional strategies in terms of its structure and strategies as a musical comedy (Miller 224).

Although it did deal with issues such as Neo-Nazis, objectified beauty, stereotyped gay characters and commercialized theatre community, most of the audience members certainly enjoyed the show without worrying about those issues.[2] It had everything that a typical work of American musical comedy had during the first half of the twentieth century, and thus revived the culture of watching a musical simply for enjoyment and a night of good music and dance. It also spoke to those who wanted to see a new work of old-fashioned American musical comedy back on Broadway, as Nathan Lane explains (Maslon and Kantor 427). With ecstatic reviews by the audience and critics, it continued on Broadway for more than six years and closed in 2007, after a little more than 2,000 consecutive performances.

Encouraged by the success of the musical in the United States, Seoul & Company, the company responsible for the 2001 Korean production of *The Phantom of the Opera*, opened the Korean production of *The Producers* in Seoul in 2006. In addition to its stunning credentials from the American production history, *The Producers* had an extra advantage in opening in Korea: Korean audiences have always been generous to backstage musicals with spectacles such as *42nd Street* and *Chorus Line*. *The Producers* opened in January, a month that is usually associated with poor ticket sales, because that was the only time that the company was able to secure a theatre for the show, and ran for about a month in a large and prestigious theatre in Seoul. After its month-long engagement in Seoul, the production toured different parts of Korea closing its tour in March 2006. While the overall production did not generate much profit, the reviews from the critics were generally positive, as the Korean production staff had expected.[3] Moreover, most of the audience enjoyed the show and found it to be one of the most genuine "Broadway musicals" to be introduced to Korea in months. As for the changes made during the translation process, *The Producers* went through only minor changes in terms of the script, because it was contracted to be an exact replica of its original Broadway production. In other words, all the sets and costumes for the entire production were made in the United States and shipped to Korea, and the script was translated into Korean and was translated back again, into English, to make sure that there would be hardly any changes in the script. Because of this stipulation and these conditions, there was not much that a translator or a director could do to make the production more accommodating to Korean audiences. This particular restriction in its transfer process not only served as a hindrance for the show's bigger success in Korea, but also affected how the audience responded to the show, especially considering that *The Producers* is a musical comedy that is very self-referential to Broadway musical theatre conventions and culture.

As noted above, *The Producers* was a new musical comedy that relied very much on the old conventions of traditional musical comedy. In other words, the show consisted of a number of scenes where a specific cultural frame of reference was needed. However, because there was a strict restriction on the range of changes that the producers could make in its transition to Korea, not all the messages and jokes had the same implications to Korean audiences. For example, that Max and Leo are Jewish is completely lost among the Korean audience because it is not explicitly stated by the characters; most of the audience saw Max and Leo solely as Americans, and that was all they saw in terms of their ethnic and religious distinctions. Also, in Act I, scene 3, when Max sings "We Can Do It" to Leo, Max gives a list of examples of situations where confidence matters. In this particular song, because of the contract, the Korean production had to keep the original text, which includes Lewis and Clark's expedition and Washington's crossing of the Delaware River. Also, when Roger De Bris appears on stage wearing a dress, not all of the audience members recognized that the dress was meant to look like the Chrysler Building. While the Chrysler Building in New York might be a little better known than what George Washington did more than two hundred years ago, most of the audience members had to give up on picking up the details such as those.

Nevertheless, the Korean audience still enjoyed *The Producers*, even with all the cultural gaps and the details that could have been explained better were it not for the restrictions in its transfer process. The most obvious reason for the positive response was that *The Producers* was a well-made musical comedy. Knowing that it was a musical comedy, the audience was more predisposed to enjoy the show, despite the obvious lack of complete understanding of some-details. However, I would further argue that the gaps and the cultural barriers helped the audience to enjoy the show even more, by supporting a particular representation of the United States: "America" as a place where desires and dreams can come true and the American Dream can be realized, no matter who you are and where you are from.

This particular response from the audience is initially triggered because the plot of *The Producers* develops through individual characters that bend and circumvent the rules of the society that they belong to. Max and Leo fabricate their account books for the show and take advantage of old women. However, the fact that they actually break the law to achieve their goals is brushed off because their dream comes true, after all. By the end of the show, Max and Leo end up in prison for their scam that has gone wrong, but they are soon released, because they bring joy and songs to the minds of the prisoners at Sing Sing Prison. The America which Max and Leo belong to is where their desires and dreams are recognized and embraced, even if they break the law and go against the social norms and rules. This is also true with non–American characters within the show: Ulla, who barely speaks English, finds her love, Leo; and Franz, the Neo-Nazi, gives up his allegiance to Hitler and becomes assimilated in the United States as an American. Because there is a substantial amount of explanation for each character, the majority of Korean audience members were able to sympathize with the characters and identify themselves with the characters. Thus, at the end of the show, the audience was directed to focus on the individual characters and to rejoice with the characters, without any concerns regarding legal issues or social norms.

This image of the United States was even further strengthened in the Korean production, as I argued, because the cultural gaps and missing details disengaged the audience from the physical setting of the show and created a sort of a fantasy world where anything could happen without reasonable explanations. Because *The Producers* is a musical about Broadway, a venue that is so undeniably American, the audience naturally associated everything they saw on stage with images of the United States. Thus, the audience clearly knew that the setting of the musical was the United States, and the portrayal of the United States in the show was where social norms and rules existed without much authority over individuals. One could have easily criticized the unrealistic plot development of *The Producers*, but the Korean audience was already too disengaged from the setting to take the portrayal seriously. Furthermore, most of the audience members were rather satisfied with the given portrayal of the United States, because it fitted their preconception of the United States being the land of opportunity and the idea of the American Dream. In other words, the portrayal of the United States in *The Producers* allowed the audience to keep their preconceived notion of the American Dream. The cultural barriers actually made it easier for the audience to rely on their preconceived notion of the United States as an imagined and idealized country of opportunity and success.

Above all, it is an undeniable fact that most of the audiences and critics enjoyed *The Producers* because it was a musical comedy; there were typical musical tunes such as "Keep It Gay" and "Betrayed," a brilliant choreography with beautiful girls, and stunning spectacles that amused the eyes of the audience. In addition to that, I believe that the audience was willing to respond to *The Producers* because there was not much contradiction that needed to be resolved in their heads. *The Producers* did not focus on the problems of American society, but made the audience focus on each character who got their share of the pie at the end of the show. For the Korean audience who wanted to keep their romanticized view of the United States, *The Producers* was exactly what they needed.

Assassins, however, was an altogether different show from *The Producers*, because it revealed a more realistic and bleak aspect of the United States to the Korean audience. A story of 13 successful and unsuccessful assassins who attempted to kill different American presidents, the production history of the show was quite different from that of *The Producers*. A musical collaboration of Stephen Sondheim and John Weidman, *Assassins* opened as a workshop production at Playwrights Horizons in New York, in December 1990. While most people were familiar with the unconventional choices that Sondheim had made for shows such as *Pacific Overtures* and *Sweeney Todd*, *Assassins* was staged with yet another unexpected subject, the extreme choices that the social underdogs named in the title had made.[4] Even more troubling was the fact that this musical almost sounded as if the creators were siding with those assassins, who were and still are viewed as losers and crazy minds of American society. In delivering the story of the assassins from their own perspectives, Sondheim revealed the dark side of the United States and the potential falsity of the values it holds on to: freedom, happiness and the American Dream. This is clearly depicted when Charles Guiteau, who shot President James Garfield, sings of the American Dream as he marches on to be hanged for his crime. After a few bars, Balladeer responds to him.

Here, "president" or becoming president of the United States of America, does not literally mean that every assassin-to-be wanted to become president. Rather, becoming president is the ultimate epitome of the American Dream, which is all about living a better life and having opportunities that will lead to the realization of individual American Dreams. The wishes and dreams of the assassins varied; Zangara wanted to stop his stomach pain by shooting Franklin D. Roosevelt; John Hinkley's poor attempt to assassinate Ronald Reagan was to impress Jodie Foster, with whom he was obsessed; Leon Czolgosz shot William McKinley because "no one cared about the poor man's pain" (80). Regardless of these differences, one thing that all of the assassins had in common was that their wishes and dreams never came true, no matter how small or big their dreams were. Thus, the "bright side" that Balladeer sings of was never really a bright side for them; after all, Guiteau ends up being hanged for what he has done. This individual falsity of the American Dream that eventually becomes a curse for all the assassins is a continuing theme of this piece. The only alternative answer for the desperate ones was to change the world by firing guns as they sing together in the "Gun Song."

By bringing all the assassins together on one stage, regardless of the temporal and spatial backgrounds of the characters, Sondheim made sure that the story of these assassins can transcend the background limits and that these assassins still exist in our society. The subject matter of the musical and its striking relevance to current society offended most of the audience, especially because the audiences were concerned, thinking "that [Sondheim and Weidman] were going to trivialize the subject" (Gottfried 183). The theme of the show stood out even more because of the Gulf War that the United States was engaged in at that time; the country simply had too much at stake. Thus, with the bad timing and the concerns that continued haunting the show, Assassins finished its month-long workshop engagement in New York.

Although it did not start off smoothly in New York, Assassins was actually popular at regional and college level theatres across the country.[5] In 2001, a decade after its Off-Broadway debut, it almost had its second chance in New York, but was cancelled again due to the 9/11 attack. The musical finally came to Broadway in 2004, and the timing could not have been better; while the theme remained the same, all the issues and questions that Americans had with the United States Government's campaign against terrorist forces helped the audience have a different perspective in looking at Assassins. It opened at Studio 54, successfully ran for about four months, and won five Tony Awards including Best Revival of a Musical.

It was right after this revival production that OD Musical Company, one of the most prolific musical production companies in Korea, announced that Sondheim's Assassins was to be produced in Seoul in July 2005. While the announcement generated a great sense of excitement among the critics and few Sondheim fans, there were also concerned voices over how it would be adapted and how the audience would receive the show, because Assassins was as much American in its theme and contents as The Producers. Thus, when the show opened in Seoul, on July 9, at a more intimate venue than did Th

Producers, critics, along with fans, were eager to see how the show turned out. The production ran for a little less than a month, closing on July 31. Although it had a pre-arranged schedule with the theatre, the fact that every night the house was only sixty to seventy percent full did not help. The reviews from the audience revealed rather mixed feelings about the show; those few who knew about the piece and went to see the actors enjoyed the experience, while most of the audience who had no background in musical theatre came out confused and, mostly, extremely bored.

There were a few obvious reasons why the majority of the audience found *Assassins* to be boring and confusing. First of all, *Assassins* was not a typical Broadway show musical, which Korean audiences were more accustomed to at the time; it did not have a stunning spectacle or a tune that one can dance to. The bigger issue, however, was the same problem that *The Producers* faced: the Korean audience did not have the frame of reference in understanding the historical events that they were seeing on stage. Other than Abraham Lincoln, Franklin D. Roosevelt, and John F. Kennedy, all the other presidents were not very well-known among Koreans, nor were some of them among Americans, for that matter. The translated script did attempt to help the audience to remain more connected to the show by taking out some of the minor details that Koreans would not understand.[6] As for the casting choices and the setting, there were not too many noticeable changes made from the original work, except small details of some of the actors' costumes. The Korean production of *Assassins*, as a result, was almost a copy of what was produced on Broadway the previous year, and the audience had to grapple with the names of presidents and historical events as they sat through the performance. What caused even more confusion was that the messages about the falsity of the American Dream resounded in the Korean production, as they did on Broadway. While its fundamental problem was similar to what *The Producers* faced, in that Korean audiences were unable to relate themselves to the work, what was even more problematic was that the projected image of the United States in *Assassins* challenged Koreans' pre-conceived notions of the United States and American people.

Assassins revealed and focused on the dark side of the United States from the perspectives of the underdogs of society. In other words, through the marginalized characters, *Assassins* depicted the United States as a society where inevitable problems and issues were present, just like any other place in the world. Granted, there was a possibility that the audience could have been more sympathetic to the characters and focused on their personal issues, given the distraught condition that each character was in. However, Sondheim and Weidman chose to make the piece evolve as a historical document with little dramatization or character development. Thus, most of the audience members were directed to look at the structure of the broken and dark society, rather than the issues that each character was dealing with.

As mentioned earlier, this idea of a broken society was particularly problematic to the Korean audience because the American Dream is still a valid idea in Korea. The ways that people achieve their dreams might have changed over the years, but for many Koreans, the United States is still a land of opportunity where one can build a better life for oneself. In other words, for many Koreans, the United States was a country where *Assassins* could be created, staged, and acclaimed for the message, a place where radical ideas were accepted and embraced. With their romanticized vision of the United States being shattered and with individual characters that contradict what the United States stands for among Koreans, *Assassins* was not an easy subject for the audience to digest. Furthermore, while detachment from the setting helped the audience to maintain their romanticized vision during the performances of *The Producers*, it exacerbated the confusion created among the audience in *Assassins*. The detachment created a safe place, but this time, it was not so safe because the representation of the United States in the show was challenging and subversive of the audience's preconceptions of the United States. With all these issues and concerns interrupting their expectations, most of the Korean audience could not help but find the show confusing. Thus, when the assassins sang of the "Free country" at the end of the show, not only was it ironic, but it required audiences to deliberately remind themselves of the fact that this story is about the United States, although it was a radically different place from the audiences' expectation.

Thus, the different responses from the Korean audience toward two very different American musicals show how Korea understands the United States and its culture. The United States as a country is often viewed as a fantasized or idealized concept, and individuals in the United States usually achieve whatever they wish for, even if they bend the rules a little bit. For this reason, when *Assassins* presented the bleak side of the United States and the American Dream as a mere deception, Korean audiences could not process it through their pre-conceived and invented entity called America. Also, the fact that the musical was presented by the characters who did not represent the success story of Americans did not make this process any easier for Korean audiences. With *The Producers*, however, it was a very different experience. The individual characters led the show, led the story, and achieved their victories, and everything was back in order at the end of the show. On top of the fact that Koreans are easily amused by musical comedies, *The Producers* communicated with the audiences in a very effective way, too; the issues and problems were framed in a highly camped-up setting, and thus audiences were able to distance themselves from what was being portrayed on stage.

In the reviews for both shows, there was one idea that was shared by many critics. To many Korean critics, both *Assassins* and *The Producers* portrayed the freedom and possibility allowed in the United States, whether within the show or in reality (Kim So Yeon). The negative images of United States displayed in *Assassins* were often glossed over by the critics, and the artistic freedom in the United States was appreciated and discussed more often. Also, with *The Producers*, the values of freedom and possibilities were displayed through the offensive aspects of the show and through the fact that they were actually enjoyed by many Americans. The critics and the audience also shared their appreciation for the happy ending of *The Producers* in which everyone is satisfied.

Many years have passed since Korea started being exposed to United States culture, and it seems that despite its weaknesses and faults as a society and a nation, the United States is still regarded as a country that grants opportunities to people. Broadway musicals, in particular, are expected by the general public to reveal the United States and the values and ideas it stands for. In other words, despite the changes in social and political circumstances, the Great White Way revived in Seoul still stands for the same thing as the original Great White Way that Americans once experienced in its inception — a booming economy and society in which one is granted with a value and individual possibility that allow one's dream to come true.

NOTES

1. In an interview, Mel Brooks tells us how he has seen and worked for a producer whom he created Max's character from, and implies that the show was sort of his ode to the musical theatre. See Michael Kantor and Laurence Maslon, *Broadway, the American Musical* (New York: Bulfinch Press, 2004), 425.

2. As a matter of fact, it seems that the show's political incorrectness captured the hearts of the audience. Ben Brantley, writing his review for the show in the *New York Times*, comments that the possibly offensive jokes lost their fangs, basically because the show is too funny (review of *The Producers*, *New York Times*, April 20, 2001).

3. An interview I had with one of the production staff revealed to me that people foresaw that the producers of *The Producers* would not make much profit because of the enormous cost that was spent at the pre-production stage.

4. *Pacific Overtures* was unconventional in that it was written ostensibly from the Japanese perspective (although see Kevin J. Wetmore, Jr.'s, essay "Gunboat Diplomacy on the *Kabuki* Stage" in this book for a critique of this claim), and *Sweeney Todd* was different from other musicals in that Sondheim and Hal Prince created a musical that had a serious social message to it. See Martin Gottfried's *Sondheim* (New York: Harry N. Abrams, 2000).

5. In his book *Our Musicals, Ourselves* (Lebanon, NH: University Press of New England, 2003), John Bush Jones says that there were 1,138 separate regional productions of *Assassins* between its opening in 1991 and 2000 (304).

6. For example, in scene 6, in which Moore and Fromm, who attempted to kill President Ford, talk about Charlie, the details regarding the bombing of Cambodia was omitted in the Korean Production, and the same things happened with little details that are culturally specific to the United States.

Bibliography

Aidoo, Ama Ata. *The Dilemma of a Ghost.* New York: Longman, 1987.

Allen, James Stewart. *Smash the Scottsboro Lynch Verdict.* New York: Workers' Library, 1933.

Amaya, Carlos. "Desdoblamiento y pérdida de identidad en *El gesticulador* y *A pesar del oscuro silencio.*" *Revista de humanidades* 2 (1997): 11–18.

An American Shrine in Tokyo: Memorial Meeting for Townsend Harris Held at Zempuku-ji. Tokyo: Phi Beta Kappa Japan Press, 1931.

Andrews, Elmer. *The Art of Brian Friel: Neither Reality Nor Dreams.* Basingstroke, UK: Macmillan, 1995.

Banfield, Stephen. *Sondheim's Broadway Musicals.* Ann Arbor: University of Michigan Press, 1993.

Beardsell, Peter. "Usigli's Political Drama in Perpective." *Bulletin of Hispanic Studies* 66.3 (1989): 251–261.

Beasley, W.G. *Japan Encounters the Barbarian: Japanese Travelers in America and Europe.* New Haven: Yale University Press, 1995.

Berger, Max. *The British Traveler in America, 1836–1860.* New York: Columbia University Press, 1943.

Berman, David M. "In the City of Lost Souls." *Social Studies* 86.5 (1995): 197–205.

Bert, Wayne. *The Reluctant Superpower: United States' Policy in Bosnia, 1991–1995.* New York: St. Martin's, 1997.

Bhabha, Homi K., ed. *Nation and Narration.* London: Routledge, 1990.

Bhatia, Nandia. *Acts of Authority/Acts of Resistance: Theatre and Politics in Colonial and Post-Colonial India.* Ann Arbor: University of Michigan Press, 2004.

Bhatia, Sunil. *American Karma: Race, Culture, and Identity in the Indian Diaspora.* New York: New York University Press, 2007.

Blumner, Holly A., Julie A. Iezzi, Alice E. Luhrmann and Kathy Welch, eds. *101 Years of Kabuki in Hawai'i.* Honolulu: Department of Theatre and Dance, University of Hawai'i, 1995.

Boltwood, Scott. *Brian Friel, Ireland, and The North.* Cambridge, UK: Cambridge University Press, 2007.

Booker, M. Keith. *Colonial Power, Colonial Texts: India in the Modern British Novel.* Ann Arbor: University of Michigan Press, 1997.

Bose, Neilesh, ed. *Beyond Bollywood and Broadway: Plays from the South Asian Diaspora.* Bloomington: Indiana University Press, 2009.

_____, and Sudipto Chatterjee, eds. *The Rights of Man*. Kolkata, India: Seagull, 2009.

Brantley, Ben. "Genuinely Ugly Americans, As Viewed by the Japanese." *New York Times*. 11 July 2002: E1.

Bravo Elizondo, Peter. "El concepto de la revolución y de lo mexicano en *El gesticulador*." *Texto Crítico* 10.29 (May–August 1984): 197–205.

Butler, Judith. *Bodies that Matter: On the Discursive Limits of "Sex."* New York: Routledge, 1993.

Carlson, Marvin. "The Mother Tongue and the Other Tongue: The American Challenge in Recent Drama." Keynote address, CDE Conference, Burg Rothenfels, Wuerzburg, 9 May 2002.

Carter, Dan. *Scottsboro: A Tragedy of the American South*. Baton Rouge: Louisiana State University Press, 1979.

Casey, Patrick. "How Do You Say '*I Love You, You're Perfect, Now Change*' in Mandarin?" Entertainment, AZCentral.com. <http://wwwazcentral.com/ent/articles/0509chinesemusical0509.htm>. Accessed 22 February 2008.

Castañenda, C. E. "The Oldest University in America." *Hispania* 13.3 (1930): 247–249.

Castillo, Susan. *Colonial Encounters in New World Writing, 1500–1786: Performing America*. New York: Routledge, 2006.

Cát Vũ. "*Da Cổ Hoài Lang* Trước Giờ Cất Cánh Ra Thủ Đô [*Da Cổ Hoài Lang* Before the Flight to the Capitol]." *Người Lao Động*. August 26, 1995.

Chalmers, Allan Knight. *They Shall Be Free*. Garden City, NY: Doubleday, 1951.

Chambers, Lilian, Ger FitzGibbon and Eamon Jordan, eds. *Theatre Talk: Voices of Irish Theatre Practitioners*. Dublin: Carysfort, 2001.

Chatterjee, Minoti. *Theatre Beyond the Threshold: Colonialism, Nationalism, and the Bengali Stage, 1905–47*. New Delhi: Indialog, 2004.

Chatterjee, Sudipto. *The Colonial Staged: Theatre in Colonial Calcutta*. New York: Seagull, 2007.

_____. "From 'Vanguard' to 'Avant-Garde'? Questioning the Progressive Theatre of Kolkata." In Harding, James M., and John Rouse, eds. *Not the Other Avant-Garde: the Transnational Foundations of Avant-Garde Performance*. Ann Arbor: Michigan University Press, 2006.

_____. "The Nation Staged: Nationalist Discourse in Late Nineteenth-Century Bengali Theatre." In *(Post) Colonial Stages: Critical and Creative Views on Drama, Theatre and Performance*. Ed. Helen Gilbert. London: Dangaroo, 1999.

_____. "South Asian American Theatre: (Un/Re) Painting the Town Brown." *Theatre Survey* 49.1 (May 2008): 109–117.

_____. "Utpal Dutt." Unpublished manuscript, n.d.

Chattopadhyay, Debesh, ed. "Special Edition: Bangla Theatre in the Reflection of Theatre Criticism, 1944–78." *Sanskriti* 3 (August 2000).

Choudhury, Mita. *Interculturalism and Resistance in the London Theatre, 1660–1800: Identity, Performance, and Empire*. Lewisburg, PA: Bucknell University Press, 2000.

Clay, Carolyn. "Babes in Belgrade." Rev. of *Family Stories*, by Biljana Srbljanović. *The Boston Phoenix*. 1 Feb. 2008 <http://www.bostonphoenix.com/boston/arts/the ater/documents/02249642.html>.

Cohan, Steven. "Case Study: Interpreting *Singin' in the Rain*." In *Reinventing Film Studies*. Eds. Christine Gledhill and Linda Williams. London: Arnold, 2000.

Coker, Niyi, Jr. *Ola Rotimi's African Theatre: The Development of an Indigenous Aesthetic*. Lewiston, NY: Edwin Mellen, 2005.

Colgan, Gerry. "Friel's Bloody Sunday." *The Irish Times*. 24 April 1999.

Conceison, Claire. *Significant Other: Staging the American in China.* Honolulu: University of Hawai'i Press, 2004.

Conrad, Earl, and Haywood Patterson. *Scottsboro Boy.* Garden City, NY: Doubleday, 1950.

Corbett, Tony. *Brian Friel: Decoding the Language of the Tribe.* Dublin: Liffey, 2002.

Coria-Sánchez, Carlos. "El gesticulador: contextualización del 'yo' mexicano." *Cuadernos Americanos* 75 (1999): 208–214.

Covin, Kelly. *Hear That Train Blow.* New York: Delacorte, 1970.

Cregan, David. "'Badness. Good, Isn't It? A Bit of Badness': Frank McGuinness's Dramaturgy of 'Deviance' and the Irish Theatrical Tradition." Diss., Trinity College Dublin, 2004.

Cronin, Maura. "The Yankee and The Veteran: Vehicles of Nationalism." *Journal of American Drama and Theatre (JADT)* 13.2 (Spring 2001): 51–70.

Cullingford, Elizabeth Butler. *Ireland's Others: Gender and Ethnicity in Irish Literature and Popular Culture.* Cork: Cork University Press, 2001.

"*Dạ Cổ Hoài Lang:* Cổ Mà Không Cổ [*Dạ Cổ Hoài Lang:* Old but Not Old]." *Việt Báo.* December 31, 2004. <http://vietbao.vn/Van-hoa/Da-co-hoai-lang-co-ma-khong-co/10893528/181/>. Accessed 15 November 2008. Originally published in *Thế Giới Mới* newspaper.

Dalmia, Vasudha. *Politics, Plays, and Performances: The Politics of Modern Indian Theatre.* New York: Oxford University Press, 2006.

Danatanus, Ulf. *Brian Friel: The Growth of an Irish Dramatist.* Göteborg: Göteborg University Press, 1985.

De Almeida, Hermione, and George H. Gilpin. *Indian Renaissance: British Romantic Art and the Prospect of India.* London: Ashgate, 2005.

deGraft, J.C. *Through a Film Darkly.* London: Oxford University Press, 1970.

Delaney, Paul, ed. *Brian Friel in Conversation.* Ann Arbor: University of Michigan Press, 2000.

Dharwadker, Aparna. *Theatres of Independence: Drama, Theory, and Urban Performance in India Since 1947.* Iowa City: University of Iowa Press, 2005.

Diamond, Elin. *Unmaking Mimesis.* New York: Routledge, 1997, Sharpe, 1998.

Doan, Mary Ann. "The Voice in the Cinema: The Articulation of Body and Space." In *Film and Criticism: Introductory Readings.* Eds. Leo Braudy and Marshall Cohen. New York and Oxford: Oxford University Press, 1999.

"D'oh!" *Los Angeles Times.* 4 August 2007: A16.

Drudy, P.J., ed. *The Irish in America: Emigration, Assimilation and Impact.* Cambridge, UK: Cambridge University Press, 1985.

Duffy, Susan. "Hughes' Move to the Left: *Scottsboro Limited.*" In *The Political Plays of Langston Hughes.* Ed. Langston Hughes. Carbondale: Southern Illinois University Press, 2000.

Dunlap, William. *History of the American Theatre.* New York: J & J Harper, 1832.

Dunton, Chris. *Make Man Talk True.* London: Hans Zell, 1992.

Ellis, Caroline Burlingham. "*Family Stories:* A Slapstick Tragedy." Rev. of *Family Stories,* by Biljana Srbljanović. <http://www.theatermania.com/content/news.cfm/story>. 26 April 2002.

Fehrenbach, Heide, and Uta G. Poiger. "Introduction." *Transactions, Transgressions, Transformations: American Culture in Western Europe and Japan.* Eds. Heide Fehrenbach and Uta G. Poiger. New York: Berghan, 2000.

Felsenstein, Frank, ed. *English Trader, Indian Maid: Representing Gender, Race, and Slav-*

ery in the New World; An Inkle and Yarico Reader. Baltimore: Johns Hopkins University Press, 1999.

Fisher, Kimberly. "Locating Frames in the Discursive Universe." *Sociological Research Online* 2.3 (September 1997). <http://www.socresonline.org.uk/2/3/4.html>. Accessed 28 January 2008.

Freeman, James. *Hearts of Sorrow: Vietnamese-American Lives*. Stanford, CA: Stanford University Press, 1989.

Frick, John. "Staging Scottsboro: The Violence of Representation and Class-Race 'Negotiations' in the 1930s." *New England Theatre Journal* 6 (Fall 1995).

Friel, Brian. *American Welcome*. In *More Ten Minute Plays from Actors Theatre of Louisville*. Ed. Michael Bigelow Dixon. New York: Samuel French, 1992.

_____. *Give Me Your Answer, Do!* London: Penguin, 1997.

_____. *The Loves of Cass Maguire*. New York: Samuel French, 1966.

_____. *Selected Plays of Brian Friel*. London: Faber and Faber, 1984.

"'GEISAI-2' Ôza Kunrin!!; gyakushû no hasha tachi GEISAI-3 e no yabô ôi ni kataru!? ['GEISAI-2' Champions Rule!!: Champions of a Counterattack Discuss Their Ambitions for GEISAI-3!?]." *BT* 827 (2002): 154–156.

"Gero." *VOX Diccionario Ilustrado (Latino-Español/Español-Latino)*. Barcelona: Bibliograf, 1999.

Gerould, Daniel C., ed. *American Melodrama*. New York: Performing Arts, 1983.

"Gesticulate." *Webster's New World Dictionary: Second College Edition*. New York: Simon and Schuster, 1984.

"Gesticulor, -ari." *Cassell's New Latin Dictionary (Latin-English/English-Latin)*. Ed. D.P. Simpson. New York: Funk and Wagnalls, 1959.

Ghosh, Nemai. *Dramatic Moments: Photographs and Memories of Calcutta Theatre*. Kolkata, India: Seagull, 2000.

Gist, Jerry W. *The Story of Scottsboro, Alabama*. Nashville: Rich, 1968.

Goffman, Erving. *Frame Analysis: An Essay on the Organization of Experience*. Boston: Northeastern University Press, 1986.

Goodman, James. *Stories of Scottsboro*. New York: Pantheon, 1994.

Gordon, Joanne. *Art Isn't Easy: The Theater of Stephen Sondheim*. New York: Da Capo, 1992.

Gottfried, Martin. *Sondheim*. New York: Harry N. Abrams, 2000.

Gow, James. *Triumph of the Lack of Will: International Diplomacy and the Yugoslav War*. New York: Columbia University Press, 1997.

Gowon, Herbert H. *Five Foreigners in Japan*. Freeport: Books for Libraries, 1936.

Gregg, Stephen. "Representing the Nabob: India, Stereotypes, and Eighteenth Century Theatre." In *Picturing South Asian Culture in English: Textual and Visual Representations*. Eds. Tasleem Shakur and Karen D'Souza. Liverpool, UK: Open House, 2003.

Griffis, William Elliot. *Townsend Harris: First American Envoy in Japan*. Boston: Houghton Mifflin, 1895.

Gryphius, Andrea. *Ermordete Majestät oder Carolus Stuardus*. In *Trauerspiele*. Ed. Hugh Powell. *Gesamtausgabe der deutschsprachigen Werke*. Vol. 4 Tübingen: Max Niemeyer 1964.

Gunawardana, A.J. "Theatre as a Weapon: An Interview with Utpal Dutt." *The Drama Review* 15.3 (1971): 224–237.

Hall, Brook. "A Discussion with the Director Brook Hall." <http://www.infine-art com/smokeyjoes/englishindex.html>. Accessed 28 December 2008.

Harada, Yuki. "Maddonesu aidoru [Madness Idol]." *Dazed and Confused Japan* (2003) 25.

Harris, Susan Cannon. "Watch Yourself: Performance, Sexual Difference, and National Identity in the Irish Plays of Frank McGuinness." *Genders* 28 (1998).

Harris, Townsend. *The Complete Journals of Townsend Harris.* Ed. Mario Emilio Cosenza. 2d rev. ed. Rutland, UT: Charles E. Tuttle, 1959.

Hays, Arthur G. *Trial by Prejudice.* New York: Covici, Friede, 1933.

Hays, Michael, and Anastasia Nikolopoulou, eds. *Melodrama: The Cultural Emergence of a Genre.* New York: St. Martin's, 1996.

Henshall, Kenneth. *A History of Japan.* New York: Palgrave Macmillan, 2004.

Hentea, Calin. *Balkan Propaganda Wars.* Trans. Cristina Bordianu. Lanham, MD: Scarecrow, 2006.

Herndon, Angela. *The Scottsboro Boys: Four Freed, Five to Go!* New York: Workers' Library, 1937.

Hien Duc Do. "The Dispersion Policies." In *The Vietnamese.* Ed. Michele E. Houle. Detroit, MI: Greenhaven/Thomson Gale, 2006.

Hisamatsu Senichi. *Biographical Dictionary of Japanese Literature.* Tokyo: Kodansha, 1976.

Hoàng Kim. "Thành Lộc và *Dạ Cổ Hoài Lang* [Thành Lộc and *Dạ Cổ Hoài Lang*]." *Thanh Niên.* July 26, 2006. <http://www.thanhnien.com.vn/2006/Pages/200630/156 878.aspx>. Accessed 15 November 2008.

Honour, Hugh. *The European Vision of America.* Cleveland: Cleveland Museum of Art, 1975.

_____. *The New Golden Land: European Images of America from the Discoveries to the Present Time.* New York: Pantheon, 1975.

Hulme, Peter. *Colonial Encounters: Europe and the Native Caribbean, 1492–1797.* New York: Routledge, 1989.

Humphreys, David. *The Yankey in England, a Drama in Five Acts.* Boston?, 1815.

Hunter, Melanie R. "British Travel Writing and Imperial Authority." In *Issues in Travel Writing: Empire, Spectacle, and Displacement.* Ed. Kristi Siegel. New York: Peter Lang, 2002.

Igarashi, Yoshikumi. *Bodies of Memory: Narratives of War in Postwar Japanese Culture, 1945–1970.* Princeton, NJ: Princeton University Press, 2000.

"I Hip Hop, Therefore I Am." *Taiwan Culture Portal.* <http://www.culture.tw/index. php?option=com_content&task=view&id=645&Itemid=157>. Accessed 17 January 2009.

Iida, Yumiko. *Rethinking Identity in Modern Japan: Nationalism as Aesthetics.* London and New York: Routledge, 2002.

Inouye Masanao. "Foreword." In *The American Envoy.* Okamoto Kidō. Trans. Masanao Inouye. Kobe: J.L. Thompson, 1931.

Ivy, Marilyn. Rev. of *Little Boy. The Journal of Japanese Studies* 32.2 (2006): 498–502.

Jantz, Harold. "Amerika im deutschen Dichten und Denken." In *Deutsche Philologie im Aufriss.* Ed. Wolfgang Stammler. 2d ed., vol. 3. Berlin: Erich Schmidt Verlag, 1959.

Jaynes, Nanette. "Celebrating with Godot." *Taiwan Review.* 1 September 1999. <http://taiwanreview.nat.gov.tw/site/Tr/ct.asp?xItem=1460&ctNode=119>. Accessed 14 February 2008.

Jones, Eugene H. *Native Americans as Shown on the Stage, 1753–1916.* Metuchen, NJ: Scarecrow, 1988.

Jones, John Bush. *Our Musicals, Ourselves—A Social History of the American Musical Theatre.* Lebanon, NH: University Press of New England, 2003.

Jones, Kenneth. "Chinese Staging of *I Love You, You're Perfect* Will Play in Rep Off-Broadway." *Playbill*. 29 March 2007. <http://www.playbill.com/news/article/106929.html>. Accessed 22 February 2008.

Jones, Marie. *Stones in His Pockets* and *A Night in November*. London: Nick Hern, 2000.

Jordan, Eamonn. *The Feast of Famine: The Plays of Frank McGuinness*. Bern: Peter Lang, 1997.

Keene, Donald. *Dawn to the West: Japanese Literature of the Modern Era, Volume Four: Poetry, Drama and Criticism*. Rev. ed. New York: Columbia, 1999.

Khan, Lin Shi, and Tony Perez. *Scottsboro, Alabama: A Story in Linoleum Cuts*. New York: New York University, 2002.

Kim So Yeon. "7 Reasons Why Musicals Cannot Help but Succeed." *HanKyung Business Magazine*, 24 April 2006. <http://www.kbizweek.com/article/printarticle.asp?vol_no=542%26art_no=26617>. Accessed 27 November 2008.

Kimura, Satoru. "Imadoki no 'odoriko' no yûmorasu de setsunai shukumei" [Humorous Yet Painful Destiny of Showgirls of Today]. *BT* 841 (2003): 180–181.

Klepac, Richard L. *Mr. Mathews at Home*. Leicester: Blackfriars [The Society for Theatre Research], 1979.

Klinger, Friedrich Maximilian. *Sturm und Drang. Klingers Werke in Zwei Bänden*. Vol. 1. Weimar: Volksverlag, 1958.

Knapp, Raymond. *The American Musical and the Formation of National Identity*. Princeton, NJ: Princeton University Press, 2005.

Kristeva, Julia. *Nations without Nationalism*. Trans. Leon S. Roudiez. New York: Columbia University Press, 1993.

_____. *The Powers of Horror: An Essay on Abjection*. Trans. Leon S. Roudiez. New York: Columbia University Press, 1982.

Kruger, Loren. *The National Stage: Theatre and Cultural Legitimation in England, France, and America*. Chicago: University of Chicago Press, 1992.

Lederer, William J., and Eugene Burdick. *The Ugly American*. New York: Norton, 1958.

Lefebvre, Henri. *The Production of Space*. Trans. Donald Nicholson-Smith. Malden, MA: Blackwell, 1991.

Leibowitz, Robert. *The Defender: The Life and Career of Samuel Leibowitz, 1893–1933*. Englewood Cliffs, NJ: Prentice-Hall, 1981.

Leiter, Samuel L. *Kabuki Encyclopedia*. Westport, CT: Greenwood, 1979.

Lessing, Karl Gotthelf. *Die Mätresse: Lustspiel*. Heilbronn: Behr, 1887. Rpt. Wiesbaden: Kraus Reprint, 1968.

Lohenstein, Daniel Casper von. *Cleopatra*. In *Afrikanische Trauerspiele*. Ed. Klaus Günther Just. Stuttgart: Anton Hiersemann, 1957.

_____. *Sophonisbe*. In *Afrikanische Trauerspiele*. Ed. Klaus Günther Just. Stuttgart: Anton Hiersemann, 1957.

Lojek, Helen. "Stage Irish-Americans in the Plays of Brian Friel." *The Canadian Journal of Irish Studies* 17.2 (December 1991).

_____. *The Theatre of Frank McGuinness: Stages of Mutability*. Dublin: Carysfort Press, 2002.

Lukac, Aleksandar. "Invitation to an Exorcism." Rev. of *Family Stories* by Biljana Srbljanović. *Toronto Slavic Quarterly* 9 (Summer 2004): <http://www.nowtoronto.com/issues/2005-09-29/stage_theatrereviews7.php>.

Marks, Peter. "Sondheim, Gaining Much in the Translation" *Washington Post*. 5 September 2002: C1.

Martin, Carol. "Lingering Heat and Local Global J Stuff." *TDR* 50.1 (2006): 46–56.

Maslon, Laurence, and Michael Kantor. *Broadway: The American Musical.* New York: Bulfinch Press, 2004.

Mathews, Charles. *Memoirs of Charles Mathews, comedian.* Ed. Mrs. Mathews. 5 vols. London: Richard Bentley, 1839.

Matsui, Midori. "Beyond the Pleasure Room to a Chaotic Street: Transformations of Cute Subculture in the Art of the Japanese Nineties." In *Little Boy: The Arts of Japan's Exploding Subculture.* Ed. Murakami, Takashi. New York: Japan Society, New Haven: Yale University Press, 2005.

Maxwell, D. E. S. *Brian Friel.* Lewisburg, PA: Bucknell University Press, 1973.

McClintock, Anne. *Imperial Leather: Race, Gender, and Sexuality in the Colonial Contest.* New York: Routledge, 1995.

McDonagh, Martin. *The Cripple of Inishmaan.* London: Methuen, 1997.

McGuinness, Frank. *Plays 2.* London: Faber and Faber, 2002.

Mehta, Binita. *Widows, Pariahs, and Bayederes: India as Spectacle.* Lewisburg, PA: Bucknell University Press, 2002.

Mesick, Jane Louis. *The English Traveler in America, 1785–1835.* New York: Columbia University Press, 1922.

Mestrovic, Stjepan G. "Beginning to Clean the Air." *Theater* 31.1 (2001): 26–34.

_____. *The Conceit of Innocence: Losing the Conscience of the West in the War against Bosnia.* College Station: Texas A&M University Press, 1997.

Michener, James. *Sayonara.* New York: Random House, 1954.

Midgette, Anne. "Wacky Love in Translation." *New York Times.* 18 May 2007. <http://theater2.nytimes.com/2007/05/18/theater/reviews/18perf.html>. Accessed 22 February 2008.

Miller, Arthur. *"Salesman" in Bejing.* London: Metheun, 1984.

Miller, Scott. *Strike Up the Band—A New History of Musical Theatre.* Portsmouth, NH: Heinemann, 2007.

Mission/K. Videocassette. 2002.

Mitra, Dinabandhu. *Nil Darpan* (The Indigo Mirror). Calcutta: Indian Publications, [1860] 1972.

Morash, Christopher. *A History of Irish Theatre, 1601–2000.* Cambridge, UK: Cambridge University Press, 2002.

Munk, Erika. "Before the Fall: Yugoslav Theaters of Opposition." *Theater* 31.1 (2001): 4–26.

_____. "Beginning to Clean the Air." *Theater* 31.1 (2001): 32.

_____. "Munk's Interview of Two" *Theater* 31.1 (2001): 32.

Murakami Takashi. *DOB in the Strange Forest.* Tokyo: Bijutsu Shuppansha, 1999.

_____. "Earth in My Window." In *Little Boy.* Ed. Takashi Murakami. New York: Japan Society, New Haven: Yale University Press, 2005.

_____. "Introduction." In *Tokyo Girls Bravo.* Ed. Takashi Murakami. Tokyo: Kaikaikiki, 2002.

_____. "Revolutionizing Art in the 21st Century." In *The GEISAI.* Ed. Izumi Karashima. Tokyo: Kaikaikiki, 2005.

_____. "Superflat Trilogy: Greetings: You Are Alive." In *Little Boy.* Ed. Takashi Murakami. New York: Japan Society, New Haven: Yale University Press, 2005.

_____. "A Theory of Super Flat Japanese Art." In *Superflat.* Ed. Takashi Murakami. Tokyo: Madora Shuppan, 2000.

Muramatsu Shunsui. *Shimoda ni okeru yoshida shoin.* Tokyo: Heibonsha, 1930.

Murphy, Tom. *The House.* London: Methuen, 2000.

_____. *Plays Two*. London: Methuen, 1993.

_____. *The Wake*. London: Methuen, 1998.

_____. *A Whistle in the Dark and Other Plays*. London: Methuen, 1989.

Murray, Christopher. *Twentieth-Century Irish Drama: Mirror Up to Nation*. Manchester, NH: Manchester University Press, 1997.

_____, ed. *Brian Friel, Essays, Diaries and Interviews: 1964–1999*. London: Faber and Faber, 1999.

The Musical Database. Clipservice. 2000. <http://www.themusical.co.kr.? Accessed 26 October 2007.

Nelson, Richard. *Some Americans Abroad*. London: Faber & Faber, 1990.

Nguyễn Thị Minh Ngọc. "Đi Tìm Người Yêu [Searching for a Lover]" Gió O. <http://www.gio-o.com/NguyenThiMinhNgocDTNY.html>. Accessed 15 January 2009.

Nguyễn Thị Minh Thái. "*Dạ Cổ Hoài Lang*: Vở Diễn Xuất Sắc Của Sân Khấu Nhỏ TP Hồ Chí Minh [*Dạ Cổ Hoài Lang*: An Excellent Play by Ho Chi Minh City's Small Theater]." *Phụ Nữ*, 1995.

Nguyễn Vũ. "Xem Vở *Dạ Cổ Hoài Lang* [Watching *Dạ Cổ Hoài Lang*]." *Hà Nội Mới* September 10, 1995.

O'Brien, George. *Brian Friel*. Dublin: Gill and Macmillan, 1989.

Oguma, Eiji. *Tan'itsu minzoku shinwa no kigen : "Nihonjin" no jigazô no keifu* [*The Myth of the Homogeneous Nation*]. Tokyo: Shinyosha, 1995.

Okamoto Kidō. *The American Envoy*. Trans. Masanao Inouye. Kobe: J.L. Thompson 1931.

_____. "Amerika no Tsukai." In *Gendai Nihon Gikyoku Senshō*. Tokyo: Hakusuisha 1955.

Otake Tomoko. "Go! Go! Kingyo!" *Japan Times*. 13 February 2005.

O'Toole, Fintan. *The Ex-Isle of Erin*. Dublin: New Island, 1997.

_____. *Tom Murphy: The Politics of Magic*. Dublin: New Island, 1994.

Panovski, Naum. "New Old Times in the Balkans: The Search for Cultural Identity. *PAJ: A Journal of Performance and Art* 28.2 (May 2006): 61–74.

Park, Ji Hyeon, and Park Su Jin. "'I wanna be a producer!' *The Producers* will make you laugh out loud." *No-Cut News*. 14 January, 2006. <http://www.cbs.co.kr/nocut/show asp?idx=143184>. Accessed 27 November 2008.

Paz, Octavio. "Máscaras mexicanas." *El laberinto de la soledad. Postdata. Vuelta al laber into de la soledad*. Mexico City: Fondo de Cultura Económica, 1999.

_____. "Mexican Masks." In *The Labyrinth of Solitude and Other Writings (The Othe Mexico, Return to the Labyrinth of Solitude, Mexico and the United States, The Philan thropic Ogre)*. Trans. L. Kemp, Y. Milos and R. Phillips Belash. New York: Grove 1985.

Peacock, Alan J., ed. *The Achievement of Brian Friel*. Gerrards Cross: Colin Smyth 1993.

Peake, Richard B. "Americans Abroad." *Dicks' Standard Plays*. London: John Dicks, 31 Strand. No. 589.

Perkins, Kathy A., ed. *African Women Playwrights*. Urbana: University of Illinois Pres 2009.

Perry, Matthew C. *The Japan Expedition 1852–1854: The Personal Journal of Comm dore Matthew Perry*. Ed. Roger Pineau. Washington, D.C.: Smithsonian Institutio 1968.

Pilkington, Lionel. *Theatre and the State in Twentieth-Century Ireland*. London: Rou ledge, 2001.

Pine, Richard. *The Diviner: The Art of Brian Friel.* Dublin: University College Dublin Press, 1999.

Postlewait, Thomas. "From Melodrama to Realism: The Suspect History of American Drama." In *Melodrama: The Cultural Emergence of a Genre.* Eds. Michael Hays and Anastasia Nikolopoulou. New York: St. Martin's, 1996.

Powell, Brian. *Kabuki in Modern Japan.* New York: St. Martin's, 1990.

Prasad, Vijay. *The Karma of Brown Folk.* Minneapolis: University of Minnesota Press, 2000.

Price, Lawrence Marsden. *Inkle and Yarico Album.* Berkeley: University of California Press, 1987.

Prock, Stephan. "Music, Gender and the Politics of Performance in *Singin' in the Rain.*" *Colby Quarterly* 38:4 (2000): 295–318.

Rafroidi, Patrick. "The Worlds of Brian Friel." In *Perspectives of Irish Drama and Theatre.* Eds. J. Genet and R. A. Cave. Gerrards Cross: Colin Smythe, 1991.

Ragle, Gordon. "Rodolfo Usigli and His Mexican Scene." *Hispania* 46.2 (1963): 307–311.

Ramos, Samuel. *El perfil del hombre y la cultura en México.* Mexico City: Espasa-Calpe/ Austral, 1999.

Rath, Eric. "Godzilla Meets Super-*Kyogen,* or How a Dinosaur Saved the World." In *In Godzilla's Footsteps: Japanese Pop Icons on the Global Stage.* Eds. William M. Tsutsui and Michiko Ito. New York: Palgrave Macmillan, 2006.

Reden-Esbeck, Friedrich Johann Freiherrn von. *Caroline Neuber und ihre Zeitgenossen: Ein Beitrag zur deutschen Kultur- und Theatergeschichte.* Leipzig: J.A. Barth, 1881.

Requa, Marny. "Adolfo Gilly: The Long Strike at UNAM: Higher Education and the Restructuring of the Mexican State." <http://socrates.berkeley.edu:7001/Events/spring 2000/03-22-00-gilly/index.html#resources>.

Richards, Shaun, ed. *The Cambridge Companion to Twentieth-Century Irish Drama.* Cambridge, UK: Cambridge University Press, 2004.

Richtarik, Marilynn, J. *Acting Between the Lines: The Field Day Theatre Company and Irish Cultural Politics 1980–1984.* Oxford: Clarendon Press, 1994.

Robertson, Jennifer. *Takarazuka: Sexual Politics and Popular Culture in Modern Japan.* Berkeley: University of California Press, 1998.

Roche, Anthony. *Contemporary Irish Drama: From Beckett to McGuinness.* Dublin: Gill and Macmillan, 1994.

Rosana Scarano, Laura. "Metateatro e identitdad en 'Saverio El Cruel' de Roberto Arlt y 'El gesticulador' de Rodolfo Usigli." *Alba de América* 6.10–11 (July 1988): 199–207.

Rothstein, Edward. "A Japanese View of an American View of Japan." *New York Times.* 1 September 2002: 3.

Rotimi, Ola. *Our Husband Has Gone Mad Again.* Ibadan: University Press, 1977.

Rugg, Rebecca Ann. "Shout Theater in Crowded Fire." *Theater* 30.1 (2000): 4–6.

Rutledge, Paul. *The Vietnamese in America.* Minneapolis: Lerner, 1987.

Sakabe Megumi. *Kagami no naka no nihongo: sono shikô no shushusô [Japanese Language in Mirror: Its Various Thinkings].* Tokyo: Chikuma Shobô, 1989.

Sakurai Keisuke. "'Kodomo no kuni no dansu' dayori — gijutsu no 'zenyô' ni tsuite [Newsletter of 'Dance in Children's Country'— On 'Making Good Use' of Skills]." *Butai Geijutsu [Performing Arts]* 5 (2004): 204–213.

_____. "'Kodomo no kuni no dansu' dayori: tadashii 'darashinasa' ni tsuite [Newsletter of 'Dance in Children's Country': On Correct 'Sloppiness']" *Butai Geijutsu [Performing Arts]* 7 (2004): 177–188.

_____. "Kodomo shintai to iu koto: kontenporarii dansu ni miru rekishi to kioku (?)

["What Is 'Child Body': History and Memory in Contemporary Dance (?)"]. *Butai Geijutsu [Performing Arts]* 4 (2003): 29–42.

Salz, Jonah. "Super-*kyōgen*: Radically Traditional Utopian Comedies." In *Modern Japanese Theatre and Performance*. Eds. David Jortner, Keiko McDonald and Kevin J. Wetmore, Jr. Lanham, MD: Lexington, 2006.

Sasaguchi Rei. "A Musical that Rewrites History." *Japan Times*. 23 October 2002: 27.

"Screen Comedy and Our National Identity." *La Trobe University Bulletin* January/February 2006. 7. <http://www.latrobe.edu.au/bulletin/archive/010206/research1. html>. Accessed 7 January 2008.

Shih, Sandra. "Troupe Recasts U. S. Musical in Taipei's Dating Environment." *Taiwan Journal*. 1 November 2007. <http://taiwanjournal.nat.gov.tw/ct.asp?xItem=24858& CtNode=118>. Accessed 7 January 2008.

Shih, Ying-Ying. "East of Broadway." *Taiwan Review*. 1 November 2007. <http://taiwan review.nat.gov.tw/ct.asp?xItem=24775&CtNode=128>. Accessed 13 January 2008.

Shimakawa, Karen. *National Abjection: The Asian American Body Onstage*. Durham, NC: Duke University Press, 2002.

Shirō, Okamoto. *The Man Who Saved Kabuki: Faubion Bowers and Theatre Censorship in Occupied Japan*. Trans. Samuel L. Leiter. Honolulu: University of Hawai'i Press, 2001.

Siegel, Ed. "An Effective and Affecting *Family Stories* at the Market." *The Boston Globe*. 26 April 2002, C15.

Siegel, Kristi. "Travel Writing and Travel Theory." In *Issues in Travel Writing: Empire, Spectacle, and Displacement*. Ed. Kristi Siegel. New York: Peter Lang, 2002.

Singer, Jane. "The Dream World of Takarazuka." *Japan Quarterly* 43.2 (1996): 162.

Singh, Jyotsna. *Colonial Narratives/Cultural Dialogues: "Discoveries" of India in the Language of Colonialism*. New York: Routledge, 1996.

Singleton, Brian, and Anna McMullan. "Performing Ireland: New Perspectives on Contemporary Irish Theatre." *Australasian Drama Studies* 43 (2003): 1–16.

Singin' in the Rain. Dir. Gene Kelly and Stanley Donen. 1952. DVD. Turner Entertainment Co. and Warner Home Video, 2000.

Sischy, Ingrid. "Selling Dreams." *The New Yorker*. September 28, 1992: 88.

Smith, Michael, and Tarallo, Bernadette. "The Second Wave." In *The Vietnamese*. Ed. Michele E. Houle. Detroit: Greenhaven/Thomson Gale, 2006.

Sondheim, Stephen, and John Weidman. *Assassins*. New York: Theatre Communication Group, 1991.

Sorgenfrei, Carol Fisher. *Unspeakable Acts: The Avant-Garde Theatre of Terayama Shuji and Postwar Japan*. Honolulu: University of Hawai'i Press, 2005.

_____. "Victory in Defeat; Mimetic Transformation and the Performance of National Identity in Postwar Japan." American Society for Theatre Research. Allegro Hotel, Chicago. 18 November 2006.

Soyinka, Wole. *Before the Blackout*. In *African Theatre: Soyinka*. Eds. Martin Banham, Judith Greenwood and Chuck Mike. Trenton, NJ: Africa World, 2005.

Srbljanović, Biljana. *Belgrade Trilogy*. Trans. Ellis. In *Eastern Promise: Eight Plays from Central and Eastern Europe*. Eds. Sian Evans and Cheryl Robson. London: Aurora Metro, 1999.

_____. "Diary of a Defiant Serb." *The Guardian*. 31 July 1999.

_____. *Family Stories*. Trans. Rebecca Ann Rugg. Reprinted in *Theatre* 30.1 (2000): 6–48.

Stackman, Will. "Aisle Say." 26 April 2002. <http://www.aislesay.com/MA-FAMILY STORIES.html>.

Statler, Oliver. *Shimoda Story*. New York: Random House, 1969.

Symons, Emma-Kate. "Coming Home: Look Who's Making Vietnam Hip." *Wall Street Journal.* December 12, 2008.

Takaki, Ronald. "Why the Vietnamese Came to America." In *The Vietnamese.* Ed. Michele E. Houle. Detroit: Greenhaven/Thomson Gale, 2006.

Takashima, Miki. "Multiple Reflections Across the Pacific." *Yomiuri Shimbun* 17 October 2002: 13.

Thanh Hoàng. *Dạ Cổ Hoài Lang* [*She Yearns for Her Husband Upon Hearing the Sound of the Midnight Drum*]. Play manuscript, Association of Theater Artists, Ho Chi Minh City, Vietnam, 1994.

"Thanh Hoàng: 'Tôi là người sống hướng nội'" ["Thanh Hoàng: 'I Am an Introspective Person'"] *Vietnam Express.* July 21, 2003. <http://www.vnexpress.net/GL/Vanhoa/San-khau-Dien-anh/2003/07/3B9C9DB3/>. Accessed 20 November 2008. Originally published in *Thanh Niên* newspaper.

"Thanh Hoàng Viết Kich Bản *Dạ Cổ Hoài Lang* Tập 2" ["Thanh Hoang Writes the Sequel to *Dạ Cổ Hoài Lang*"]. *Việt Báo.* February 26, 2007. <http://vietbao.vn/Vanhoa/Thanh-Hoang-viet-kich-ban-Da-co-hoai-lang-tap-2/40188657/181/>. Accessed 15 November 2008. Originally published in *Người Lao Động Newspaper.*

Thomas, Joe. *Ethnocide: A Cultural Narrative of Refugee Detention in Hong Kong.* Aldershot, UK: Ashgate, 2000.

Thu Nguyệt. "Quê Hương Ở Đâu? [Where is Homeland?]." Văn Của Những Người Cùng Thời Trong va Ngoài Nước [Literature of Contemporary Vietnamese and Diaspora]. <http://tranxuanan.writer.2.googlepages.com/thu_nguyet_quehodau.htm>. Accessed 5 January 2009.

Torao, Toshiya, and Delmer M. Brown, eds. *Chronology of Japan.* Tokyo: Hitoshi Haga, 1991.

Tyler, Royall. *The Contrast: A Comedy in Five Acts.* New York: AMS, 1970.

Tymms, Ralph. *Doubles in Literary Psychology.* Oxford: Bowes and Bowes, 1949.

Uchino, Tadashi. "Globality's Children: Thinking through the 'Child's' Body as a Strategy of Flatness in Performance." *TDR* 50.1 (2006): 57–66.

_____. "KATHY." *Eureka* 7 (2005): 206.

Usigli, Rodolfo. *El gesticulador.* Ed. Daniel Meyran. Madrid: Cátedra, 2004.

_____. "Ensayo sobre la actualidad de la poesía dramática." Mexico City: Editorial Syltlo, 1947.

Vingerhoets, A. J. J. M., and Randolph R. Cornelius. *Adult Crying: A Biopsychosocial Approach.* Hove, UK: Psychology Press, 2001. <http://books.google.com.tw/books?id=MfDEsYSBbgC&dq=Adult+Crying:+A+Biopsychosocial+Approach&printsec=frontcover&source=bn&hl=en&sa=X&oi=book_result&resnum=4&ct=result>. Accessed 22 February 2008.

Wang, Jing. "I Love You." CRIENGLISH.com. 19 July 2007. <http://english.cri.cn/4026/2007/07/19/1361@251310.htm>. Accessed 26 December 2007.

Wetmore, Kevin J., Jr. "From *Scaretto* to *Kaze to tomo ni sarinu*: Musical Adaptations of *Gone with the Wind* in Japan" in *Modern Japanese Theatre and Performance.* Eds. David Jortner, Keiko McDonald and Kevin J. Wetmore, Jr. Lanham, MD: Lexington, 2006.

White, Edgar. *Lament for Rastafari and Other Plays.* New York: Marion Boyers, 1983.

Widgery, Lord. *Bloody Sunday: Lord Widgery's Report of Events in Londonderry, Northern Ireland, on 30 January 1972.* London: Stationery Office, 2001.

Wiley, Peter Booth, with Korogi Ichiro. *Yankees in the Land of the Gods.* New York: Viking, 1990.

Williams, David, ed. *Peter Brook and the Mahabharata: Critical Perspectives.* New York: Routledge, 1991.

Wilmeth, Don B., and Christopher Bigsby, eds. *The Cambridge History of American Theatre: 1870–1945, Volume II.* Cambridge, UK: Cambridge University Press, 1998.

Winkler, Elizabeth Hale. "Brian Friel's *The Freedom of the City*: Historical Accuracy and Dramatic Imagination." *Canadian Journal of Irish Studies* 7 (June 1981): 12.

Wollen, Peter. *Singin' in the Rain.* London: British Film Institute, 1992.

Wood, David. "World Opinion of U.S. Sinking." *New Orleans Times-Picayune.* 17 May 2006. <http://www.nola.com/base/news-5/114784654160150.xml>. Accessed 26 December 2008.

Young, Robert. *Colonial Desire: Hybridity in Theory, Culture and Race.* London: Routledge, 1995.

Young, William C., ed. *Famous Actors and Actresses on the American Stage: Documents of American Theater History.* Volume 1, A–J, and Volume 2, K–Z. New York: R. R. Bowker, 1975.

Zach, Wolfgang. "Criticism, Theatre and Politics: Brian Friel's *The Freedom of the City* and its Early Reception." In *Irish Literature and Culture.* Ed. M. Kenneally. Gerards Cross, Buckinghamshire, UK: Colin Smythe, 1992.

Zantop, Susanne. *Colonial Fantasies: Conquest, Family, and Nation in Precolonial Germany, 1770–1870.* Durham, NC: Duke University Press, 1997.

About the Contributors

Nobuko Anan is a Ph.D. candidate in the Department of Theatre and Performance Studies at UCLA. She is completing her dissertation, which explores parody and resistance in contemporary Japanese women's theatre and dance troupes from 1990 to the present. Her research interests include gender/sexuality studies and popular culture studies.

Neilesh Bose is completing his doctorate in history at Tufts University, where he specializes in Indian political movements, culture and identity, with a focus on performance. He was a fellow at the Center for Citizenship, Race, and Ethnicity Studies at the College of St. Rose and is the Riley Scholar-in-Residence at Colorado College.

Thomas B. Costello teaches acting, directing and theatre history at the University of Pittsburgh. He writes and lectures on Irish theatre and has directed and designed in Dublin, New York, Prague, and elsewhere.

Jessica Hester is an assistant professor of theatre at SUNY Oswego, where she directs the history/criticism/dramaturgy degree track. She has a Ph.D. in theatre from the University of Texas at Austin.

Maura L. Jortner received her doctorate from the University of Pittsburgh in theatre and performance studies in 2005. She is a lecturer at Baylor University, where she teaches composition and introduction to British Literature. She's had articles published in *Nineteenth Century Theatre and Film* and *The Journal of American Drama and Theatre (JADT)*.

Sabine Macris Klein is an assistant professor of English with a focus on theatre and drama at Westfield State College. She has a Ph.D. from CUNY Graduate Center and her research interests are on eighteenth-century German drama.

Jessica C. Locke is an assistant professor of Spanish at the University of Mary Washington. She has a Ph.D. from El Colegio de México and has written extensively on Mexican drama.

Khai Thu Nguyen is completing her doctorate in performance studies at the University of California, Berkeley. Her dissertation focuses on the function of melodrama in constructing political subjecthood and national identity in Vietnam. She co-founded NEWS, an intercultural performance troupe in Ho Chi Mihn City, and has presented her work at several national and international conferences.

Nenad "Neno" Pervan is a native of Sarajevo, Bosnia and Herzegovina. His career in theatre, film and television started twenty-five years ago in the former Yugoslavia. In 1993, following the breakup of Yugoslavia, Pervan moved to the United States. In 1997, he earned his MFA in performance from the University of Tennessee in Knoxville. He is visiting assistant professor of theatre at Loyola Marymount University in Los Angeles, California.

Melissa Rynn Porterfield is pursuing her Ph.D. in theatre arts and performance studies at the University of Pittsburgh. She has an M.A. in theatre arts from Miami University and a BFA in acting from Long Island University, C.W. Post Campus. She is currently working on her dissertation on the use of Shakespeare as cultural capital by American Shakespeare companies.

Llyn Scott is a professor emeritus of English and theatre at Fu Jen Catholic University in Taiwan. She is a professor in the department of foreign languages and literature at Aletheia University. She is the editor of *English Onstage* and has directed over fifty productions at FJCU. Her Ph.D. is from Louisiana State University and she has also written plays for Radio Taiwan International.

Kevin J. Wetmore, Jr., is an associate professor of theatre at Loyola Marymount University. He is the author of four books, including the McFarland-published *The Athenian Sun in an African Sky*, *Black Dionysus*, and *The Empire Triumphant*, and the editor or co-editor of another four, including *Modern Japanese Theatre and Performance*, *Suzan-Lori Parks: A Casebook* and *Revenge Drama in Renaissance European and Japanese Theatre*. His research interests include Japanese theatre, African theatre, and early modern drama.

Ji Hyon (Kayla) Yuh received her M.A. in theatre at the University of Illinois at Urbana Champaign and is a doctoral candidate in Theatre at CUNY Graduate Center. Her research is in Korean theatre and foreign theatre in Korea.

Index

239